Globe Law
and Business

Managing Talent for Success

Talent Development in Law Firms
Second Edition

Consulting Editor **Rebecca Normand-Hochman**
on behalf of the International Bar Association

Consulting editor
Rebecca Normand-Hochman on behalf of the International Bar Association

Managing director
Sian O'Neill

Managing Talent for Success: Talent Development in Law Firms, Second Edition
is published by

Globe Law and Business Ltd
3 Mylor Close
Horsell
Woking
Surrey GU21 4DD
United Kingdom
Tel: +44 20 3745 4770
www.globelawandbusiness.com

Printed and bound by CPI Group (UK) Ltd, Croydon CR0 4YY, United Kingdom

Managing Talent for Success: Talent Development in Law Firms, Second Edition

ISBN 9781787423749
EPUB ISBN 9781787423756
Adobe PDF ISBN 9781787423763
Mobi ISBN 9781787423770

Table of contents

The keys to building a successful talent strategy

Rebecca Normand-Hochman
Institute of Legal Talent & Leadership

1. Introduction

Ten years ago, at the end of a meeting, a managing partner of an international law firm looked at me with despair and said, "You can't imagine how difficult it is to motivate lawyers!" Those words struck me at the time as being symptomatic of what many law firms were facing: they were reaching a dead end in the way they managed talent.

Today it is less likely that the same managing partner would express the same astonishment, as appreciation of the complexity of the challenges that firms face has significantly increased. Now, every leader and experienced lawyer I meet grasps the many factors that are capable of affecting motivation and success, both at an individual and a collective level.

The acceleration of the profound transformations that the world is going through with digitalisation, artificial intelligence, globalisation, significantly higher levels of competition and more recently the Covid-19 pandemic, have meant that the legal industry is having to deal with rapid change as never before. A large number of law firms now consider talent management as a strategic driver of competitiveness, and this trend is not likely to be short term.

Because of the direct link between great talent and a firm's ability to compete for and win work, it is an absolute imperative to align talent with strategy. Unless talent management activities are directly linked and aligned, horizontally to HR management and vertically to the firm's strategy-making process, their impact will be less than optimum (see Figure 1).

Moving talent management up to the next level of maturity is a strategic process.

Strategic flexibility is increasingly important as firms must be able to adapt to changing business conditions and revamp their talent approach when necessary.

Lawyers are naturally driven and motivated professionals. The challenge that law firms have is therefore to create the conditions for them to keep their natural drive, motivation for excellence, sense of direction and achievement as the years go by.

No one would argue that managing and leading talent in the legal

Figure 1. Alignment of talent management with strategy[1]

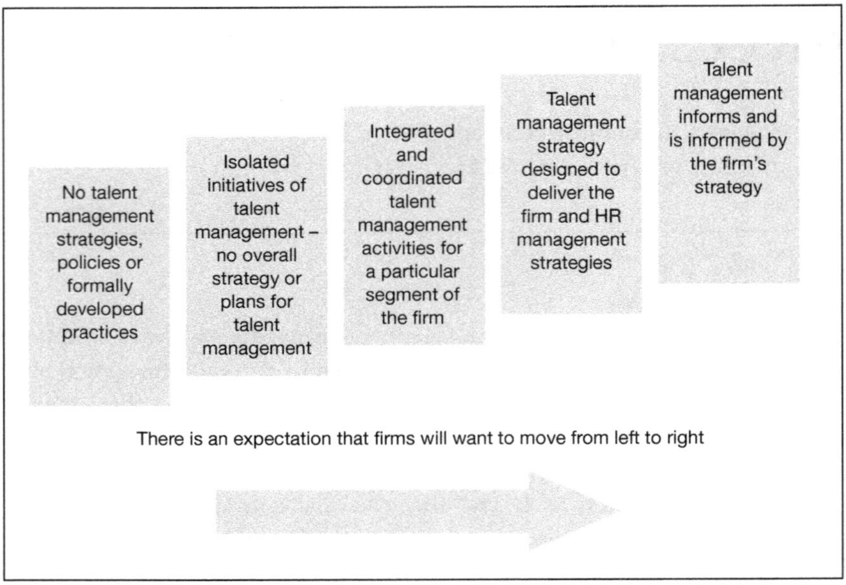

Source: Author.

profession is straightforward. On the contrary. There are inherent specific challenges linked to both lawyers' personalities and the law firm model which explain why the profession can often seem behind the curve at an organisational level.[2] It is, however, possible to create a framework and a culture to achieve great results. Although every firm's approach varies because of its specific strategic goals, challenges, culture, history and leadership, when a talent strategy is successful the foundations are invariability built around the same principles.

This chapter explores what these principles are and is designed around the three strategic needs that all firms have in order to be in a position to face the competition and thrive:

- the need to attract and select lawyers;
- the need to develop and retain key talent; and
- the need to manage exits and alumni networks.

1   Adapted from CIPD, "Talent Management: Understanding the Dimensions", 2006. Available at: www.libraryservices.nhs.uk/document_uploads/Talent_Management_Toolkit/CIPD_TM.pdf.

2   Jay W Lorsch and Thomas J Tierney, *Aligning the Stars: How to Succeed When Professionals Drive Results*, Harvard Business Review Press, 2002.

2. Attracting and selecting lawyers

The unprecedented competition for talent described in *The War for Talent*[3] two decades ago has now become a reality which requires law firms, like all other knowledge-intensive industries, to be highly strategic in how they attract and select their talents.

It used to be – not that long ago – that talented lawyers would be knocking at the firms' doors but it is no longer the case and today, law firms across the globe are competing to recruit the best and brightest lawyers in their field.

2.1 What attracts great talent?

The first step to being able to attract the right type of talent is to have an employee value proposition (EVP) that reflects what the firm is offering but that is also aligned with the needs and aspirations of today's best talents.

An EVP is perceived by three types of people:

- lawyers in the market – potential recruits;
- lawyers inside the firm; and
- clients.

These perspectives need to be aligned otherwise a number of problems arise.

The traditional implied promise, of partnership opportunities in exchange for excellent work, long hours and loyalty, is no longer what law firms can offer. Neither is it what many in the younger generation of lawyers find appealing.

Understanding what attracts today's best lawyers, not just around financial rewards and benefits, but across all aspects – career development, type of work, international opportunities, flexible work–life balance – has become critical. How do your people grow through the firm both personally and professionally, and how can you support them in doing so?

Having a powerful EVP is without a doubt the most effective response to both recruitment and retention issues.[4]

Based on how EVPs are evolving in other industries and how some of the leading law firms have recently reshaped their EVP, there are three core elements on which firms should focus to attract today's best lawyers:

- personal growth and development;
- collaboration and teaming; and
- impact.

(a) Personal growth and development

Instead of an implied promise around partnership promotion, EVPs now focus

---

3   E Michaels, H Handfield-Jones and B Axelrod, *The War for Talent*, Harvard Business School Press, 2001.
4   Rebecca Normand-Hochman, *Recruiting and Retaining Lawyers: Innovative Strategies to Attract, Develop and Retain Legal Talent*, Globe Law and Business, 2017.

on offering outstanding developmental opportunities. In other words, what law can firms offer to the best and brightest in the market is to support them in developing their full potential – not the promise that they will be made partner "if everything goes well". Since the 2008 financial crisis, many of the most established large law firms have stopped being in a position to promise partnership opportunities to their best talents, and at the same time the young talents' aspirations and expectations have shifted – partnership roles are no longer considered to be attractive to everyone, nor the single goal for a successful lawyer career. These two major concurrent trends require law firms to significantly change their EVPs. A number have done so and many are in the process.

(b) ***Collaboration and teaming***
Young (and less young) lawyers are also increasingly valuing opportunities to collaborate and work in teams. Lawyers need high levels of autonomy and independence but the younger generation tends to favour collective working approaches, where the focus is on both collective and individual performance.

(c) ***Impact***
A growing number of young lawyers have a desire to contribute to creating a positive impact, either through environmental awareness, social justice or other causes that produce transformation in society at a deep level. So, creating clear messages indicating the firm's values around positive impact has become an important criterion when choosing whether to join an organisation.
This is an example of an EVP that is capable of attracting great talent:
Do what you love: a career at Latham & Watkins will give you the opportunity to do some of the best work of your life.
Another example is from Bain & Company's career page:
Picture yourself at one of the world's best places to work, surrounded by teams and people who challenge you, support you, and inspire you to be extraordinary.
The company goes on to emphasise the opportunities to collaborate with diverse teams across various departments and offices around the world. Tellingly, the consultancy has been listed as number two on Glassdoor's "Best Places to Work 2020" list and is a known leader in collaboration.[5]

2.2 The imperative to deliver on the EVP
EVPs need to be lived by all the partners across the firm; in other words, what is promised needs to be delivered. Increasingly, any gap between what law firms communicate and the behaviours that partners demonstrate is poorly tolerated. As one managing partner recently told me, "It's not enough to talk the talk;

---

5   Available at: www.glassdoor.co.uk/Award/Best-Places-to-Work-LST_KQ0,19.htm.

partners are now expected to walk the talk and deliver on the firm's value proposition consistently."

2.3 Selecting the right talent

Hiring the right people may be among the most important decisions law firms can make. It is estimated by some experts that 80% of turnover in companies is due to bad hiring decisions. Often these choices are made because people hired the person they liked the best. Instincts are an important part of the decision-making process, but should not be the only part.

(a) Behavioural interviews

When partners interview candidates, they have an opportunity to assess whether the person will be a good fit for the firm or not.

Behavioural interviewing is a technique now commonly used in recruiting to help evaluate a candidate's future performance. It involves asking questions about the candidate's behaviour in past situations that are similar to the ones required in their future role, in order to predict future behaviour, good or bad.

Behavioural questions ask the candidate to describe past behaviour in context. By contrast, traditional questions such as, "What are your strengths and weaknesses?" and "How do you define success?" are more generic, with straightforward answers.

By asking behavioural questions, partners can gain insight into a candidate's personality, skills and abilities. The questions require candidates to share specific stories that highlight their strengths and skills, providing the opportunity to assess how the candidate will be once they have joined the firm. They also provide valuable comparisons between candidates, and ultimately avoid wrong decisions based on gut feeling.

Instinct is important, but it should not be the sole consideration, as evidenced by Daniel Kahneman's work.[6] Many candidates come across as excellent, but when you dig into their past experience you may discover, for example, that they have had constant friction with previous colleagues and don't work well in teams.

Examples of good behavioural interview questions include:

- "Tell me about a time when you handled a challenging situation."
- "Tell me about a time when you made a mistake. What did you do to correct it?"
- "Tell me about a time when you were in conflict with a peer and how the situation was resolved."
- "Tell me about how you work under pressure."
- "Tell me about a goal you set and how you achieved it."
- "Tell me about a goal you failed to achieve."

---

6   John Baldoni, "What Daniel Kahneman Knows About Your Gut (Decisions)", *Forbes*, 2019.

(b) Assessment tools

In 2015 about 76% of organisations with more than 100 employees relied on assessment tools such as aptitude and personality tests for external hiring, and that figure continues to climb.[7] The more senior the role, the more likely the employer is to use assessments to identify candidates with the right traits and abilities.

Interestingly, recruitment assessments have been around at least since the Han dynasty in the third century. Chinese imperial leaders used them to gauge knowledge, intellect and moral integrity when selecting civil servants. Modern personality and intelligence tests were introduced in the United States and Europe during World War I, to aid in military selection, and after World War II companies started adopting them to select applicants.

Sophisticated assessment tools help firms measure three critical elements of success on the job:

- competence;
- work ethic; and
- emotional intelligence.

Like behavioural questions, assessment tools look at how someone is likely to behave in a given environment. They help to predict performance but also to understand the complex interaction between someone's specific mental framework and the environment/culture in which they operate.

Once the types of behaviours that are needed for the culture of the firm are identified, the talents, competencies and potential that should be sought for particular roles and levels of seniority can be determined.

Being able to recruit lawyers with the right talents, competencies and potential who are likely to adopt the behaviours that the firm needs is the foundation of any solid approach to talent in today's law firm. Taking advantage of tools to bring greater predictability and increase the chances of success in the recruitment process is a simple and pragmatic option.

3. The art of developing and retaining lawyers

I'm using the word 'art' because this is an aspect that requires a high degree of mastery to get good results.

3.1 Motivation

It's important to understand what motivates and drives lawyers, and the question we hear most often is, "Do lawyers have internal drivers of motivation that are different from those of other intensive knowledge workers?"

Motivation derives from the Latin word *movere*, 'to move'.

It can be defined as the set of forces that causes people to engage in one

---

7   Tomas Chamorro-Premuzic, "Ace the Assessment", *Harvard Business Review*, July–August 2015.

behaviour rather than some alternative behaviour. Abraham Maslow developed the Hierarchy of Needs model on human motivation and personal development in the 1940s–50s, and the theory remains valid today.[8] According to Maslow, organisations are responsible for providing an environment in which people are encouraged to fulfil their unique potential, described as 'self-actualisation'.

In his book *Drive*,[9] Daniel Pink argues that on the edge of the economy, old-fashioned ideas of management are giving way to a new-fangled emphasis on self-direction. He labels the three elements of motivation Autonomy, Mastery and Purpose.

In his chapter in this book on the role of personality, Larry Richard explains the personality traits and motivations that set lawyers apart from other professionals in the workplace, and that make managing legal talent more challenging. In particular, lawyers have these traits in common:

- They need constant challenge and have high expectations of their careers.
- They are independent-minded and reluctant to follow procedures.
- They need to be highly motivated to perform well.

Lawyers have many motivational drivers, but at their core is the need to achieve and to perform.[10]

Based on their motivational drivers, lawyers need:[11]

- *Challenging work:* This is the most fundamental motivator for achievement-orientated personalities who self-select into professions. For them, solving challenging questions for clients is motivating.
- *Clear, timely and actionable feedback:* Individuals who have a high need for achievement have a much greater need for feedback that do other professionals. This is because they want to perform as well as possible. They need positive as well as constructive feedback to stay motivated.
- *Autonomy and control over task parameters:* Having the autonomy needed to do their work free of constraint is itself a motivating force for professionals who have a high need for achievement. As a corollary, they become frustrated and demotivated when limitations are imposed that interfere with their ability to deal directly with the problems or when these barriers reduce their freedom.
- *Coaching and mentoring:* The more senior high-need-to-achieve professionals become, the more they want the kind of mentoring that addresses the questions, "What does it take to make it at the firm?" Lawyers need and expect coaching and mentoring.

---

8   See AH Maslow, *Motivation and Personality*, Harper & Bros, 1954.
9   Daniel H Pink, *Drive*, Penguin Group, 2009.
10   TJ Delong, JJ Gabarro and RJ Lees, *When Professionals Have to Lead*, Harvard Business School Press, 2007.
11   *Ibid.*

- *Recognition:* The kind of recognition that best motivates lawyers includes acknowledging or recognising that they have done extraordinary work on a client project, have gone the extra mile or have significantly enhanced an engagement team's performance. This kind of recognition occurs during personal interactions that may take a few minutes or less but are very powerful. Recognition is the most underused source of motivation in professional services firms.

So, if the nature of the required motivation is understood, why do most law firms still fail to build the appropriate systems and cultures to achieve it?

Senior professionals with a high need for achievement are rarely disposed to give feedback to, or to coach and mentor, others, because they are impatient with anything that distracts them from the 'real' work of serving clients and enhancing the book of business.

For many partners, on-the-spot feedback, coaching and mentoring are still not considered as central to their responsibility for getting a deal done, and are still often ignored. These partners fail to recognise and acknowledge the link between great talent development and business performance.

This is, however, changing. More and more firms are integrating ongoing feedback, periodical development feedback, coaching and mentoring, challenging work and recognition in the way they develop talent at all levels of seniority. Development doesn't happen through training, however sophisticated – it happens through a combination of all of these components and needs to be tailored to the specific needs of individual lawyers as they develop.

Table 1. The changing approach to talent development

Traditional	New
Development just happens.	Development is woven into the fabric of the firm.
Development means training.	Development primarily means challenging experiences, feedback, coaching and mentoring.
Only poor performers have development needs.	Everyone has development needs and receives coaching.
A few lucky people find mentors.	Mentors are assigned to every high-potential person.

3.2 Factors affecting retention

Retention is a critical issue as firms compete for talent in an increasingly tight economy. The cost of turnover has also risen to as much as 2.5 times salary depending on the role. Additionally, there are of course side costs such as decreased engagement, loss of knowhow and cultural impact.

Modern psychology has long shown that financial reward is not the most important element in retention of the best talent. Research supports the increasingly widespread view that intrinsic human emotion and behaviour cannot be positively affected by monetary reward in any sustainable way.[12]

The most critical contributions to retention, particularly for those with supervising partners and peers, are:

- development;
- career development;
- relationships; and
- respect.

Given lawyers' specific motivations and personality, some of the most effective retention approaches in law firms involve elements that relate to the culture that firms build around their people, such as:

- leaders and partners modelling cultural norms and behaviours;
- giving everyone an opportunity to grow;
- providing more positive feedback and recognition;
- fostering respect;
- cultivating trust; and
- encouraging individual creativity and contribution.

4. Managing exits and alumni networks

The way in which people leave their firm has a lasting impact on how they perceive their whole experience in the organisation. For the reasons detailed below, it has become increasingly important for law firms to make sure that lawyers who leave have a positive experience in their transition out of the firm.

In addition, law firms, like a number of other professional services, are now paying more attention to building and managing a strong alumni community, benefiting both the firm itself and former employees.

4.1 Why exit interviews matter

Of all talent-management processes, a strategic exit interview process, one that is designed to yield ongoing, long-term benefits, may be one of the most powerful, yet least utilised, in law firms.

A decade ago, organisations were less concerned about how people leaving

---

12   Daniel H Pink, *Drive, supra.*

their firm felt about their exit management process. However, today, law firms who wish to remain attractive to top talent cannot afford not to think strategically about their exit management approach.

By conducting structured exit interviews, law firms have the opportunity to learn from their best lawyers:

- why they stay;
- why they leave; and
- how the firm needs to change.

A thoughtful exit interview process can create a constant flow of feedback on all three fronts.[13]

Done well, an exit interview, whether it be a face-to-face conversation, a questionnaire, a survey or some combination of those methods, can catalyse leaders' listening skills, reveal what does or doesn't work inside the firm, highlight hidden challenges and opportunities, and generate essential competitive intelligence. It can also promote engagement and enhance retention by signalling to associates that their views matter. It can turn departing lawyers into ambassadors for life.

Some of the benefits of a well-managed exit process include:

- the conversion of exiting lawyers into brand ambassadors, sources of referrals and clients;
- the rebuilding of trust in the system and the psychological contract between the firm and the other lawyers;
- an opportunity to show the firm's commitment to people wellbeing; and
- an opportunity to position the firm as an employer of choice, ultimately attracting top talent.

4.2 Effective exit interviews

To get the most out of an exit interview – for both parties – it is important to ask the right questions (see Table 2).

4.3 The value of an active alumni network

In the same way that lawyers leverage their experience to get new roles, increasingly large law firms are leveraging their alumni for future business. Through sometimes elaborate networking programmes, law firms are keeping track of the talent and creating a community culture.

Carol Sprague, the New York City-based director of talent acquisition and attorney engagement at Skadden, Arps, Slate, Meagher & Flom, which has had an alumni program in place for over 20 years, has this to say:

It takes some firms a bit longer to say these things out loud. Not every associate

---

13   Everett Spain and Boris Groysberg, "Making Exit Interviews Count", *Harvard Business Review*, April 2016.

Table 2. Exit interview questions to ask

Category	Question
Reasons for leaving the firm	What prompted you to start looking for another firm? What was the biggest factor that led you to accept a new offer? What makes your new role more attractive than the one you currently have?
Satisfaction	What did you like most about your time with the firm? What did you dislike the most about your time with our firm? Did you have all the tools and resources you needed to effectively do your work?
Learning and development opportunities	How would you evaluate the quality of the training you received? Was the feedback you received about your performance timely, helpful and specific? Do you feel like you've had enough opportunities for growth and development at our firm?
Firm culture and work environment	How would you describe our firm's culture? What could be done to make this firm a better place to work? Is there a culture of teamwork and collaboration at our firm?
Employee brand ambassador score	Would you recommend our firm to your friend as a great place to work? Why? Would you consider working with us again in the future? On a scale of 1 to 10, how would you rate your experience in our firm?

wants to be a partner at their organization. We are more realistic. We would rather facilitate and have them work [with] our clients than have them go off and disappear.[14]

McKinsey & Company led the way in valuing the importance of building an alumni community. When recruiters for the firm visit business school campuses or meet with prospective applicants, they talk about the extensive impact of being McKinsey alumni. According to Sean Brown, former global director of alumni relations:

We will talk about not just the great training you'll get and the great problems you'll work on and the wonderful clients you'll work with, but also the fact that the firm does celebrate those lifelong connections and how we keep our alumni connected.

Alumni from the firm have gone on to become CEOs of global companies, start entrepreneurial ventures, or transition into the nonprofit or government sectors.[15]

McKinsey's investment in maintaining the network is remarkable. In almost every one of its offices, the firm has at least one individual responsible for alumni engagement. The directory, the knowledge events and the worldwide conferences are all funded by the firm. McKinsey's alumni network does produce new clients, but that isn't the biggest payoff. According to Sean Brown:

That's a very frequent assumption. In fact, we're much more focused on client impact and people impact. The firm believes that by building a worldwide network of former consultants, it's better able to serve the needs of current clients. It's better equipped to recruit the best talent, but also better positioned to attain the knowledge needed to keep delivering outstanding service to clients.

In the last decade, the most advanced law firms have been following McKinsey's example, building and managing increasingly active alumni networks. There are both business and human reasons to do so:

- *Lawyers frequently refer significant business to each other:* Whether due to a conflict of interest, a practice area that is not covered by the firm or the need to co-counsel with a niche expert, lawyers often refer business to each other.
- *Lawyers who move firms gain experience and contacts:* Lawyers who leave to go to other law firms get more experience and insight and can occasionally come back as boomerang hires into more senior positions with new perspectives and clients.
- *Lawyers move in-house and can become clients:* Alumni can become clients, bringing their business, introducing potential clients and making helpful connections.

---

14   Janan Hanah, "Old Firm Ties", *American Bar Association Journal*, May 2011.
15   David Burkus, "Why McKinsey & Company's Alumni Network Is Crucial To Its Success", Forbes, July 2016.

- *Lawyers start businesses:* Lawyers who leave to start businesses are potential clients. With referrals being the largest source of new business for most service companies, having alumni who are now in the entrepreneurial community is a great way to access a potential innovative client base.
- *Lawyers can become sector experts:* In the case of lawyers moving into business or indeed starting and growing businesses, alumni offer direct access to people creating companies of the future and those creating and dictating market trends can offer invaluable information and insight useful to any law firm, either for commercial strategy, training or lectures.
- *Alumni make great mentors:* Alumni are a useful source of mentoring for current employees. With an understanding of the corporate culture they came from yet no longer working under that roof, they can provide useful career advice through a more independent lens to graduates, rising stars and those wanting some professional support.
- *Good leavers are ambassadors:* Lawyers who leave the firm with a positive experience have the potential to be ambassadors for the rest of their careers.

All of us intuitively recognise the power of networks and being connected.

5. Conclusion

Managing and leading the human side of organisations has never been so important.

Although business leaders and talent professionals have long known intuitively that investment in talent management drives business results, measuring the impact of talent management on business outcomes can prove to be difficult. Deloitte has found that organisations with higher levels of talent management maturity tend to perform better on critical talent and business outcomes.[16] Historical approaches that see talent management as a collection of initiatives (for example conducting annual appraisals or training), fail to provide competitive advantage to today's firms and are therefore no longer enough.

There are clear signs in law firms of all sizes and cultures, not only of an awareness of the great challenges that exist around managing talent, but also of a shift in mindset that has opened up opportunities for new approaches in the future.

Law firms now need to plan for, integrate, develop and engage lawyers with the capability to deliver what they do today as well as what they will do tomorrow; and that is likely to be significantly different to what they did

---

16   Deloitte, *Talent Matters*, Deloitte University Press, 2017.

yesterday. As law firms continue to navigate the transition from traditional law to new law, they will increasingly require to be expert at managing talent.

As Terri Mottershead has observed, "If we have heard it once, we have heard it many times: People are our greatest asset. The difference between then and now is that we need to mean it."[17]

---

[17]   Terri Mottershead, "Innovating Talent Management in Law Firms", *Law Practice Today*, 2016.

Driving business results through talent

Marc Bartel
Korn Ferry
Caroline Vanovermeire
Effra Consult Ltd
Dentsu International

1. Introduction

The term 'strategy' has strong corporate connotations and hence is often perceived as something which is less relevant to smaller law firms. However, it remains essential in today's highly competitive legal market to know where one is going and why one has decided to become an independent adviser.

When a couple of lawyers decide to set up a new firm, establishing a strategy is not usually an initial concern. Yet their efforts to launch their new enterprise are nonetheless the first step towards establishing a strategy. They must ask themselves how they wish to differentiate their offering and what kind of clientele they are targeting.

2. A focused strategy

Historically, factors such as bar regulations that restrict business development and high demand for quality advisers in certain sectors fuelled an assumption that clients would come knocking on firms' doors to seek their help. Indeed, this might still be the case in a few limited situations. However, this reactive attitude can no longer be considered a viable way to develop a sustainable client base in today's challenging market. In the not so distant past, some even suggested that lawyers should not respond to clients too quickly, for fear that such quick turnaround times would come to be expected as a matter of course. At a session at the International Bar Association's 2012 annual conference in Dublin, by contrast, a US partner revealed that his firm now has a 20-minute return phone call policy.

A coherent strategy is crucial to ensure success in this demanding new environment. The most common flaw when considering a strategy is to overlook the fact that its success is entirely dependent on the talent available to implement it. In a professional service organisation, whose sole assets are its people, this omission is critical and often damaging. A second common flaw is a lack of focus, where the strategy is continually adapted to fit whatever talent might be available. Another common mistake is the partners' failure to communicate their strategy clearly and consistently to all other staff members. Finally, while the partners may agree on what their strategy should be, they may be less clear on how to go about implementing it.

Considering the first problem, then, a flawed evaluation of the available talent pool too often results in a compromise on the quality of the staff leading implementation of the strategy. For example, a strategy aimed at becoming a key player in a specific sector or developing niche expertise will not materialise as hoped if it is led by lawyers without the necessary talent to implement it successfully. If plans to attract a star lawyer from another firm or to groom up-and-coming internal talent to this end fall through, less experienced people may be hired or asked to lead, resulting in at best much slower implementation, at worst failure of the strategy. The financial expectation to return profits over the short term may thus result in a loss-making operation, putting pressure on profitability. Management will often argue that the market turned out to be more challenging than expected, when in fact it was poor talent planning that caused the losses. This resembles a situation where a company hopes to tap a potentially lucrative market and seeks the necessary equipment to profitably build and sell a product, but on discovering that such equipment is unavailable or unaffordable, still persists in its plan by investing in old technology which will not deliver the expected profits – or any profits, for that matter.

Those in smaller firms may think that a focused talent plan is unrealistic at this stage of their evolution. However, even a single-partner firm should consider how it intends to grow and whether or how available talent could help achieve its goals. In smaller firms especially, it is crucial that all lawyers share a common vision and purpose. Building synergies around skills and clients will deliver results and unify the partners. It is also much easier to develop work from existing clients than to win new ones. Once again, a simple plan or common objective should be determined, based on the specific talent which the firm can afford, access or attract.

An unfocused approach of accepting any talent that happens to come along is common, but is frequently problematic. The temptation to hire talent with a solid book of business or revenues is understandable, but not optimal. Depending on the size of the firm, this may be regarded as a way to boost overall revenues or counterbalance a risky or challenging revenue stream. There is often a false sense that the new hire will mean success for all, as he will make an immediate contribution to the bottom line. But if this were so simple, all or most such lateral hires – and even promotions – would end in success. By contrast, history has shown that, like all other professionals, lawyers who move firm rarely deliver the anticipated contribution in the short term. A study published by Heidrick & Struggles in collaboration with Winmark revealed that it "takes lawyers longer to bring their so-called following along, which normally ends up being about a third of that they said they would bring".[1] Too often, great expectations become disappointments on both sides and the bottom line may be endangered as a result.

Such hires can also undermine synergy in the firm, as partners focus on individual revenues instead of working together towards a common purpose. The most commonly overlooked issue, despite what firms may claim, is the importance of cultural fit. Too often in the rush to consider a potential lateral hire, or even an internal promotion, billing ends up being the decisive factor. In many jurisdictions, this is driven by an aggressive recruitment market or the fear of losing out on future talent. No one could disagree with the statement that the success of any business depends on quality. The impact of quality – or lack thereof – is quickly felt in the legal sector, where you are only as good as your last advice. Furthermore, a firm or individual's career will span several decades, and a short-term view on quality thus has the potential to seriously damage the firm's brand, clientele and very survival. Despite this, however, for many firms internal promotions and lateral recruitment are still driven by existing or potential revenue. I have rarely heard management say that someone is a brilliant lawyer who delivers outstanding quality and hence will be promoted or hired despite a lack of revenues or clientele. I would not venture to say that the reverse is true, but billing or billing potential is too often the decisive criterion.

As mentioned, another common mistake is the partners' failure to communicate strategy clearly and consistently to all other staff members. Inevitably, a firm's primary focus tends to be on its lawyers, and thus strategy may be discussed at length within the partners' forum. However, firms tend to underestimate the importance of support functions in ensuring that lawyers can thrive and perform effectively. It is therefore crucial to familiarise all staff members with the strategy and how they can contribute towards achieving it.

Even once a strategy has been clearly articulated and consistently understood, the partners may not be aligned as to how it should be implemented. There may be disagreements about pace and timing, as well as 'softer' elements such as values which are reflected in daily client and colleague interactions, as well as in decisions made on behalf of or within the partnership.

3. Building a brand

There are numerous definitions of the term 'brand'. In some ways it can be equated to the culture of a firm, which can be hard to describe. It may be easy to intuit, but difficult to describe beyond basic adjectives such as 'collegiate' or 'client-centric'. Essentially, the brand reflects the culture of the people working within the firm, and hence is a blend of their values, styles, personalities and aspirations.

---

1 Heidrick & Struggles and Winmark, "Bridging the Gap: Talent strategies to align law firms with client needs", September 2011.

From this perspective, then, a firm's strategy should include the objective of building or preserving a coherent brand. This could mean reinforcing the existing culture, ensuring that people can articulate the culture and identify with it, or reshaping the culture to facilitate implementation of the new strategy. A famous quote from Peter Drucker sums it up: "Culture eats strategy for breakfast." If the culture is not aligned with the strategy, implementation will be difficult and may ultimately come to naught.

One of the main principles highlighted by culture consultant firm Senn Delaney is that the firm is a mirror of its own leadership. In other words, a successful firm that is making great progress in line with its strategy will have partners who behave in line with the brand and culture. All too often, where this is not the case, firms try to solve the issue of culture by reviewing their structure. A leading law firm once approached us with the aim of increasing cross-selling activities as part of its growth strategy. However, we quickly established that we first had to tackle a lack of trust among partners and the absence of a common set of values. In other words, the partners needed to decide whether they wanted to operate as a real team or as franchisees. Both options work; however, they each require a different strategy and reflect a different culture and brand position in the market.

It is difficult to dissociate a firm's brand from that of each individual member. When developing or acquiring talent, this issue should not be overlooked. No partner would be happy to hear that a colleague delivers poor quality, lacks ethics or is not pleasant to work with when pitching to a client. Word of mouth about a bad experience with one partner may mean that the others are suddenly ignored by existing or potential clients. Sadly, such experiences generally arise post-promotion or recruitment, and are hard to predict. However, while we all tend to question, check and run simulations on portable revenue streams, we rarely invest the same energy in assessing the reputation or values of individual partners; and if there is any doubt, strategic needs and billing will inevitably take priority. The misperception is that the firm's culture and procedures will improve and correct some of the individual's perceived flaws.

4. Differentiating the firm in the market

Clients instruct a firm due to the perceived quality of its service, which makes it stand out from the crowd. Consolidation on the legal services market is continuing and more work is now being undertaken in-house – factors which have served to make this environment more competitive. Market positioning, brand building and differentiation are thus becoming increasingly important for law firms of all sizes. Admittedly, the 'friendship factor' does still apply at some level and can carry significant weight in certain cultures and countries. However, if the competition can offer a better service at the same price – or even at a higher price – even hitherto loyal clients may eventually move on.

A sole practitioner defines the brand by their actions. As soon as two lawyers begin to work together, their individual actions will reflect on one another. Even if the firm's name is just a basic combination of their surname, that name will develop a brand of its own in the market. Clients' perceptions will also be informed by the type of work and advice provided. There is nothing worse – except a reputation for poor quality, which may eventually prove fatal – than confused market perceptions about the types of services on offer. If clients do not understand what services the firm is offering and how good it is at providing them, they will not consider even asking it for more information about what it does. It is therefore essential to identify the clientele that the firm will target and what is required to serve and please that clientele. Clients and the market should have a clear understanding of what they can expect from the firm. In deciding on how the firm will differentiate itself, the partners must consider what kind of service they wish to offer and therefore what kind of talent they need. In a smaller firm, one person may be so well known that he effectively *is* the brand – the magnet that attracts more work. This situation may create unrest among other more entrepreneurially aspirational lawyers or those seeking a greater say in the firm's day-to-day or future plans.

5. Developing a dynamic talent strategy

5.1 An evolving partnership

The economic landscape is changing increasingly rapidly. Client demand for services and advice is mirroring this dynamic as new markets, products and issues emerge. In an ailing economy there is heightened need for restructuring skills and hence talent who can offer these skills. In some emerging markets, on the other hand, new legislative regimes may develop quickly and clients will need up-to-date advice to support and protect them in entering those markets.

A static partnership – that is, a group of partners with few synergies or little desire to cooperate, or with rigid or siloed views of clients' needs – risks misreading or simply missing these economic changes altogether, or failing to adapt its offering accordingly.

It is thus essential that lawyers, like all other professionals, accept that the era of a single job or skill for life is over. We will all have to change jobs, position or function several times during our working careers. Lawyers cannot expect to be the exception to this rule and must commit to continual learning in order to stay agile, flexible and adaptable. Equally, firms must support the continued development of their lawyers, to ensure that they are well equipped to deal with the increased complexities and ambiguities of the sector and to promote their employability. At times, internal talent will need to be complemented by the acquisition of new talent, and offices or practices may need to be opened or closed. It is imperative to keep a finger on the pulse of the market and to anticipate trends in a proactive manner. Those who truly care about their clients' business challenges must pick up on early signs of change. However, inertia may make it difficult to adapt the talent and skills within the partnership sufficiently quickly to keep pace with market changes. Successful firms and partners will know how to break out of siloed thinking and develop talent with a wider skillset. Indeed, for smaller firms or in some jurisdictions, it is already a basic requirement to be more versatile.

5.2 Identifying the necessary talent to achieve the strategy

The law firm's strategy must be clear, realistic and focused. It must further be dynamic and reviewed regularly – although not excessively, as this will mean it is neither focused nor realistic, and will further blur the brand and confuse clients. The strategy must rely on existing or easily accessible talent. As market opportunities are identified and regularly reviewed and refined, it is thus critical to conduct in-depth analysis of the firm's talent and ensure that this talent is capable of adapting to market and demand changes. Lawyers tend to be resistant to the notion of developing new skills, which requires that billable time be set aside as an investment towards the future. But each professional should commit to keep learning – and not just by attending interesting presentations. Learning also involves humility and a willingness to accept new challenges. Lawyers often have abundant potential to learn, but less motivation to do so. A positive attitude towards learning is even more important in smaller firms, where a sudden drop in work and hence revenues will have a quicker, more dramatic impact on the firm as a whole, rapidly creating tension between the partners and possibly isolating the weakest link.

5.3 Support professionals are a vital asset

As previously observed, there is a common misconception that a firm's sole talent is its lawyers. They generate billable hours (many of which, in fact, are unbillable or of poor quality), and hence revenues. But whatever the size of the firm, one cannot deny the added value of support professionals. Some still feel that it is easier to find a good secretary than a good lawyer, and thus show little interest in the recruitment and development of this talent. Lawyers for the most part sell their time, packaged up in a quality service; so ensuring that they can optimise this time will help to ensure success. A great professional support team will assist in implementing the strategy, as it can facilitate the delivery of a quality service. On the business development front, professionals can also help lawyers to identify new opportunities. Some firms have understood this strategic advantage and have invested in their support professionals well beyond the salary element.

6.   Integration

One word which is always used following the hiring of new talent is 'integration'. Many firms have thought at length about the issues and challenges facing new recruits, and have designed integration programmes in response. In most cases, however, such programmes suffer from three major flaws. First, they are condensed: the vast majority of the information is usually shared in the first week that the new hire joins. Second, they cover only objective rules and procedures, neglecting unwritten rules or key aspects of the firm's culture. Third, where the programme is extended over several months, it is rarely fully implemented as originally intended, because all parties are too busy, do not prioritise it or forget about it all together.

Any new recruit who does not quickly grasp the culture or who thinks they can impose their own culture on the firm will face a rude awakening. Resistance is futile, as ultimately the prevailing culture will win out. Anecdotal data shows that one of the mains reasons why external hires do not work out is cultural misalignment.

The standard approach to integration seems to involve touring the office, reading the firm's rules and procedures, possibly signing an elaborate code of conduct and attending a couple of lunches with various members of the office. The IT manager will stop by to explain briefly how to use the computer system and other devices, and will provide the helpdesk phone number. It also seems that the more senior the new recruit, the quicker the process. The attitude is that the new recruit has joined to sell their time, and enough billable hours have already been invested in the recruitment process, so the priority is to get down to work and start making a return on that investment. What is forgotten is that the recruitment process is effectively a kind of courtship, in which both parties tend to oversell their qualities and potential, and fail to assess objective and/or subjective criteria with rigour. To complicate things further, many head hunters enthusiastically exaggerate the candidate's abilities and the firm, charmed by the promised revenues on offer, feels obliged to promise more than it can deliver.

By structuring the integration process over several months, and past the classic 90 or 100 days, unspoken rules can be clearly iterated over time and answers given to any unfulfilled expectations. The process can be compared to a training session for a newly acquired software program. A lot of information is thrown at the user, of which only a fraction is understood and assimilated. Those functionalities which are not used within a few days are easily forgotten, and suddenly the helpdesk telephone number provided earlier becomes so much more useful. Slowly, over time, one comes to learn the basic applications. Refresher courses are essential.

7. **Selling and cross-selling**

As outlined elsewhere in this book, successful cross-selling requires a culture that supports cross-practice collaboration and talent which has the necessary skillsets to do so.

Adding new talent to the firm without a common interest or potential synergies is unlikely to deliver the benefits of collaborative working. The end result may be a group of talented attorneys who share nothing more than costs and a coffee in the morning. The ultimate goal in creating a firm should be to help each other and chase, share and advise common clients, thus cross-pollinating both skillsets and potential and existing client bases. Cross-selling skills should always be considered when creating or growing a law firm. This might be more challenging for someone who is just starting out on a legal career or who has always worked by him/herself. However, it is nonetheless an essential skill. Aside from the obvious additional value it creates by increasing the flow of work from clients and hence strengthening the firm's client base, it further ties the client more closely to the firm and reduces the risk of defection to the competition. The client will also take comfort from the fact that two partners are clearly involved in protecting each other's clients and trust in each other's abilities to provide a quality service.

8. **Transition management**

A partnership is a living structure in many ways: over the years, new partners are hired or appointed, while others are asked to leave or retire.

Significant investments in terms of effort and money are made in order to attract the best possible talent, and to promote business development activities aimed at protecting or developing a profitable client base. In today's challenging economic climate and increasingly competitive legal market, some firms are further investing in chasing down alumni in the hope that they may send on work to their old firm, or at least say a few good words about it. A much easier way to secure future revenues or the firm's brand is to help partners transition out of the firm and prepare them for the next stage of their journey in life. Some partners who have retired may wish to utilise their knowledge or experience for the benefit of charities; others may still need to work to support their family; other may wish to continue working in a different position; and still others may wish to become non-executive directors. Firms should start investing time in understanding what their partners may wish to do later in their careers and offer advice or external help to prepare them for life after leaving the firm. These partners will only be thankful for the help they have received and will speak highly of the human qualities of their former firm – valuable word-of-mouth praise for the firm.

9. Conclusion

Talent is vital for the successful implementation of any strategy. However, this issue is normally considered only after a strategy has been determined, which can lead to the acquisition of sub-optimal talent and to failures or tensions between partners. Other industries have realised that their main competitive advantage is their talent, its adaptability and its ability to help realise a strategy – law firms need to do likewise.

This chapter remains the same as published in the previous edition.

Managing talent in global law firms

Jay Connolly
Dentons

1. Introduction

In any size of law firm, attracting, leading, developing, retaining and incentivising talent – the only resource – is critical, and never more so than today. While these tasks can be more or less challenging for global compared to smaller law firms, in many cases they offer similar opportunities, albeit amplified by scale, geography, culture and expectations.

This chapter sets out some of these challenges and opportunities, along with tools and strategies that are used in many global firms today. It shares insights into current practice and provides ideas that can be scaled to suit firms of any size.

2. The global landscape

Successfully deploying impactful talent approaches in a global organisation requires an understanding and recognition of the differences in various markets. Approaches that work well in one office may need to be refined to ensure the same positive impact in another location. Equally, it is important to achieve some consistency in talent practices, with a common framework to help ensure alignment, in areas where that is beneficial and appropriate. For example, talent attraction campaigns can be more impactful when they leverage the firmwide messaging and global branding, yet there may be some elements tailored to the specific market.

Operating in multiple locations and across cultures will also highlight the similarities and differences that exist. The opportunity here is to leverage the areas of similarity and be sensitive to, and learn from, the areas of difference. Erin Meyers' book, *The Culture Map*,[1] provides a great insight into how people think, operate and lead across cultures. To be successful working across borders, either within a firm or indeed with clients, building the skills to navigate a more globalised and virtual world requires a greater understanding of cultures. Therefore, any of the talent approaches need to be viewed from different

---

1 Erin Meyer, *The Culture Map: Breaking Through the Invisible Boundaries of Global Business*, PublicAffairs, 2014.

perspectives and considered from the viewpoint on the ground many miles from where you may presently be sitting. The key is a successful talent management approach ensuring the firm achieves the desired business goals, and not an identical template mandated everywhere.

3. Defining 'talent' in a global law firm

Talent management has long existed in large law firms, although the definition and focus that exist today are relatively new phenomena. Large firms in the 1970s and 1980s were significantly different in size and reach, and thus adopted far less sophisticated approaches to talent management. Existing talent at large law firms served as a magnet to attract other talented lawyers, and competition from respected, challenging, career-building employment options, while beginning to grow in wider professional services, were not the same as exist today.

Fast-forward 40 years and the global legal market has developed significantly as a result of technological advances, changing client needs and law firm consolidation. In the last few years, large firms have focused on coming to terms with the evolving new normal in which they operate. This includes:

- a willingness among clients to disaggregate matters (ie, outsourcing);
- a growing expectation of pricing alternatives;
- greater availability of detailed information about law firms and their practices; and
- a changing role for in-house general counsel and the downstream impact on firms.

These market changes have increased the need to build talent and key capabilities within firms, not only to enable them to meet client expectations but also to allow them to lead the way forward.

The changes in the industry have also affected the answer to the question, With reference to whom do you define talent in your firm? There are a number of possible answers:

- Lawyers – in some firms, talent management is focused purely on the lawyers as revenue generators. The legal minds in any firm are necessarily a key part of the talent pool that needs to be nurtured. However, there is recognition today in global firms that meeting client expectations, delivering innovation and reinventing how transactions can be structured depend on multiple roles within the firm.
- Potential partners – within the population of lawyers in any firm, either explicitly or implicitly, there will be some who are seen to be on track for partnership. Many firms now have a competency model in place for lawyer development which can make measurement of this clearer, but it

will not necessarily focus solely on the route to partnership. Non-traditional roles also exist in firms today and, for example, staff associates often fulfil valuable, but non-partnership track roles. Alternative roles and more flexible career path options are an important part of talent retention.

- Partners – within some firms, the primary focus when discussing talent is on the partnership. This is more likely the case in areas of high specialism – and therefore typically lower-leverage environments. It is essential to build the legal skillsets and wider business development capabilities of partners in such firms.
- A firm-recognised sub-group – many firms have implemented talent development programmes targeted at defined sub-groups – for example, selection of senior associates against pre-agreed criteria for access to additional training or coaching. This can be a powerful and key element of a talent management strategy, but cannot be the only approach.
- Everyone – today there is an understanding that everyone in the firm is part of the talent pool. Firms have become more systematic about gathering feedback from key clients on their performance, and such feedback often includes comments on the rapport and relationships with other staff at the firm – for example, the partner's assistant who remembers the client and is proactive when the client calls, the reception desk staff or the conference support team who pay attention to detail and resolve any issues that arise on-site.

When you consider talent management, whom do you think of within your firm? Where are you focusing attention? Identifying talent is important, but the more important question is how to develop the variety of talent that exists in your organisation, and to do so in a truly inclusive manner.

4. Leveraging inclusion and diversity

When considering talent and the focus for firms, it is also essential to consider the diversity across all groups and the whole firm. The expectation of clients, potential talent and people within organisations have changed; firms need a strategic and business focus on diversity and inclusion. Although the topic has received increasing attention in the wider business community in recent years, changes in the legal profession have been limited.

Clients are driving the diversity agenda, taking an interest for a variety of reasons:

- As they drive successful diversity agendas and goals in their own businesses, there is a desire to make an impact on their suppliers.
- GCs have been driving towards more diverse teams in their organisations and expect it from their law firms.

- In a sea of legal suppliers, clients find it difficult to distinguish between the offerings of different firms. Legal ability, finesse and skill are obvious prerequisites; clients have thus been looking beyond these criteria for a number of years and are now doing so in a systematic way.
- The path from senior associate or law firm partner to in-house counsel at a client offers an opportunity for those frustrated with progress in the diversity arena to help drive change by demanding it as a client.

It would be wrong to suggest that it is purely clients that have driven the change in focus in recent years. They have played an important role, but we have also seen change across professional service firms and from individuals within firms. Diversity committees, affinity groups and specific initiatives have moved beyond event and sponsorship planning and are engaging in a more challenging, meaningful debate about structural change.

Bar associations, regulatory bodies and law schools and universities are focused on the need for greater diversity in the profession, and the pressure for firms to play their part continues to grow. Improving diversity and access to the profession needs to be a common goal for all firms. Discussing the topic internally, supporting external initiatives and building a truly inclusive culture within the firm – for example, by reviewing policies, being clear on expectations and recognising biases – are all steps that can easily be taken to achieve these goals.

For global firms discussion is now firmly on inclusion – how to ensure the diverse talent in the firm feels truly included and empowered to perform. Inclusion is the differentiator in firms today, as the ability to manage diverse teams and unlock the greater creativity of thought, input, ideas and experience to develop leading solutions will make the difference.

5.   Attracting talent

Approaches to attracting talent currently take many forms. Entry routes into firms are diversifying, while firms are more accepting of different career paths and are focusing on different markets in order to attract the best talent. The employer proposition and the firm's ability to explain, portray and deliver on its promises are thus becoming ever more important.

Firms are facing increased competition for the best talent at entry level and beyond. Lawyers are increasingly prioritising skills and capability development over loyalty or longevity. Increased client sophistication in procurement of legal expertise is changing the nature of work and resourcing at many firms. These and other factors have put significant pressure on the traditional law firm model, demanding greater productivity and utilisation to maintain or improve profit levels.

The changes within the market and the need to attract talent in a variety of ways have created new entry routes to the legal profession, thereby modifying the career model in many firms. The once-linear route from university or law school to partnership now has many additional pathways.

5.1 Trainee

This was once the sole entry point to most large global firms, offering the prospect of partnership in return for hard work, commitment, dedication and legal excellence. However, for many of the reasons noted above, this is no longer the case. The Law Society's trend reports show that the number of training contracts registered in the United Kingdom between 1 August 2009 and 31 July 2010 fell by a record 16.1%. After a slight increase the following year, the 12 months up to 31 July 2012 saw a 10.5% decrease. This pattern was repeated in the United States, with firms hiring far smaller summer classes.

Although there has been an upswing in recent years, the lower recruitment levels have helped to open up alternative routes into firms via paralegal positions and other legal executive roles, and off-track associate positions.

5.2 Paralegal

While the drive to reduce costs has seen a reduction in training contracts in the United Kingdom, opportunities for paralegals in firms have increased significantly. Paralegal positions have doubled in the last 10 years, whether in more traditional roles within firms or in new centres outside expensive hubs.

Firms are now using this resource option in more diverse ways, whether through career paralegal roles, opportunities with the potential for progression to a training contract or shorter-term paralegal positions.

5.3 Lateral associate

The market for lateral associates is expanding, affording them greater post-qualification opportunities and mobility.

5.4 Staff associate

The staff associate role can take a number of forms: it may represent an off-partnership-track position, provide individual flexibility or be temporary in nature. Easier access to high-quality talent on a short-term basis, coupled with the challenges of meeting client demands and cost constraints, have contributed to eliminating any stigma associated with this resource pool.

5.5 Lateral partner

Once almost non-existent in certain markets, today movement of partners between firms is increasingly the norm. The meaning of 'partnership' has evolved and it is no longer a ticket for life. Over the past two decades, the number of lateral partner moves, tracked by *The American Lawyer* since 2000, has ranged from just above 2,000 to more than 3,000 a year. Integration into the partnership is the biggest and most consistent indicator of satisfaction for lateral partners.[2]

5.6 Implications

It is important to consider all of these different routes into firms, as a targeted approach is essential to attract the best talent. Who are you looking to attract? What approaches are most likely to succeed with this target group? What offerings will be the most attractive for the target audience? Lateral partner recruitment differs greatly from entry-level recruitment, yet even firms that grasp this difference continue to employ ill-suited tactics.

6. Talent development

To compete in a people-oriented business, it is essential for a firm to develop its talent. A talent development offering initially helps to attract staff and also ensures that the needs of highly sought-after clients – which may have been equally hard to attract – can be met.

Global firms are focused on the wider development offering for lawyers and talent throughout the firm. Over recent years we have seen increased efforts in this space as there is growing recognition that the capabilities of their people will make the difference. One example of this is NextTalent, which was launched by Dentons to reinvent talent development, leverage behavioural science and take an innovative approach that is essential in firms today to better respond to client needs. Emotional intelligence is one capability that forms an essential part of NextTalent and also brings a data-driven, future-focused approach, recognising that human and social skills will play an increasing role in the law firm.[3]

Figure 1 shows the weighted importance of the three areas of learning and development: in-role, formal and targeted. While the intersections of these areas are where the most beneficial development happens, the challenge is not to reach point B, but rather to ensure that what is in place intersects to some degree. As you consider any formal or targeted training, ensure that it is timely and there is opportunity to practise new skills through in-role experience.

---

2   Major, Lindsey & Africa, 2020 Lateral Partner Survey. Available at: www.mlaglobal.com/en-gb/knowledge-library/research/2020-lateral-partner-satisfaction-survey.
3   See Thomson Reuters Legal Executive Institute, "Dentons' NextTalent Strategy: A Radical Investment in its Next Gen Talent", July 2019. Available at: www.legalexecutiveinstitute.com/dentons-nexttalent-strategy/.

Figure 1. The three areas of learning and development

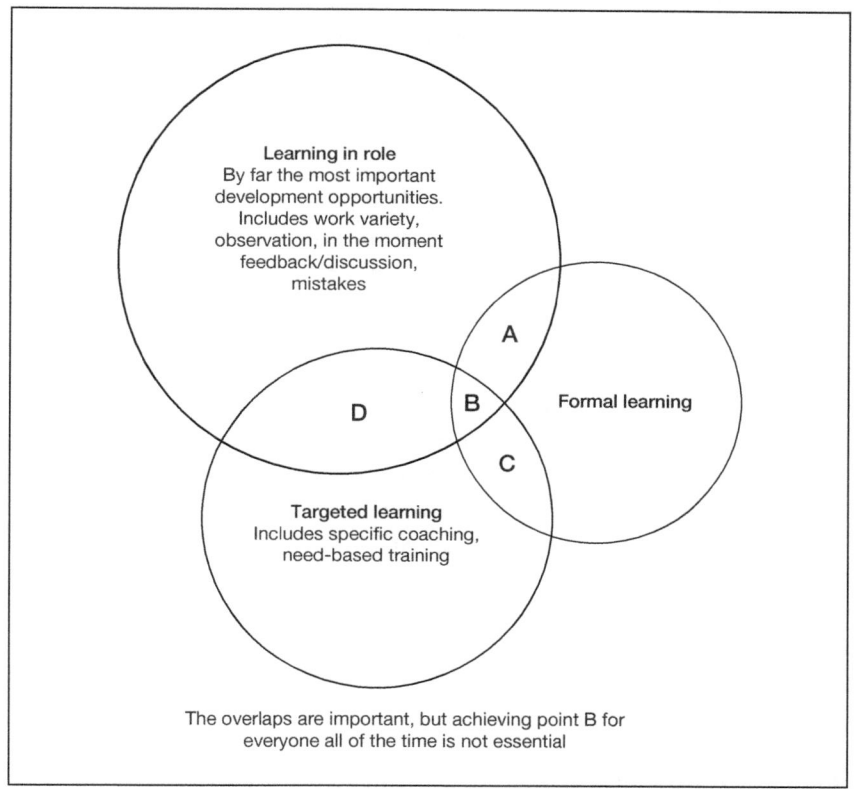

Source: Author.

6.1 Work allocation

Development occurs in a multitude of ways. One of the most effective is proactive work allocation that takes into account the development needs of a particular lawyer. This approach is often the most powerful and timely way to develop talent within a firm. In order to allow for active development over a period of time, elements of a transaction, matter or case must be allocated in a considered manner, not least with a focus on inclusion and diversity. A number of common situations that frequently arise in large global firms – in part due to the nature of the work – must be avoided for this development approach to be effective.

(a) The easy route

Today's firms face time and volume pressures driven by client needs and demands in a faster work environment. It is thus often easier for the partner managing a transaction to delegate elements to an associate who she knows can handle the piece of work and deliver a quality product, with limited review.

Delegating the drafting of a sale–purchase agreement to an associate who has done this before will be easier than explaining the process to, and reviewing the work of, a less-experienced junior associate.

Consider how and why you are allocating work within the team.

(b)   *Financial metrics*

Financial metrics within a firm can inadvertently drive unintended behaviours. Allocating work to an associate for whom the task is new often results in more time recorded than would be the case with someone who has the benefit of previous research and experience. This often results in the recording of a time write-off that can impact on the partner's financial metrics.

Consider whether metrics may be impeding talent development.

(c)   *Lack of visibility of development needs*

In larger firms with multiple partners, the understanding of individual development needs arising from performance review discussions and other interactions is inevitably diluted. Such firms may rely on formally implemented 'practice adviser' or 'career development partner' relationships, rather than the one-partner firm mentor/mentee relationship with an associate. Formal relationships may not be as productive, resulting in the loss of some of the positive development aspects of proactive work allocation.

Consider whether you have clarity about the development needs of all those in your firm.

(d)   *Changing nature of work*

Significant changes in the work undertaken in global firms today create challenges for work allocation. These include the following:

- **Commoditisation of work:** Client pressure and improvements in knowledge management systems and template management have commoditised work once considered to suit junior lawyers. Clients often will not pay for time to be spent on template creation or drafting.
- **Offshoring or outsourcing of low-value work:** A growing trend is for commoditised or lower-value work to be completed in lower-cost locations, either set up by firms themselves (eg, Allen & Overy and Herbert Smith in Northern Ireland, Orrick in West Virginia) or outsourced. The global market for legal process outsourcing is projected to grow at a staggering 18.9% compound annual growth rate over the period 2020–27.
- **A focus on higher-value, challenging matters:** Clients are now more likely to split their legal spend across panel law firms, based upon the level of technical expertise needed, type of work and cost. Large firms may see more specialised, higher-value work.

- **Fewer smaller matters:** Many of the above factors have created a trend towards fewer smaller matters, where associates have historically been able to take the lead and build experience.

Consider opportunities to enable individuals to run elements of a project on their own.

On-the-job, work-based development requires one other critical element: feedback. Within the fast-paced, technology-enhanced workplace of today, finding time to provide constructive feedback and discuss performance is often seen as a barrier. However, providing valuable, developmental feedback is not about finding a free hour to sit down for a discussion; rather, it is about developing a routine to provide this frequently.

Successful talent development requires feedback, recognition and encouragement. Time spent going over feedback in a straightforward fashion can be invaluable. Elements to consider include the following:

- When – be specific about the situation, context and time.
- What – describe what was done or not done.
- Result – articulate the impact, positive or negative.
- Next time – identify what should be repeated or changed.

Consider whether feedback is being delivered in the above manner.

6.2   Rotations

Movement of talent can take a number of forms and, even within a single location, can be a powerful way to develop an individual's skillset early on. This model has been adopted for some time in the training contract for trainees joining large firms in the United Kingdom. In the United States, the approach is more mixed: some firms adopt a rotation system for their first-year associates, in part as an attraction tool for individuals leaving law school who have not yet decided upon, or had enough exposure to, different practice areas.

While it is easier to move trainees and junior associates between practices in a firm, creating flexibility to maximise mobility at other levels can enhance development. This is not to suggest that a white-collar litigator should transfer to capital markets, but rather that proactive sharing and movement of resources between certain practices, or even within areas in large practices, can benefit the firm, as well as the individual.

The next level of resource movement is on an international scale. With changes in the nature of work as noted above, working across borders is commonplace. There is significant benefit in having talented lawyers with an in-depth understanding of other jurisdictions, appreciating local challenges and having connections and relationships in place.

Such experience can be built in a number of ways:

- In the past, global or international firms typically set up two- or three-year secondments in overseas offices. However, the financial impacts of such an approach have come under close scrutiny, particularly as the total cost for a secondee is normally around three times his or her annual salary.
- Transfers from one office to another – on the basis of local employment terms – are increasing as a result of growing trends, such as dual careers, acceptance of greater mobility and the desire to gain experience in the face of fewer secondment opportunities.
- Client secondments provide excellent opportunities for individuals to grow their networks, improve their understanding of clients and develop their skills. Adopting a flexible approach – for example, by considering part-time secondments, shorter placement periods or different approaches to cost management – can help to lower the costs associated with such opportunities.
- Opportunities can also arise for secondments to other firms, on a limited basis. Careful arrangements are needed in such circumstances, and normally an individual should leave his or her home firm for the period of the secondment.

6.3 Formal training

Formal business and legal skills training has an important place in the development of talent in a global firm. Such development needs to focus on the skills and capabilities that will be essential moving forward. The continued impact of technology is changing how work is done, the shape of roles and the capabilities that will be critical for success.

There are many ways to deliver the training; it is not always necessary to use external trainers to run programmes in-house. Firms can consider offering business skill training through a number of mechanisms, as below.

(a) Partners/senior associates

It can be extremely productive when a respected partner or senior associate discusses tools and techniques on various topics – for example, giving presentations or negotiating – and shares specific relevant experiences. This approach has the benefit of being tailored to the firm and audience. It is important that the person delivering the session can share key messages clearly and provide examples, and is recognised for his or her ability in the area under discussion. There is often a misconception that such sessions need a significant amount of time (eg, a half or full day); in fact, they may be short, with additional follow-ups, if required.

(b) *Panel discussions*

Many of the topics that fall under business skills training do not have one right approach or answer. Consider business development as an example: this can vary across clients, practices and sectors, albeit with some common techniques underpinning different approaches. A panel discussion with a number of senior lawyers provides the opportunity to share and discuss multiple approaches and debate a variety of experiences. A well-moderated session, along with participation from those attending, can yield meaningful results. This approach works well for new and existing partners. An adaptation is to invite clients to talk about their experience from the other side; they are often prepared to share a wealth of valuable information.

(c) *E-learning*

The quality and accessibility of e-learning options have greatly increased in recent years. E-learning is cost effective and provides a resource that can be reviewed – for example, ahead of an important presentation. Global firms have implemented e-learning to varying degrees: the spectrum ranges from partnerships with external providers to training on specific topics developed in-house. Any e-learning will be more impactful when it is targeted, relevant and part of a wider programme.

(d) *Bar associations*

These are an excellent resource that can often be forgotten. Proactively using them, and reminding individuals in the firm about what is available and its value, can add to the overall development offering.

(e) *Experiential opportunities*

Formal training opportunities, in whatever format, are a small part of any integrated learning and development offering. Indeed, it is thought that individuals gain the majority of their development through experiential, on-the-job learning – hence the earlier discussion about proactive work allocation. As part of business skills development, it is important to encourage lawyers to maximise opportunities that can be all too easily passed by, including:

- **Networking opportunities:** Client, industry, sector, alumni and bar association events are a selection of opportunities that can arise in any given year. Unless the skills that are desired, discussed and read about are actively used and tested, they will not be developed.
- **Presentations:** Internal opportunities are excellent low-risk scenarios for individuals to build confidence, practise skills and receive feedback. Bar association opportunities, joint continuing legal education presentations and industry groups can all provide stepping stones before making presentations to clients, at seminars or at larger gatherings.

7. Talent retention

Keeping high-quality talent in a firm is more challenging today, for a multitude of reasons. Career development now takes a variety of forms, and it is accepted that these may include moving to another employer – for example, another law firm or client – or changing roles for a period of time, in order to build skillsets and capabilities while gaining exposure to a broader variety of work. Expectations of individuals have also changed, so it is important to place an active focus on the careers of associates. Similarly, the availability of career options and willingness of individuals to change careers are far greater. With the industry facing questions about the future of the law firm model and firms grappling with different approaches and roles, the conveyor belt of advancement is slower and more unpredictable.

Analysis of employee opinions has greatly helped efforts focused on retention. At a minimum, exit surveys provide helpful guidance; today's approach is more robust and analytical in many firms than the short confidential discussion of the past, which used to be the only source of feedback. While such discussions still have value, the ability to capture views from departing individuals against specific criteria that can be analysed and measured over time is extremely valuable to direct and guide retention programmes and further internal discussion.

A number of notable changes have been implemented in recent years, with the intent of addressing the challenges in retention.

7.1 Development partner role

All partners in a law firm are leading people. So, developing that talent and ensuring high performance is a key business goal. One application of this has been to ensure that all in a firm have a partner who is responsible for their individual development. While the design of this role varies, it is broadly intended to capture a partner's responsibilities for managing feedback, supporting development opportunities through work allocation, providing formal training, ensuring high utilisation levels and ensuring that career goals and progression are actively managed. An annual review and formal follow-up during the course of the year also sit within the role scope.

The role does not place sole responsibility for career development in the hands of the appointed partner – there is a continued expectation of proactivity from the individual – but it does ensure that there is a dedicated point of contact for these important elements.

7.2 Career structures

The movement among large firms to define different levels of associate roles has, in large part, been driven by a need to stem attrition rates in the productive mid-levels. Surveys revealed that this attrition was primarily rooted in a feeling that partnership was still a long way off – if achievable at all – and that there was no goal or recognition of progress beyond the 'badge' of being one more year beyond law school or qualification. Prior to becoming associates, high-achieving individuals in the legal industry have specific, achievable goals which fall within shorter time horizons – for example, a three-year degree, one-year legal practice course and two-year traineeship. Upon reaching full associate status, suddenly the time horizon expands to a minimum of eight years – today, typically over 10 years – to potential partnership.

The introduction of associate levels has affected many firms in a number of ways:

- It has created a career path with shorter time horizons, which supports the sense of achievement and progression that is important for high-performing individuals in law firms.
- It enables firms to review the development of associates in a formal manner at certain gateways – for example, between associate and managing associate roles. Often a formal review and/or attendance at a development workshop (typically an off-site event aimed at benchmarking certain skills and providing feedback to the associate) is required ahead of advancement.
- Progression is now based on the individual's development, rather than on the amount of time that has elapsed since graduating from law school or university, as has been the norm historically.
- Expectations concerning the skills required at differing levels within a firm are now clearer. These are often articulated through role descriptions and competency models that describe the skills and behaviours at each level.
- Clients can be confident that firms are taking development of their lawyers seriously and not merely charging higher rates for lawyers who have witnessed the passage of another year.

7.3 Alternative roles

A greater number of alternative roles exist in firms today to help retain talent. These include:

- **Counsel/director roles:** These are typically for specialised, subject-matter experts where a business case for partnership is not feasible or an individual does not wish to pursue promotion.
- **Off-track lawyer roles:** These may involve a different contribution expectation, but demand the same level of quality. Professional support lawyers may also fall under this category.
- **Management roles:** These offer opportunities for talented individuals to step into alternative management roles within a firm, in recognition of the need for professional leadership and management of all aspects of

that firm's operation (eg, leading a knowledge management function, taking responsibility for practice management or managing large projects for a period of time).

7.4 Flexibility

In order to retain the best talent, and as part of diversity efforts, firms have recognised the importance of providing greater working flexibility. Although challenging due to client demands and the nature of the work, this is possible to achieve on both sides.

Policies and procedures around flexible working (eg, reduced hours, part-time, compressed schedules) and agile working have been scrutinised and revisited in recent years, and a change in mindset is reflected in the drive to remove negative connotations from existing terminology (eg, 'balanced hours' instead of 'reduced hours', 'flexible working' instead of 'part-time'). While this has helped to signal a change in attitude, clients are often ahead of law firms in this area and are expecting to see greater commitment to making changes.

Flexibility is also improving the ability of firms themselves to ramp up resource needs for particular pieces of work, without carrying an ongoing cost. Parts of a matter or transaction may be better handled by a flexible, on-tap workforce that is trained and led by a team of lawyers from the firm. This flexible resourcing approach is being developed through improved alumni programmes that enable firms to maintain contact with former employees and so-called 'on-/off-ramp' policies that allow those wishing to leave a firm for lifestyle reasons to remain in contact, have access to training and have their bar dues paid for by the firm.

7.5 Performance management

Today's large international or global law firm is a different place from that which existed 10 years ago. The economic landscape has changed, resulting in greater pressure on firms to address inefficiencies and maintain standing. Clients are more sophisticated in how they go about procuring legal services, whether through the use of request for proposals, procurement teams, e-billing, panels or a stronger focus on rates and who is conducting the work.

In the post-Lehman landscape, the large number of forced partner departures from firms was seen by many as a watershed. The safe haven of partnership ceased to exist, affecting the mindset of many within firms, such as the recently promoted partner, the mid-career service partner or the highly productive senior partner. Partner performance management – often discussed, but never truly implemented in the way that is commonplace in the corporate world – arrived in law firms and is here to stay. This development is generally a positive one and supports the retention of talent in a number of ways:

- Firms have improved their ability to support and guide partners, in order to avoid any damaging or irrevocable effects of underperformance.

- There is greater clarity regarding the division of partnership talent (eg, between revenue producers, service partners, the next generation and transitioning partners).
- It has created a mechanism for managing transitions – whether into different internal roles, through retirement or to clients – which enables firms to create the required space for upcoming partner talent.
- It fosters stronger, more robust partnerships that are better able to adapt to the new normal.

Clarity regarding talent is important at all levels within any firm. Active performance management needs to cover the full spectrum, from high-performing individuals to those who require active exit management from the business. All too often, both ends can be neglected – for different reasons – until it is too late.

For rising stars – whether junior associates, those closing in on potential partnership or partners themselves – discussions need to be held on a regular basis to identify what support, opportunities and further development are needed to maximise potential and ensure retention. Firms that have truly embraced this concept will be undertaking some or all of the following:

- using the performance review process to support the identification and management of talent;
- proactively agreeing actions for identified talent, covering:
  - experience that the individual should gain in a defined time period;
  - introduction to clients or business development opportunities;
  - assignment of a mentor; and
  - training and development opportunities; and
- scheduling regular discussion and follow-up, with summaries recorded.

Even with the changes currently underway, the law firm model is still founded on the premise that talent will leave; not everyone is going to, or indeed can, make partner. Importantly, this provides an excellent opportunity to generate new clients, through those former employees who had a positive experience with their firm and were appropriately handled during their transition to an in-house role. It is essential to provide transition approaches or programmes at more senior levels, in order to maximise this potential opportunity. While recognising that transitions may occur for a variety of reasons, the key elements remain the same and include the following:

- early identification of a successor for client work;
- development of plans to seamlessly handle these client relationships and any ongoing work;
- provision of personalised support to the individual transitioning out of the firm;

- clarity on both sides about the parameters and what is on offer; and
- supporting frequent dialogue throughout the process.

Years of positive feelings about a firm can be undone in exceptionally short periods of time when these basic steps are not followed. The lawyer who becomes a new potential client is unlikely to feel inclined to engage the firm that just ostracised him or her for the last six months, damaged his or her confidence or failed to provide even basic help. Those remaining at the firm also watch transitions keenly.

8. Conclusion

In summary, there is a great deal of change with regard to how large firms manage and develop talent. It is critical that firms respond to the needs of today and anticipate the themes of tomorrow as the critical capabilities are changing. This chapter's discussion of programmes, initiatives and tools at global firms has highlighted a number of areas for consideration by anyone focusing on talent within a law firm:

- What are the market and client demands and direction?
- How does internal talent need to adapt and develop to address these needs?
- What needs to be implemented to support different approaches to attraction, development, retention or performance management of staff?

This chapter has aimed to share insights and spark ideas around what can be undertaken or considered in any firm. Talent needs attention. Your limited time can be most meaningfully utilised by addressing the questions posed in this chapter and implementing appropriate strategies.

New approaches to performance management

Laure Carapezzi
Jean-Baptiste Lebelle
Allen & Overy Paris

1. Introduction

For many years, performance management in law firms was not seen as a strategic priority.

Until recently, the legal industry had a very traditional approach to career management. The only way for lawyers to progress was to improve their skills under the supervision of a more senior lawyer who had also learned from a former mentor. This approach worked well for small law firms where exclusive relationships between partner and associate were the norm, but it became problematic with the development of big law firms. In those structures, where large teams with different expertise have to work together, the need to manage performance became more and more important.

How many times have we heard the claim that if nobody talks about our performance in a law firm, it means that all is well? The traditional path to partnership was relatively unstructured, with associates not experiencing a formal performance management process until, after years of demanding work, they were told either that a partnership was in the pipeline or that they should think about a future outside the firm. Of course, this absence of a feedback culture necessarily led to a huge misalignment between the expectations of associates and those of their firms.

This was obviously a challenge for a sector where developing technical and managerial and business development skills was critically important. Other professional services industries had a significant advantage in terms of performance management, conducting wholesale reassessments of their performance management approach long before the legal sector. However, little by little, law firms have professionalised their support functions, especially, given the critical importance of people to their business success, the HR function. Over the last fifteen years, many large firms have been hiring HR professionals from the consulting sector with a view to incorporating best practice into the profession.

One of the biggest challenges in HR is to retain and engage the workforce, and part of the solution was to set up robust annual appraisal systems. Most law firms set up systems involving the collection of feedback, self-reviews and annual review meetings. However, over the years the process became a nightmare for both partners and associates. The road to hell, as they say, is paved with good intentions.

Frustration was the feeling most associated with annual appraisals. Partners and associates viewed performance management as time-consuming, subjective, discouraging and ultimately unhelpful. In many cases, it did not improve the performance or development of associates. It might even have weakened their performance as they struggled with ratings, worried about their bonuses, and tried to understand feedback. Numerous studies confirmed that the appraisal system had the opposite effect to that for which it was designed.

Historical and economic context has played a large part in the evolution of performance management. The appraisal system can be traced back to the US military's 'merit rating' system, created during World War I, to identify and track poor performers for discharge or transfer. Such a system was particularly efficient during periods of strong economic growth with a booming labour market. The focus was on who to let go, who to keep and who to reward, and the traditional appraisal system – in a context where employees were uniquely responsible for their professional development – of feedback collection and a single annual review meeting at the end of the financial year, was considered sufficient.

However, in the last decade organisations have started to review their priorities in the context of a competitive market for talent, where the focus shifted to the professional development of their employees. Several leading companies, such as front-line technology companies and big consulting firms, as well as Deloitte and General Electric (the long-time role model for traditional appraisal) decided to drop the traditional annual appraisal system after reviewing their performance management approach.

What influenced the change? Beyond the need to better engage and retain talent in an increasingly competitive marketplace, these companies studied the time spent on performance management and found that completing the forms, holding the meetings and creating the ratings consumed a huge amount of resources (close to two million hours a year in the case of Deloitte), and eye-watering sums of money. Consulting firms also discovered that leaders used those hours to discuss the outcomes of the process behind closed doors – effectively, they talked amongst themselves instead of having honest and constructive discussions with their people.

It was clear that such a huge investment of time and money could be more productively focused on people performance and career development.

With growing numbers in the legal industry conscious that the traditional cycle of annual appraisals was a waste of time and energy, particularly in a business where time is so difficult to find, a new approach was required. The more forward-looking law firms led the way and now, with the benefit of hindsight, others can understand what works best for everyone – and what are the challenges.

A new approach to performance management will see a change from an inefficient, cumbersome and time-consuming process to one with a competitive edge that will improve not only retention and engagement but also the overall performance of a firm. In the following pages we focus on the associate population; however, many of the insights are equally appropriate for partners.

2. Sustainable performance management

2.1 A culture of feedback

During a presentation we organised with successful people from various backgrounds, one speech about feedback changed the minds of an audience of lawyers. The goal of the presentation was to encourage the audience to open their horizons.

We welcomed a female fighter pilot who had led the French aerobatic flight display team. While she explained the importance of teamwork and mutual trust to success in such a dangerous activity, her speech focused on the importance of having a true culture of feedback. After each flight, she would organise a debriefing with her team in order to give and receive feedback on the display. That feedback, she said, was extremely important to ensure that every small, imperfect detail could be discussed and improved next time.

It was important to raise any issues immediately and not to postpone the discussion. Everyone came to treat the debriefing as routine, and it became a powerful tool in addressing any issues. She underlined that she needed to be sure her team was able to debrief on all the topics that might arise, so that everyone would be 100% focused on what they had to do on the next flight. This was very important in a job where every little mistake could have lethal consequences. It was another example of how the military was leading the way in performance management.

The pilot's testimony was a revelation to a number of the lawyers present. All expressed the view that it was equally important in their job to be able to give and receive feedback, but it became obvious to them that waiting for months for an annual review meeting to discuss their performance on a specific matter was the wrong approach. A fighter pilot was giving management lessons to lawyers, but at the end of the day everyone was convinced that it was the right thing to do – or at least worth a try.

By developing a culture of ongoing feedback, you change the paradigm: performance management is no longer just about holding people accountable for past behaviour, but also about improving performance and developing talent for the future.

2.2 Adopting best practice from consulting firms

Assessing performance is challenging for consultants as they work on complex, long-running and cross-disciplinary projects. A one-off exercise at the end of the year hardly reflects the realities of the business. Performance requires to be evaluated at least at the end of every project, and at regular intervals during long-running projects.

If conversations take place when milestones are reached as well as when projects are finished, people will be able to solve problems in real time while also developing skills for the next stage of their career.

This applies equally to law firms, where teams are working hard on complex and high-level matters. Associates need feedback on their performance on a regular basis – not just when the matter is finished but at different stages of progress in a long-running project. The new appraisal system should follow the natural work cycle of law firms. In this way, associates are challenged throughout the year and develop their careers and professional competencies faster and more effectively.

Table 1. The new approach to performance management

Old/classical elements	New/ideal elements
Annual appraisal meeting	Ongoing feedback and regular discussions
Bureaucratic paperwork	Easy to use application, agile and mobile
Focus on past behaviour	Focus on future improvement and development
Goals set once a year, with top-down approach	Flexible goal-setting in line with the team's objectives
Mechanical remuneration system based on chargeable hours	Remuneration based on different indicators that capture the whole performance
Process managed by HR	Process owned by people with the support of HR

The key point is that annual reviews should be replaced by regular conversations – future-oriented check-ins providing guidance about what someone needs to improve on or do differently to get them to the next level. An important switch in terms of culture is that associates must take ownership of their careers and be proactive in seeking feedback, if necessary organising check-ins themselves. This is a real cultural change in a sector where lawyers are used from their first internship to being heavily supported on all the time-consuming aspects that could divert them from their chargeable hours; but it allows associates to take better ownership of their development, to stay motivated and to perform to a high level throughout the year.

That said, if we can't get partners to have good conversations with their associates once a year, how can we expect them to do so more frequently?

(a) Convince, train and motivate

The biggest challenge is to convince, train and motivate managers and partners to accept this new approach – constant and consistent communication by partners is critical. Change should be driven from the top and it's illusory to expect associates to follow a process that is not embraced by the leadership.

Partners generally find it difficult to discuss performance with associates, give feedback on the job done and, in particular, talk about remuneration and career plans. Paradoxically, while partners are notoriously deficient in this area, associates have high expectations about more regular feedback and better career conversations.

Partners must therefore be trained to talk more about personal development and career paths to the associates in their teams. The conversations need to be held by the partners, not by HR, but HR has a responsibility to train partners and to provide clear and concise guidance on how to give feedback and manage performance in a way that drives business results. This requires an appreciation of why feedback matters and what makes it effective. Guidance should include the following:

- Focus on behaviours and not personal characteristics; focus on what the other person can control.
- Include specific examples.
- Provide feedback as soon as possible and on a regular basis.
- Ensure feedback is accurate, fair, honest and straightforward.
- Seek to provide more praise than criticism; focus on strengths rather than weaknesses.

(b) Assess the process and its evolution annually

There is no end to building a new approach to performance management. It is work in progress that management and HR teams must continually keep under review. Taking stock of what has worked and what has not – and on what needs improvement – is critical. A process that does not evolve and is not questioned based on experience is doomed to failure.

The opinions of evaluators and assessors must be gathered, and the obstacles that prevent some people from making full use of the tools or adhering to the culture of continuous feedback identified, population by population, so that appropriate targeted developmental actions can be taken.

Figure 1. Performance management implementation cycle

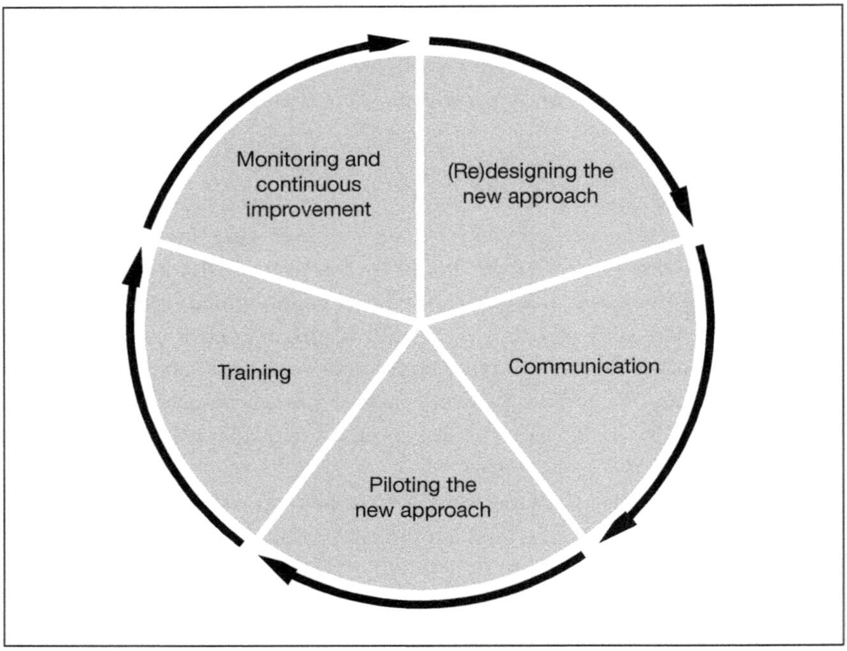

Source: Authors.

(c)   *Assemble the data*

Chargeable hours: Considering a new approach to performance management necessarily involves an analysis of the data available, and the most relevant source of data, easily accessible and part of the DNA of every law firm (with some minor variations as to definition), is chargeable hours. In many cases it is still the only form of data used to measure a lawyer's performance, and while the practice of charging clients by the hour has been challenged in recent years, it remains the most widely used billing method across the sector.

Billable hours is potentially the best and worst index available, depending on your perspective. The best, because it is completely objective, directly linked to economic performance, where figures don't lie (often in a team it is the most talented and efficient lawyers who are the busiest and naturally they capture a larger share of the work available thanks to their professional quality and the trust they have earned from their partners); the worst, because it can contribute to inefficient and unethical behaviour – billable hours may penalise the most talented and expeditious of lawyers, and the data is not always accurate because most lawyers put down what they think their time spent was or what it should have been, rather than what it actually was. For these reasons, some firms have decided to get rid of this indicator completely; however, the few experiments carried out by major international firms have not yet been generalised and the only environments where the change is relevant are those that have adopted alternative methods of fee payment combined with other pricing models.

For the vast majority of firms that continue to base their business model on fees charged by the hour, it is illusory think that they can do without this metric altogether.

Other contributions: Billable hours, however ubiquitous, is just one of the metrics available to measure performance. It is important to have a fair appreciation of the other contributions a lawyer is expected to make, and clear data on which to base the appropriate reward.

Imagine how frustrating it is for associates who have worked on more than client matters – perhaps given time to the recruitment of trainees – to find that at the end of the day their bonus is only linked to their level of chargeable hours!

It is, of course, the same for partners and if your performance management process does not take into account such contributions as people management, training and development, marketing and business development and *pro bono* work, then these areas will be considered unimportant right across the firm.

A new approach to performance management must in one way or another have the ability to capture and reward those contributions. There are different ways to achieve this, depending on the specific behaviour you want to reward. It is important to ask first what behaviours need to be taken into account in the assessment of performance. Once a list has been established (without going into too much detail), try to find the best metrics for measuring performance in that behaviour. Establishing the appropriate metrics is a first step in objectively discussing performance, although it is important to be able to take into account external factors that may have influenced the results.

Contributions in the following areas should be taken into account:
- financials (actions that contribute to profitability);
- clients (actions that contribute to gaining or retaining clients);
- people (actions that contribute to attracting, recruiting, developing and retaining people); and
- firm (actions that contribute to the firm's reputation, internally and externally).

(d) ***Use of software to deliver data and insights***

Let's be clear: performance management should not be an IT process, nor an app that has to be used at all times by everyone. Performance management is about a new way to give feedback, focusing on development and retention of people. Software is a tool that can facilitate your performance management process; it is never the process itself. If it were, people would focus on the app and performance management would be a box-ticking process at risk, eventually, of abandonment.

On the other hand, it is extremely important to have good software to support performance management. The software must meet the specific needs of the legal sector, one of the most important being the ability to integrate different assessors from various practices or offices. In large firms, the evaluation of an associate is rarely in the hands of a single partner. The system must be able to take into account a multitude of interlocutors.

A user-friendly interface and integration with the data used to evaluate performance are also crucial. As discussed above, the right sources of data are important to capturing an associate's performance and to complementing the feedback received along the way. In order for the partner to have a global view, it is essential that these different forms of data (chargeable hours, other contributions, *pro bono*) can be identified in a single overview. Similarly, relevant information on particular individuals can be included so that a complete picture is available.

Partners already have many different IT elements to juggle on a daily basis – timesheets, conflicts of interest checks, billing, CRM and many others. It is therefore important to ensure that the IT tool used in performance management is not seen as a constraint but as a source of additional help. The important thing is adherence to the new approach and the feedback culture – not the use of an IT solution.

3. Other performance levers

Performance management is about much more than just appraisal, although in the minds of many it is considered to be the same thing. It should be seen as something much wider and more efficient.

Performance management is a varied collection of actions designed to develop people and, by extension, the firm's performance. It includes levers that should be used in a tailor-made effort to maximise individual performance. For each individual, it is important to find the appropriate levers and the right support that will allow them to maximise their potential and progress in their career. A feedback culture and regular discussions allow precisely that.

In short, the purpose of performance management is to align individual efforts to achieve organisational goals.

3.1 Coaching

With a fresh approach to performance management, where associates take ownership of their careers, external coaching is a must-have and an excellent way to develop lawyers' skills and proactivity as part of their career plan.

The law firm culture is decisive in making engaged leaders. A strong management coaching programme is necessary at every step of a lawyer's career, first in learning to manage interns and personal assistants, then in managing a small team of junior lawyers. An effective way to develop lawyers as good managers is to create accountability for the management of others.

Lawyers should be assessed at every stage of their careers on their capacity to take more advanced management roles, and should be given upward feedback on their management ability – all linked to discussions around remuneration.

3.2 Mentoring and reverse mentoring

Big law firms have had in place mentoring and reverse mentoring programmes for several years now. Research on the power of mentorship is pretty clear: people with mentors perform better and advance faster in their careers. In addition, mentoring programmes benefit the mentors.

If you ask partners and HR how they have managed their associates' growth and careers, they will inevitably say that mentoring has been an important tool. However, the image of a wise old sage teaching a junior employee how to be successful in his or her career is out of date.

In the new approach to performance management, mentoring should reflect the need for an agile way of thinking. Rigid mentoring programmes with no link to the law firm's culture make no sense and are not efficient.

However, while the concept of mentoring has changed, the need for career counselling is greater than ever. Career discussions are usually carried out by one partner of the team, but it is important to emphasise that they stand as part of a complementary approach to a mentoring culture consisting of a robust but flexible pool of mentors.

Rather than have a single assigned mentor, juniors should be encouraged to be part of a wider mentoring culture within the firm. Such a mentoring constellation helps to promote a culture where all members of the organisation seek opportunities within the framework of daily interactions to develop or grow junior colleagues and peers. It leads to better retention, more loyalty and commitment among associates, stronger succession planning and a better way of managing performance.

Reverse mentoring programmes have also been widely introduced in large firms. In a reverse mentoring relationship it is the less experienced person who takes the position of mentor and helps his or her more experienced colleague.

The main benefits of reverse mentoring are as follows:

- It makes for increased retention of junior talent. Reverse mentoring programmes provide junior associates with the transparency and recognition that they're seeking from management.
- It drives cultural change.
- It promotes diversity. Some law and consulting firms have piloted reverse mentoring programmes in order to improve leadership's understanding of minority issues, including those affecting their LGBT+ and ethnic minority workforces.

3.3 Diversity and inclusion

One of the benefits of the new approach to performance management is that it embraces diversity and creates an inclusive environment. Diversity and inclusion must be considered at every stage in the development of a performance management programme.

When assessing performance, the goals set and the contributions expected must be expressed clearly and objectively. It is important to ensure that assessment is based on objective criteria and is not affected by factors not linked to performance, such as gender or ethnicity. Ongoing and frequent feedback prevents biased reviews and provides the opportunity to gain feedback from a multiplicity of reviewers.

In addition, a diversity and inclusion culture must be linked to accountability. The new performance management approach must set diversity and inclusion goals at each step of a lawyer's career within the firm. Such an approach must be actively supported by partners and management, who must be beyond reproach in this respect. It is essential to ensure that a partner is assessed on, and accountable for, the diversity of his or her team and that the promotion process within the team is fair. Goals linked to diversity must also be set for senior associates by ensuring that they get involved in D&I events and training and that they are role models for the more junior associates.

Strong mentoring and reverse mentoring programmes also play a fundamental role in promoting a better understanding of the challenges faced by minorities. With the new approach to performance management, associates are invited to take control of their careers. However, they must be supported in this approach, and this applies especially to minorities, who are less likely to feel at ease or able to talk, for example, about remuneration or promotion. To this end it is essential to offer appropriate coaching and training in parallel.

The best way to ensure that your new approach to performance management is fair and inclusive is to build a clear, objective and formalised career and promotion process.

4. Reinforcing the impact of performance management

4.1 Career development

One of the obvious objectives of a new approach to performance management is to develop your associates, maximise their talents and above all prepare them for the future. And having a career plan with formal milestones is clearly something that helps people project themselves into the future and set achievable goals in the short term.

The idea of having a different status after a formalised promotion process is now quite common in law firms. The benefits are numerous, both internally and externally. If we start from the principle that to become a successful partner it is necessary to master three fundamentals of the profession – legal expertise, management (of teams, files, financial performance) and business development/ client relationships – then it is easy to articulate a career path as shown in Figure 2.

Figure 2. The career path to partner

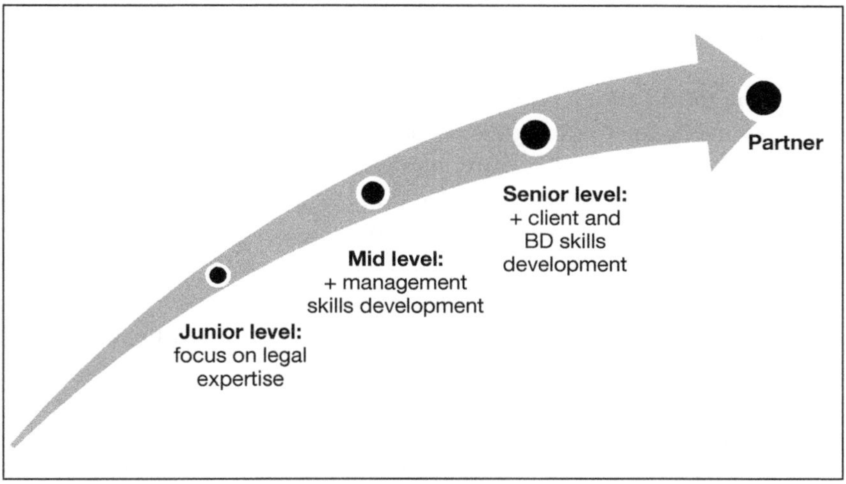

Source: Authors.

Given the rapidity of careers in law firms, these three steps may be more than sufficient before joining the partnership. Communicating clearly about these steps and what is expected at each level gives even more meaning to the performance management process and in particular to the setting of individual objectives.

Moreover, these milestones are a very powerful tool for managing the pyramid and the expectations of the associate population. Not everyone will master them all, but through formal steps you can engage in constructive discussion with associates and enable them to better understand and take ownership of their career plans.

4.2 The promotion process

The promotion process should not be taken lightly. It must be objective, independent, robust and in line with the firm's values. It is also necessary to find the right balance between input from the performance management process (which can be used to identify the potential candidates) and a selection method that involves nomination papers and formal interviews. The more selective the process is, the more rewarding it is for the associate and the greater the contribution to a culture of excellence and a sense of belonging.

Promotion criteria must be applied to all candidates, irrespective of their educational background, their diversity, the team they are a part of or the input of the partner who supports them. This is obviously the only way to ensure that diversity of profile (if it exists at the time of hiring) is maintained at all levels of seniority.

Beyond the professional aspects, the promotion process is a key element in ensuring that the firm's values are respected. If behaviour and adherence to the values/code of conduct of the firm are not important elements in the promotion decision, or even prerequisites, they will be considered as nothing more than empty rhetoric.

4.3 The role of the sponsor

Formalised career progression necessarily implies that the candidate has a sponsor. Having a sponsor is a proven stepping stone to success and is critical for career development. Associates with sponsors, as opposed to those without, are more likely to be satisfied with their rate of progression. A sponsor should be someone who truly believes in his or her associate's potential and is willing to take a bet on him or her, as well as someone who takes primary responsibility for actively supporting the lawyer's career, creating client opportunities, giving honest/critical feedback on skills gaps and driving success through key transitions like promotions and changes in personal circumstances.

From a people perspective, it is at these moments that the role of a partner is most critical to the development of his/her associates, with a potentially huge positive impact on loyalty and performance.

For a successful outcome, the partner must fully understand the role of sponsor. The sponsor must understand the significant impact he or she will have on the career progression of his or her sponsee. For this reason, the sponsor must be trained to understand exactly what is expected of him or her, doing everything possible to help the sponsee to advance, to maximise his or her full potential, and to remain and succeed within the firm. The associate, in turn, will better understand where he or she needs to improve in order to progress, and will be successful more quickly where such support is provided.

4.4   Transparent remuneration policy

Partners are famously reticent about money, and avoid remuneration discussions with their teams at any cost. They get round this by delegating those discussions to HR.

But it is essential to put in place a transparent remuneration policy, with clear rules and a direct link to performance, in order to avoid problematic, time-consuming and often frustrating discussions.

Numerous studies have shown that keeping salaries secret is associated with diminished employee performance. When employees know where they stand and how to advance to the next level, they will be more likely to improve their performance. A compensation grid must be clearly set out in order to avoid any discrimination between associates on the same grade, and to prevent conflict between them.

However, if the remuneration policy is too transparent there is a risk that individuals will focus on comparing pay rather than elevating performance. The best solution, therefore, is to give maximum information to associates regarding fee earner salaries and bonus schemes, without disclosing detailed figures for individuals.

Bonus schemes must be strongly founded. Bonuses are often used as deferred salary to flatten demands for salary increases and so do not correspond to well established performance objectives. Schemes must be transparent for all associates – albeit total transparency must be mitigated, as a bonus is by definition discretionary – and in the new approach to performance management associates must know what is expected of them and what they can receive if they achieve the goals set.

4.5   The role of HR

HR has a role to play in coaching partners to be at ease with the remuneration policy in place by providing them with the knowledge and arguments with which to explain and defend it to their teams.

Remuneration policies should be assessed annually as to their coherence across the firm and across the market. A 'reward commission' drawn from partners, HR and finance is an effective mechanism for assessing the fairness and objectivity of every decision made, in terms of both coherence across the firm and the gender pay gap.

Also best HR practice is an annual benchmark exercise among other firms in the market to establish, before retention problems arise, whether the remuneration policy remains competitive and up to date.

4.6   Other types of reward

Incentives are not just financial – especially in big law firms, where remuneration schemes may not differ substantially from one to another.

To retain the best talent, law firms must rethink their incentive policies and develop strong professional development programmes. To place greater emphasis on non-monetary rewards is to reinforce intrinsic motivation and loyalty to the firm, and the new approach to performance management should be aligned with incentives for associates' development opportunities like client and international secondments.

Client secondments are a great opportunity for associates. They become better acquainted with the sectors in which their clients operate, they develop their understanding of how clients work and what they expect from law firms, and they acquire a more business-oriented view of legal matters.

International secondments are equally valuable for rewarding talented associates. Associates are generally keen to spend time in countries in which they have a personal interest, and secondments are a unique opportunity to develop their networking skills at the same time.

There are many other ways to reward talented associates: special assignments, attending special events, high recognition in the firm and greater exposure to clients. These should be in line with the expectations of associates and their personal objectives.

5.   Conclusion

For too long, engagement, people development and wellness have been viewed as the responsibility of the HR function and not an integral part of law firm strategy. However, it is increasingly clear that people engagement has a strong impact on productivity, innovation, efficiency and, at the end of the day, the success of the firm.

It is time to adopt a new culture in the management of people performance in law firms, and to take the opportunity it affords to address the many future challenges in the legal sector, reinforce engagement and create a strong culture of excellence. A new approach to performance management that keeps associate and partner development firmly on the agenda and avoids wasted time and energy will be a game changer, both for the firm and its workforce.

A strong investment from top management and HR teams is required, in terms of both training and adherence to the task at hand, but the new approach represents an exciting and powerful way to bring to life and reinforce the firm's values, behaviours and culture and ultimately to define a new working relationship based on trust, transparency, proximity and efficiency.

Partner selection and promotion in large law firms

Tony King
AGK PSF Training Ltd

1. Introduction

Appointing partners is arguably the most important HR decision that any firm can make.

In the not too distant past, the promotion process was shrouded in mystery, often with the partner candidates not being aware they were in the process until they were told they had been promoted. There are even stories of individuals being appointed to the partnership under 'Any other business' at partners' meetings.

Over time, things have changed and now there is far greater transparency about the promotion process in firms, large and small.

This chapter looks at best practice in terms of both preparing associates for promotion to partner and the promotion process itself, including:

- what firms typically look for in future partners;
- how best to prepare associates to make the transition into the partnership;
- alternative career paths for associates who do not become partners;
- the structure of the promotion process; and
- the typical content of new partner orientation programmes.

Before looking at these issues in more detail, some caveats.

First, the legal structures through which law firms of all sizes operate (partnership, LLP, company etc) mean that there are a range of titles used for the business owners. In some firms it is 'partner'; in others, 'shareholder' or 'director'. For the sake of simplicity, the term 'partner' is used to cover all of these variants in this chapter. Furthermore, 'firm' is used to cover the business entity whatever its legal structure, and 'entering the partnership' denotes the promotion process – again, whatever the nature of the ownership the promoted associate is acquiring.

Secondly, many firms have different levels of partner for sound business reasons, each level carrying with it different entitlements and obligations as regards voting, profit share and the like. The titles given to those levels are many and varied, reflecting the status of the individuals in each level – equity partner, non-equity partner, salaried partner, contract partner and so on. The status and title of each level will often reflect the financial contribution to the firm made by the individuals within it.

This chapter largely ignores the differences between the levels and the transition from one to the next, instead focusing on the transition from associate to (junior) partner.

Thirdly, the size of law firms around the world varies considerably, from one or two partners up to hundreds, or even thousands. Clearly, the promotion processes in firms of such widely differing size will vary. A firm with one or two partners, where the identity of the partner candidate is obvious, does not need the same process as one with hundreds of partners, most of whom will know only a few of the candidates put forward at any given time. Therefore, this chapter focuses on the promotion of partners in larger firms.

2.   What do firms look for in future partners?

The nature of the leverage and profit-sharing structures operated by large firms means there will always be limited space for new partners. Therefore, firms have clear criteria for deciding which of their senior associates and counsel will join the partnership.

In essence, all firms will look for much the same things in future partners. They will want to appoint associates who have shown that they are excellent lawyers in their particular field; who have the ability to bring in business; and who will be able to contribute to the management of the firm (or their part of it at any rate) in the short and medium term as well as contributing to the long-term success of the organisation.

What qualifies as 'excellent' will depend on the lawyer's particular area of practice and the skills they need to display to be at the top of their game.

They clearly need to be knowledgeable about the law and practice in their field, but their skills need to go beyond that. They need to be:

- legal analysts;
- problem-solvers;
- drafters;
- negotiators;
- communicators;
- interviewers;
- project managers; and
- people managers.

The list can go on.

Accepting that all would-be partners need a high base level of knowledge and skills, the balance within this range of skills will depend on the nature of the associate's practice and the expectations of the firm as regards the associate's particular contribution.

Some examples of the balance required:

- A tax lawyer will need to be an excellent analyst of the legislation and relevant case law, and have the ability to capture complex issues in both writing and orally.
- An associate specialising in commercial contracts (for example, financing deals, contracts or M&A transactions) will need excellent negotiation and drafting skills along with much else.
- A litigator will need strong tactical and advocacy skills, again among many other skills.

Within large teams in the same practice area, associates may well bring a range of complementary skills to the team. The strengths of one associate may mesh with the strengths of another so that the sum of the whole is greater than the parts.

While this complementarity is a fact of professional life, it can complicate promotion decisions. The firm needs to decide which of the mix of legal skills puts one associate in a better position for promotion to partner than another.

The circumstances of a particular firm or practice area may mean that an associate who has powerful legal analytical skills, enabling them to see ways of using complex and complementary areas of law for the benefit of their clients, is preferred for promotion over a colleague who, though an excellent lawyer, has greater skills as a legal project manager; whereas a firm with a different practice or different strategic objectives may favour the project manager.

The point here is that the decision on promotion to partner is a very subjective one, as it depends on the particular skills of the individual, the current needs of the firm and the longer-term objectives of both the firm and the associate. While important, legal skills are not the only factors in deciding who will be given the badge of partner – associates need to show they have the managerial skills to contribute to the delivery of the firm's objectives.

In their lists of competencies, firms describe managerial skills in a variety of ways – indeed, volumes could be filled with law firms' lists of competencies and the underpinning descriptors.

That said, most if not all of the competency lists cover common areas (however described) including, in particular, the ability to manage in these areas:

- Business: Managing the firm's business will involve making sure that everything done in all parts of the firm aligns with the firm's vision, mission and strategy. And of course the firm needs to be managed profitably and efficiently.
- Clients: Managing clients covers everything from identifying for whom the firm wants to work, to winning the work from that client base and doing the work for the clients efficiently and to the right quality level, to maintaining relationships with the client base between mandates.

- People: Managing the firm's people covers the range of HR issues from initial manpower planning, recruitment, team & firm leadership and management to development, promotion and discipline.
- Ethical issues: Managing the firm's ethical issues covers not only being on top of all of the relevant regulatory requirements but also addressing the issues in an ethical way. (The fact that issues of risk and compliance may be overseen in many firms by a dedicated team does not alter the fact that partners and indeed associates need to have these skills under their belts.)

It is, of course, somewhat artificial to separate legal from managerial skills as they will merge in the course of any lawyer's practice. For example, an associate who is running a commercial transaction will use their legal skills to find the appropriate legal solution to the client's issues. They will also maintain the client relationship by communicating regularly, and ensure the work is done profitably for the firm by managing (as appropriate) the work of the deal team.

3.   **Preparing associates for entering the partner track**
In the (now fairly distant) past, there was almost an assumption among many young associates that if they worked hard and stayed with the firm they would become partners in due course. All that has changed as the economics of law firms have changed.

Taking into account the likely turnover of associates in the course of a typical associate career (if such a thing exists), the likelihood of any one associate making it to partner in larger firms could be quite low in percentage terms (even as low as single figures in some cases).

Associates tend to be realistic and they recognise that, statistically at least, their personal chances of making it to partner will be slim even if many hope they will be among the chosen few. To keep that hope alive, associates need to understand what factors the firm will take into account when choosing partners so they can ensure they develop the right knowledge and skills over the course of their careers. Firms are well aware of this, hence much greater transparency as to both the expectations of future partners and the process by which they are chosen.

With this in mind, firms will align the competencies for all levels of associate with their criteria for choosing partners, and will publicise that alignment. This typically means that the headline titles of the firm's competencies for associates will be the same as the list of competencies for partners. The latter will form the criteria which partner candidates must meet when they are seeking promotion.

However, this does not mean associates at every level must show partner-level skills throughout their careers. The competencies will be progressive, so that those for each level of associate will reflect the expectations of the firm for that particular level.

To illustrate this briefly, the firm might decide that its list of competencies should include client management and communication skills. While these two headings will apply to all of the lawyers working in the firm, both partners and associates, the underpinning indicators/descriptions of what the firm expects of its lawyers in each level will be different. Without replicating what can sometimes be quite lengthy lists of indicators, in essence client management for a partner might cover managing client relationships at a strategic level, while for a junior associate it might mean keeping the clients informed as necessary of progress with their matters. Similarly, communication skills for partners may mean having the ability to explain complex issues clearly and persuasively, selling the firm's expertise effectively and being a compelling speaker outside the firm. In contrast, a junior associate might be expected to write clear letters, emails and documents as well as to explain their research to their seniors.

It is not the purpose of this chapter to go into detail on the career paths of associates. However, it is common practice for firms to have in place a clear career and developmental path that associates follow.

The length of the associate career path will vary from firm to firm but in the larger firms it is typically between eight and 12 years. Given the length of that path, many firms include career milestones (in addition to the appraisal or review process) which give both the firm and the associates clear indications of how well or otherwise the associates are progressing.

While this may not universally be the case, most firms have one or two of these milestones in the career path of associates between qualification and promotion to partner. The titles vary but the categories of associates are typically associate, senior associate and, possibly, managing associate.

3.1 Promotion criteria

Whatever titles may be given to the categories, associates need developmental support, not only to ensure that they are delivering against the criteria for their current level but also to prepare them for the transition to the next (which for some will ultimately be partnership).

Firms have for many years had extensive schedules of training programmes which develop both the legal expertise and managerial skills of associates in line with the firm's competency structure. These training programmes are supplemented by the ongoing supervision, mentoring and coaching support associates receive from senior members of the firm, supported by the appraisal or review process.

Picking up the point about supervision, mentoring and coaching, whatever knowledge an individual lawyer will acquire through their academic studies or on-the-job research, that knowledge will be refined and enhanced by the support they receive from their seniors. An inexperienced lawyer will benefit from close supervision and guidance from seniors in the early stages of their career. As the individual gains experience and confidence, the guidance will become less close, moving from close management of the work product (supervision) to guidance based on experience (mentoring) and eventually to drawing out solutions to the issues (coaching).

The process for promotion from one level to the next varies. In some firms, it is the appraisal or review process outcome alone that determines whether or not an individual associate is ready to move forward to the next level. In other firms, there is some form of additional assessment process, though usually only for those moving into the highest level of associate.

Where a 'pass' in this additional assessment process is a prerequisite for progression, what does the process look like? The firms which have introduced such a process have typically also included a formal assessment element in their partner selection process. The two events are aligned in terms of structure and content (albeit inevitably the bar for the associate promotion process is lower than that for partner candidates). The logic for this is that the associates in the most senior level are the pool from which partner candidates will be chosen. Therefore, the process ensures these senior associates have a suitably high level of skills to make them, potentially at least, credible future partner candidates.

The headline promotion criteria will cover the legal, business and managerial skills the associates need to display.

Obviously, legal expertise is vitally important and that aspect of the assessment is typically overseen by those in the associate's area of practice. They will naturally have views on the nature of the business and managerial skills a would-be partner from their area needs to develop and possess – and they may be involved in overseeing that element – but as the business and managerial skills needed for the firm's partners are universal across the firm, assessment in that area is often run on a firm-wide, rather than a practice area-specific, basis.

The process might be pure assessment, and the outcome simply pass or fail, in which case an associate who fails may be allowed to try again at some later point, depending on the firm; but taking a simple pass/fail approach means the firm misses the opportunity to support the future development of its most senior associates. Given that, these events are normally a mixture of scenario-based assessment and training input, with some form of development action plan as the outcome.

Without getting into excessive detail, the event might be structured as follows:

- an introduction explaining the purpose of the event and its position in the associate's progression through the career path;
- a series of exercises aligned to the firm's key criteria for promotion to partner, including

- a strategic or financial issue;
- a client management issue;
- a people management issue; and
- an ethical issue,

  with each exercise using a range of formats – group work, written work or one-to-one discussions – and feedback provided at the end of each exercise on the individual associate's performance; and

- training input on the broad topics covered in the exercises.

At the end of the event, there will be an individual discussion with each associate by one of the assessors, at which the associate's overall performance is discussed and a development action plan agreed, focusing on capitalising on the associate's strengths and addressing any areas for development. This action plan will be sent to the associate's supervising partner who will then be able to support the associate in implementing the agreed actions both on the job and through the firm's appraisal or review process.

This kind of event does not need to be used only as a 'test' for promotion to the most senior level of associate. Firms that rely on the outcome of the appraisal or review process to decide who should be promoted can use the event as a developmental tool once the associate has been promoted. It is one way to give the most senior associates a clear insight into how their range of skills compare with what is expected of future partners – at a point in their careers when they have time to address any development needs or capitalise on any strengths.

Finally, whatever purpose such events serve – pass/fail or developmental – they will have one of four predictable results:

- a talented and highly regarded associate receives confirmation that they are, broadly speaking, on track to partnership in terms of their skills;
- a talented associate unsure of their ability to become a partner is given positive feedback which motivates them to pursue partnership;
- an associate with limited prospects of making it to partner can be given greater insight into their shortcomings, so helping with their career-related decision making; or
- an associate (whether talented or not) may decide partnership is not for them once they fully understand what is expected of partners.

Taking all this into account, these events can have a very positive impact as tools for motivation and to assist with manpower planning. However – and obviously – the reverse can apply if the firm is not very clear on both the purpose of the assessment event and the likely consequences of it.

As the firm's appraisal or review process will look at the same skills that are reviewed on these events, the messages the associates receive on the event should not be radically different from those they have received through their appraisals or reviews.

Furthermore, if the assessment event is determinative of whether associates will eventually go into the partnership track, the firm has to be prepared for those who are not put into that track leaving the firm. Conversely, if the assessment event is not determinative, the firm must accept that there will be some very senior associates who will stay on in the hope that over time they will develop their skills to the required level – which the firm may well see as unattainable for them.

Whatever process a firm may have in place for assessing an associate's suitability for promotion to the most senior level, and whatever developmental support the firm makes available in that level, it is unlikely that all of them will be promoted to partner, whether sooner or later. So, what steps should a firm take to give an indication of partnership prospects, and when should it take them? And what are the options for associates who do not make it to partner or indeed who do not want to become a partner? These points are addressed next.

4.   Career prospects discussions

A recurrent complaint of many associates is that they do not know what are their career prospects within the firm until quite late in their careers as associates. Therefore, the ones who discover that their hopes of partnership will not come to fruition when they see their peers being promoted can feel they have been misled, with damaging consequences for their careers.

It is entirely understandable from the firm's perspective for the partners not to be certain whether an individual associate will make it to partner until the moment of the promotion decision is in sight. An associate may be seen as very talented and a likely partner candidate but whether they make it to partner will be dependent on the business needs of the firm and its clients at the time, the prospects of growth in the associate's particular area of practice and/or the associate's colleagues in the pipeline to partnership.

That said, even if the partners cannot be certain very far in advance which of their associates will become partners in due course, they will usually have a clear idea of who among the very senior associates are likely to become partners.

Taking this into account, many firms have built into their career paths some form of career discussion. This will often form part of the appraisal or review discussions; and the assessment event outlined in the previous section (where it has been incorporated into the career path) can perform much the same function. Be that as it may, the key issue is to get the timing of these discussions right, and to give the right messages.

For example, if the typical time from qualification to partnership is, say, 12 years, an associate who only discovers that they will not become a partner at the end of that period may be faced with a career dilemma. Accepting that many in that position will be able to find very satisfying roles (whether in-house or at other firms, albeit sometimes at firms lower in the rankings than the associate's current firm), others may face real difficulties. If making partner after 12 years is the standard in the jurisdiction, other firms may be reluctant to take on an associate who is perceived as having failed at their current firm. Equally, the associate may be daunted by the prospect of moving to a new firm and then spending perhaps several years establishing themselves as an associate before being considered for partnership.

These career discussions should therefore take place at the point in the associate's career when there is time for them to move on if necessary, without damaging their career prospects. There is no optimum timing but after 9 or 10 years at the firm would seem to be appropriate.

The format of these discussions is a matter for the individual firm, but the core message which is usually given will be one of the following three:

- "You are on track for partnership within [1–2] years."
- "You may be considered for partnership within [2–3] years."
- "You are not on the partnership track."

While these three statements will be at the core of the discussions, they will need to be properly positioned. Aside from making it plain that any timings given may need to change, the first two statements should be clearly understood to be expectations, not promises.

The associate's reaction to the third message may be to leave the firm, and that may be the firm's intention, especially if the firm operates an 'up or out' policy.

Firms which do not operate a strict policy of up or out may be willing for the associate to stay on for a period albeit the ultimate expectation is that the associate will leave the firm. And there will be circumstances when both the firm and the associate agree the associate will stay with the firm in the longer term if there is a suitable role to fulfil. This leads into alternative career paths, discussed in the next section.

5. Alternative career paths

The term 'alternative career path' is intended to cover a role carried out by someone who is not a partner. While the role may be a non-feeing-earning one, that does not have to be the case.

With that in mind, a firm could decide that the associate who has not made it to partner will simply carry on with their current role unchanged. That approach has appeal. The cohort of very senior associates is rightly regarded as the engine room of the firm by many partners. They are very experienced lawyers and well able to run matters for clients with limited supervision from partners. As a result they can be very profitable.

However, there are two risks with taking this view. First, unless their remuneration is carefully controlled, the associates will become ever more expensive and so eat into the firm's profit margin. Secondly, these associates may block more junior (but still senior and experienced) associates from the highest level of associate work in the firm, so constraining their more junior colleagues' development. If those more junior colleagues are on lower salaries, giving them access to the senior level work will mean their contribution to the firm's profit margin will be greater.

This is not to say that a decision to allow the associate to continue in their current fee-earning role is flawed. Rather, that it has to be structured carefully to meet the needs and requirements of both the firm and the individual. Such an approach is common where the individual has voluntarily taken themselves out of the partnership track (say, because the associate enjoys legal practice but does not relish the prospect of taking on the business development and managerial functions that are so necessary for a partner). The holders of these types of role are often very expert with a wide and deep grasp of the legal issues in the practice area's field of work, so they are seen as invaluable in-house experts.

These alternative roles do not have to be fee-earning, and where the role is a business professional one the options are varied. The associate could take on a professional support role (having responsibility for knowledge and information and/or learning and development for their practice area), a business development role or a business improvement role.

Accepting that the firm's manpower planning needs will dictate how many people might perform this type of role, the likelihood is that the number who do so will be small.

The titles given to these alternative roles need to be determined by the local regulations to which the firm is subject and the structure of the firm itself. However, commonly used titles include director, counsel, senior consultant and the like.

6. The partnership selection process

The objective of any partnership selection process is to give assurance to the wider partnership that the appointed candidate will enhance the collective strengths and abilities of the firm, not dilute them.

It is, therefore, essential that the partner selection process is seen as a continuation of the associate's development path, not something which is separate from it.

The partners may on occasion face some surprises (such as when a very talented and highly regarded associate announces they are leaving the firm for whatever valid personal reason). However, and that aside, a well-structured and aligned development path should deliver a pool of skilled and experienced associates who are, broadly speaking, partnership ready, thus giving the partners the luxury of choice.

The form the partnership selection process takes must reflect the culture of the firm (including the culture of the jurisdiction in which the firm is based) and be suited to the size and structure of the organisation.

If some form of competency-based assessment process is alien in the jurisdiction in which the firm is based, introducing it may impact on retention rates. Talented associates may resent being put through such a process when highly regarded competitor firms do not impose the same requirement.

This does not mean that an innovative firm wishing to improve its selection process should avoid being first mover, but it should proceed with caution. If the firm is of a size that enables all (or at any rate the majority) of the partners to know all the partner candidates, a complex, extensive and possibly expensive process may be unnecessary. However, in large firms with hundreds of partners and multiple offices a formal process will be necessary to reassure the partnership at large that the right promotion decisions have been made.

6.1 The role of a partner selection committee

The detailed approaches taken by larger firms vary but there are some common elements.

The responsibility for managing the partnership selection process is commonly delegated by the senior management team to a committee made up of senior partners. Members may be managing partners of offices, practice areas or groups and/or partners (whether or not with formal management roles) who are respected across the firm and representative of different parts of the firm (regions, practice areas, seniority in the partnership etc).

The partner selection committee will put the partner candidates from across the firm through the firm's selection process and report to the partnership at large with their recommendations, often at the annual partners' meeting. The partnership will have the opportunity to approve or reject the recommendations; however, in most cases the committee will have dealt with any disagreements over an individual's promotion before its decision is put to the partnership at large.

6.2 Identifying candidates locally

It would obviously be administratively difficult, if not impossible, if responsibility for identifying all of the candidates for promotion in any one year were to lie with the partner selection committee.

The first step in the process each year, therefore, is for the candidates to be identified locally. How that is done will depend on the organisational structure of the firm. In large firms, either the managing partner of each office or the managing partner of each practice area will ask the partners in their office or area to put forward candidates.

The managing partner (often supported by the local management team) will then review this long list of candidates and agree which associates will be put forward for the firm-wide process. The decision on each candidate represents a balance between factors affecting the group in the office or area in which the prospective candidate works, and the personal qualities of the candidate.

Group factors will include:

- the group's strategy and how it fits with the wider office or area strategy;
- the success or otherwise of the group in terms of client base, profitability, etc;
- whether adding another partner will be accretive or dilutive of the profits of the office or group (taking into account any retirements planned or expected among the existing partners in the group);
- the quality of the pipeline of possible candidates likely to come into the frame to become partners in the next two or three years; and
- achieving an appropriate balance in terms of the numbers of candidates from each group in the office or area.

These factors will inform the decision on each individual prospective candidate but in essence the decision is whether the particular individual is the associate best able to ensure the future and continued success of the group. The explanation of why that is the case is set out in a candidate nomination form.

Personal factors covered in the form typically include:

- a summary CV of the candidate and their practice history;
- a description of their practice and contribution (hours worked, fees generated etc) over the last two or three years;
- a description of their client base;
- an explanation of why they are seen as a credible candidate to go into this year's promotion process, including how they will help the group deliver on its strategy; and
- their appraisal or review record.

6.3 Entering the selection process

Once the local lists are complete, they will be submitted to the committee along with the candidate nomination forms.

To state the obvious, the associate's sponsors, that is, the partners supporting the associate's candidacy, will be involved throughout the associate's progress through the selection process. They will answer questions about the candidate and their candidacy and be advocates for the candidate, perhaps negotiating with the partner selection committee should there be doubts about the associate progressing.

In some firms, the committee carries out the entire due diligence process; in others, the firm's central management teams have an oversight role. Typically, this will be in the form of a business case review involving scrutiny of factors similar to those for the local identification process. The review will balance the range of justifications put forward for individuals by all of the offices or areas; it is not simply a matter of confirming or rejecting locally selected candidates.

The business case review will look at a number of questions:

- Given the current state of the firm's overall business, can it afford to appoint all the candidates put forward by the offices or areas?
- Is the balance of candidate numbers between the offices or areas fair?
- Is the candidate list supportive of the firm's strategy?

An obvious outcome of such a review is that some offices or areas will be asked to trim their candidate lists.

This centralised business case review focuses on the case made by the offices or areas rather than looking at whether a particular associate is likely to be able to deliver on the business case attached to their candidacy.

The individual review of each candidate is the responsibility of the partner selection committee, which will decide on the success or otherwise of a would-be partner's candidacy in the light of their legal and managerial skills in combination.

Looking first at the candidate's legal skills, the members of the committee will probably not have the breadth and depth of knowledge of all of the practice areas of the firm to be able to judge effectively the legal skills of each candidate. In view of this, many firms put in place a system within each practice area of rigorous testing of their candidate's legal skills. Only if the candidate passes that local assessment will they be put through the firm-wide process.

6.4 Firm-wide soundings

While the partner selection committee usually does not attempt to second-guess the practice area's decision on each candidate's legal expertise, most firms have some system of taking soundings on each candidate from across the firm.

The form these soundings take can vary. In some firms this is based on a questionnaire circulated round the partnership. In others, members of the committee take on responsibility for seeking soundings from across the partnership.

What is being sought? In short, it is the views of partners across the firm on how the candidate has performed in practice over recent years. The questions asked will include:

- How well does the partner know the candidate?
- In what circumstances has the partner come across the candidate?
- What is the opinion of the partner of the candidate as a practising lawyer, a client handler, a people manager, a business manager and an ethical lawyer?

In the large firms, partners who are asked to take soundings will not know many of the candidates. This is not an issue in and of itself but a low return rate of responses can be telling. For example, if a candidate's practice should bring them into contact with a wide range of partners in the firm, a low return may raise a question mark. Why is the candidate not better known? There may be a good reason for this but it needs to be explored.

Naturally, any criticisms of the candidate will be followed up with the candidate's sponsoring office or area and an appropriate level of rational analysis will be applied to the comments. For example, a criticism dating from when the candidate was a junior associate in the firm will carry less weight than a more recent incident. Similarly, a single criticism when otherwise the candidate has had glowing comments from a range of partners will not be ignored but may not be fatal to their candidacy.

Clearly, severe criticisms highlighted in the course of the soundings process can be fatal to the candidate's candidacy. However, if the comments are more concerns about the candidate than real criticisms, these can be explored during the later stages of the process.

Some firms' processes cease at this stage. This is a legitimate approach since the business case for the candidate (both local and firm-wide) would have been reviewed and confirmed. The views of partners who have worked with the candidate would have been given and should be respected. However, it is now equally common for the selection committee to go on to the personal assessment stage.

6.5 Personal assessment

One strong rationale for this next stage is that up to this point the candidate will not have had a chance to make their own case for being a partner (accepting that they will have contributed to the information provided by their local sponsors).

The obvious format for the personal assessment is an interview with the partner selection committee. Depending on the size of the committee and the number of candidates going into the process each year, having the interviews carried out only by members of the committee could represent a considerable burden on very busy people. Therefore, it is common for the interview panels to be a mixture of members of the committee and, for example, respected retired partners.

The scope of the interviews will be tailored to the requirements of the firm both with regard to the general expectations the firm has of its partners and any specific issues relevant to each candidate.

Accepting that the following list may not be universal, the topics most often covered in these interviews are:

- the candidate's plans for implementing their personal business case;

- their knowledge of their particular market;
- their client base (covering their existing or target clients and exploring their understanding of these clients' business plans, as well as their own plans for getting more work from their client base);
- their view of the competition they face for work;
- the resources they need to deliver on their plans (including their approach to people management);
- the revenue they expect to generate over what period; and
- their wider contribution to the firm (for example, their CSR/*pro bono* activities, contributions to learning and development or knowledge and information, etc).

The outcome of these interviews, coupled with the information gathered in the earlier parts of the process, may be sufficient in many cases for the partner selection committee to decide on its recommendations for the list of candidates.

However, some firms go on to put the candidates through some form of assessment event. The firms that have followed this path have introduced events which are structured in a similar, but not identical, way to the assessment event outlined in section 3 above.

The typical structure of an assessment event forming part of the partner selection process is as follows:

- An introduction explaining the purpose of the event and its position in the selection process.
- A series of exercises aligned to the firm's key criteria for promotion to partner (so, for example, a strategic or financial issue, a client management issue, a people management issue and an ethical issue, with each exercise using a range of formats – group work, written work or one-to-one discussion) with feedback given at the end of each exercise on the individual associate's performance.

As is only to be expected, such events will be more complex and challenging than any the candidate faced as a more junior associate. However, if the event is carefully designed it will give the selection committee added evidence to assure the wider partnership that the candidate recommended for promotion has the skills necessary to function as an effective partner from day one of joining the partnership.

If there remain any concerns about an individual's candidacy by the time they get to the assessment event, the outcome of the event may give the committee the additional insight they need to refute the concern or confirm it.

This event is pure assessment. There is no feedback given, nor is a formal development action plan prepared. However, it is normal after the selection process for each candidate, whether successful or not, to have a feedback discussion covering all aspects of the selection process. For successful candidates, this usually focuses on any issues identified during the process that will help or hinder their success as new partners – so there is an element of developmental guidance in these discussions.

For unsuccessful candidates, the discussion will focus on the factors or issues which lead to them not progressing to partnership. In firms where it is possible for associates to go through the partner selection process more than once, the aspects of their candidacy on which they need to work before entering the process again are highlighted along with guidance on the support available to them.

There is a caveat to consider before introducing such an event.

A well-designed assessment event with realistic scenarios which are recognisable to both the candidates and their sponsors will give valuable insight into whether each candidate possesses the right level of skills to perform as a new partner. However, scenario-based assessment events will not necessarily be predictive of how the candidate will perform as a partner over the coming years.

For example, a client management exercise in which the candidate has to come up with proposals for dealing with a relationship problem may not give a true indication of the candidate's longer-term client management or development skills. This will particularly be the case for candidates who by virtue of their personal style and/or the nature of their practices build strong relationships over time or impress the clients with their extensive legal expertise.

There are psychometric tests which may give greater insight here, provided the use of such tests is acceptable as part of the selection process – use, and therefore acceptability, varies from jurisdiction to jurisdiction.

If an assessment event is included in the process, it should be carefully positioned as the source of additional insights, not as the deciding factor in the process. Otherwise, candidates who are not recommended may take the view that years of hard and effective work have been ignored in favour of being put through a series of artificial exercises over the course of one or two days.

By the same token, while psychometric tests can give real insight, they also need careful positioning. Using them as a source of developmental guidance is one thing; using them as part of the decision-making process is another. Given the importance (for both sides) of the promotion decision, if evidence from a test is supported by other elements of the process, the risk of a decision being challenged is lessened.

However many of these elements a firm may choose to include in its partnership selection process, it is essential that the process is seen as being rigorous by both the partnership at large and the candidates. If it is seen as biased or flawed in some way, the recommendations of the partner selection committee may not be accepted.

If rigour and fairness is achieved, the experience in many firms is that successful candidates feel they have been properly assessed against agreed and well-known firm-wide standards. Candidates and existing partners alike feel reassured that anyone who has come through the process deserves the title of partner, facilitating trust between people who may not know each other.

Furthermore, having gone through the process together, each year's cohort of new partners often feel a strong bond between them. That can have considerable benefits in terms of collegiality and future collaboration across the firm.

This section has assumed that the candidates going through the process are home-grown, whether they have spent their entire career at the firm or have been associates with the firm for the most recent years of their time in practice. However, it is now common for firms to recruit new partners laterally, and Rebecca Normand-Hochman and Tom Spence's "Lateral partner onboarding and integration" chapter looks at that process.

This chapter focuses on the process for promoting associates to partner and not the processes by which partners progress through whatever levels of partner a particular firm may have in place. Nevertheless, many firms will follow a broadly similar process – business case review, soundings, interview and, possibly, an assessment event – to support interpartner progression decisions.

7. New partner orientation programmes

As the relationships between partners and their associates have become more open and transparent, associates now have a much clearer understanding of the role and responsibilities of partners than was the case in the past. However, it is one thing to observe a partner running a practice; it is another to carry that responsibility yourself.

For this reason, many firms put their new partners through some form of event-based new partner orientation programme.

Setting aside the celebratory aspects (which are not to be underestimated), it is an opportunity for the firm to ensure that all new partners from all offices and practice areas are given common messages about the expectations the firm has of them.

The issues such an event is likely to cover are:
- a review of the firm's strategy, coupled with an opportunity for the new partners to understand how their practices fit into that strategy;
- an exploration of the firm's finances, looking at the financial management processes with which partners must comply (managing WIP, debtors, assessing bills, etc);
- the new partners' obligations to the firm (such as capital contributions);
- profit-sharing arrangements;
- client-management expectations;

- people-management obligations; and
- the firm's risk and compliance processes.

The format and speakers for the event are a matter for the firm to decide, but the in-house speakers will be members of the senior management team with the relevant firm-wide responsibilities. This group will be supplemented by the senior business professionals who, besides giving guidance on the expectations of the new partners, will be able to explain the support available to the partners when handling their various responsibilities. Many firms will bring in outsiders, such as business school professors or management consultants, to give an external view on the key issues.

The team-bonding aspect of the earlier selection process can be reinforced through these orientation programmes and associated social events, an illustration being where firms include the opportunity for the new partners to discuss among themselves the business opportunities they have identified for their practices and so explore the possibilities of jointly capitalising on those opportunities.

The key to designing an effective new partner orientation programme is to recognise that it represents the start of a career which could be decades long. Too often new partners regard having made it to partner as the equivalent of climbing Everest, whereas in fact, in terms of their longer-term career, promotion to partner means they have merely reached the foothills.

Therefore, the orientation programme needs to ensure all the new partners have the knowledge, skills, expertise and support they need to build their practices over their first few years as partners. The longer-term stages in a partner's career (from joining the partnership to retirement) are beyond the scope of this chapter. However, the foundations of that career-long development process are laid on admission to the partnership.

8. Conclusion

The key message to take away from this chapter is that the process by which a firm chooses its partners is only part (albeit a very important part) of the developmental continuum of all the lawyers in the firm, from the most junior recruits to the most senior partners.

The firm will have an agreed mission, vision and strategy, and from that flows the need to be clear on what knowledge and skills the lawyers (partners and associates) need to possess at each stage of their career with the firm. With that in mind, the firm can construct its competencies for each level of lawyer (again, partners and associates) together with its career and developmental pathways.

The firm must be open about all these aspects so there is no confusion about the firm's expectations of its people, whatever their individual roles. Equally, the firm must deal fairly with its people so no one is able to say they have been misled in any way (hence the career discussions mentioned above).

However, the associates need to understand the unavoidable business constraints under which any firm operates. The partners may have views – positive or negative – on an associate's prospects for progression, even quite early in the associate's career (albeit it is legitimate for the partners not to be able to give definitive views too early).

Competencies, appraisal or reviews, and career milestones may be common in most firms. However, the assessment event outlined in section 3 – despite the beneficial impact on associates it can represent – may be a step too far in some firms or jurisdictions and may be seen as unnecessary due to the effectiveness of the particular firm's appraisal or review process and the relationships between partners and associates.

Above all, it is essential for any firm to get the selection of its future partners right. Getting it wrong can have expensive, even catastrophic, consequences. While no process is foolproof, a process such as the one outlined in this chapter will minimise the risk of failure.

Developing partners as managers and leaders

Rebecca Normand-Hochman
Institute of Legal Talent & Leadership

1.   Introduction

When I started to write this chapter, I was in the process of researching the role that courage plays in good leadership and I came across this inspiring definition of a leader:

> *A leader is anyone who takes responsibility for finding the potential in people and processes, and who has the courage to develop that potential.*[1]

It took me a couple of minutes to think whether I agreed with that definition before I realised that this was one of the most innovative ways of looking at leadership that I had come across for some time and that it resonated particularly well with what I wanted to write about.

Leadership was until relatively recently a skill not valued in the legal profession. Like other professionals such as doctors[2] and engineers,[3] lawyers have the motivation and opportunity to develop their cerebral, analytical and technical abilities more than the skills required to be leaders. In *What Leaders Really Do*,[4] John Kotter insightfully explains that leadership is about coping with change and the reason it has become so important is that the business world is so much more competitive and volatile than in the past:

> *Major changes are more and more necessary to survive and compete effectively in this new environment. More change always demands more leadership.*

Leadership success depends on how well you manage yourself and interact with others. It depends on appreciating and accepting who you are and on knowing that self-development is a lifelong journey. As lawyers grow in seniority and have greater influence and responsibility, they increasingly need to rely on emotional[5] and social intelligence[6] skills.

---

1   Brené Brown, *Dare to Lead: Brave work, Tough Conversations, Whole Hearts*, Penguin Random House, 2018.
2   Thoms H Lee, MD and Toby Cosgrove, MD, *HBR's 10 Must Reads on Leadership for Healthcare*, Harvard Business Review Press, 2018.
3   In *Search Inside Yourself*, one of Google's earliest engineers and former Chief Happiness Officer interestingly describes how he convinced Google's engineers to train in emotional intelligence. Chade-Meng Tan, *Search Inside Yourself: The Unexpected Path to Achieving Success, Happiness (and World Peace)*, Harper Collins, 2012.
4   John P Kotter, *What Leaders Really Do*, Harvard Business Review Press, 1999.
5   Emotional Intelligence is defined by Peter Salovey and John D Mayer, the fathers of the emotional intelligence theoretical framework as "the ability to monitor one's own and others' feeling and emotions, to discriminate among them and to use this information to guide one's thinking and actions". Peter Salovey and John D Mayer, "Emotional Intelligence", *Imagination, Cognition and Personality 9*, no 3, 1990, 185–211.
6   Daniel Goleman, *Social Intelligence: The New Science of Human Relationships*, Arrow, 2007.

From my combined experience of practising law and advising and coaching leaders and partners of international law firms in the last two decades, I have witnessed the growing importance that leadership skills have assumed in the profession. It used to be that being an excellent lawyer and working hard was the path to success, but this is no longer the case. The extraordinary increase in the levels of complexity and competition at which law firms operate means that to be a successful partner in a law firm today involves significantly more competencies and abilities than in the past. Partners have to be managers and leaders alongside serving clients. They have the dual producer and manager roles described by John J Gabarro and Thomas J DeLong which inherently produces tensions and difficulties.[7] Lawyers are not professionally trained to be managers and leaders and they also can only devote a small part of their time to these roles. In addition, what attracted them to law and their need to excel technically are not the things that make great leaders.

This chapter describes the mindset, as well as the four tools, that partners need to master in order to be good managers and leaders.

2.   The mindset

If you want to build a ship, don't drum up the people to gather wood, divide the work, and give orders. Instead, teach them to yearn for the vast endless sea.[8]

Did you ever think, *This person will never have what it takes?* If so, you may have what Stanford researcher Carol Dweck calls a 'fixed mindset', which severely limits your ability to make a difference as a manager and leader.[9]

Those who operate with a fixed mindset generally believe that who they are is set in stone, that their personality, their IQ, their capabilities and their potential are all 'baked in' and cannot be altered. Such a belief can become a self-fulfilling prophecy, serve as a barrier to one's development and success, and impede a leader's ability to develop great talent in others.

The opposite of a fixed mindset is a 'growth mindset'. Those who operate with a growth mindset generally believe that people can change, learn and grow. They believe that mistakes are helpful forms of feedback that can lead to improvement. As a result, they are more likely to see their own and others' potential.

Research has shown that people can shift from a fixed mindset to a growth mindset, but doing so can be a challenge for lawyers because it requires moving away from an expert role. Knowing what is right and giving advice is how lawyers bring value to their clients, so making this shift can be counterintuitive

---

7   John J Gabarro and Thomas J DeLong, "The Producing Manager: A Double-Barreled Role", *Harvard Business Review* case study, 2008.

8   From *Citadelle* by Antoine de Saint Exupery.

9   Carol S Dweck, *Mindset: The New Psychology of Success*, Random House, 2006.

and uncomfortable. It certainly takes practice and effort to do but those who manage the shift can develop powerful leadership skills and see great results.

There follow the two main ways in which the shift from a fixed to a growth mindset can be accomplished.

2.1 Distinguish the intent from the impact

If you measure someone's performance on a task only by looking at the outcome, you won't know their intent – the driving force behind their behaviour – unless they share it with you.

When someone underperforms, there's often a gap between intent and impact, and that can lead to great misunderstanding and frustration. Helping someone learn and grow involves clarifying their intention so they can close that gap.

How? By asking them what impact they meant to have.

For instance, you might say, "I noticed that you stayed quiet at this meeting; can we discuss why?" It may be that the person didn't feel that he or she was expected to take part in the discussion, or didn't feel confident, or was afraid to be judged.

From there, you can start working on what really stopped them, and help them to do better next time.

2.2 Recognise your bias

Your own preferences can get in the way of discovering others' intent. Maybe you have difficulty dealing with certain personality types or you find it challenging to identify with fellow partners or associates whose work styles differ from yours. Whatever your biases, recognising them allows you to move past them by inquiring about intent rather than jumping to conclusions or filling in the blanks.

To spot your biases, use frustration as your guide. Think about what gets on your nerves at work and then ask a few trusted colleagues for feedback. What do they think your bugbears are? Compare their thoughts with yours; look for similarities and patterns.

3. Listening to build trust and engagement

Listening is one of the most critical leadership skills that partners can build. Managers and leaders who listen well are inspirational and influential because they build trusting relationships around them. They hear and perceive what is not being said. They build engagement and spot challenges before these start to hurt wellbeing or performance.

We tend to all think that we listen better than we actually do. More often than not, when we are listening to someone, we are thinking of what we will say next, or are listening to the inner voices in our heads at the same time.

Truly listening means understanding what someone is trying to convey with words, body, emotions. It's powerful because as well as creating better communication, it helps others feel seen, heard and valued.[10]

There are a number of ways to sharpen your listening skill. If you start to embed these techniques in your interactions every day, you'll start to see some surprising results.

3.1 Rewire yourself to listen

If you want to open the lines of communication, you have to open your own mind first.

Start by giving your full attention. Maintain comfortable eye contact and an open posture, and avoid distractions. Allow time for the other person to think and speak.

If you know the person who's talking to you, try to remove the filters that are your formed perceptions and data from your earlier interactions. Filters also include our assumptions, memories, beliefs, biases, values and expectations. These are hard-wired filters that make us hear but not listen; they block out what we need to know and perceive and they cloud our ability to listen with attention, curiosity and empathy.

Other elements that stop us listening well include human tendencies such as:

- judging/liking;
- feeling sorry for;
- wanting to understand;
- wanting to offer ideas;
- fixing/problem solving;
- comparing;
- feeling responsible; and
- needing to contribute.

Becoming aware of the existence of these filters and human tendencies is an important first step. Gradually removing these mental blocks enables us to listen in a new way.

3.2 Be genuinely curious

As a rule of thumb, ask more than you tell – aim for a ratio of 4 to 1 and be curious about what the other person is saying.

Some of my coaching clients tell me, "I am a really good listener", when the leadership assessment or feedback from colleagues says otherwise. And they go on to say, "Yes, I listen really well if I find what I'm hearing interesting" or "if I find the person interesting".

---

10   Mark Goulston, *Just Listen: Discover the Secret to Getting Through to Anyone*, AMACOM, 2009.

In other words, they are constantly selecting what they are hearing.

Being curious is the ability, like a child, to be curious about anything. To help you achieve that, you need to focus your attention on the person as much as on what he or she is saying.

You'll be surprised. The more you cultivate that curiosity, the more interesting you'll find what you're listening to.

3.3 Notice non-verbal cues

Peter Drucker said:

The most important thing in communication is hearing what isn't said.[11]

As well as hearing the words, we need to 'hear' the speaker's non-verbal messages and body language. Do the tone of voice and facial expression match what's being said? If not, comment on what you notice and ask the person to tell you more about it.

Affirm what you hear. Indicate understanding: "I hear what you are saying" or "I'm following you. Could you say more?" This simply means that you are listening closely, not that you agree.

3.4 Reflect what you see and hear

Reflect (like a mirror), the other person's emotions without agreeing or disagreeing: "You seem worried about ..." This encourages the speaker to express feelings and deepen their awareness of what they are trying to convey.

Periodically restate basic ideas to check that you grasp the key points: "If I understand, your idea is ... Did I get the essence of it? If not, please tell me more ..."

Briefly sum up the other person's point of view to check your understanding: "It sounds like your main concern is ..." or "These seem to be your main points ... is that right?"

If you are not listening well you may find yourself doing one or more of the following:

- talking more than listening (remember the rule of 4 to 1);
- suggesting solutions before the person has the chance to do so;
- interrupting;
- thinking about what you want to say next instead of focusing on what the person is saying;
- using body language that signals impatience or distraction (leaning back in your chair, checking your e-mail, accepting phone calls); and
- saying what you would have done differently in the same situation.

Always assume positive intent, even when dealing with difficult behaviour.

---

11   See Bill Moyer's interview with Drucker for Moyer's book *A World of Ideas*, Doubleday, 1989.

People usually mean well – and if you give them the benefit of the doubt, they'll be more forthcoming about their intent and more receptive to what you have to say.

3.5 Listen when someone is highly stressed

As a manager and leader, you've also got to be ready to occasionally help people to exhale emotionally and mentally. Stress isn't necessarily all bad. Research shows that it can help us to identify what's important to us, to focus, and to become determined.

But when someone's stress level becomes too high, they become incapable of thinking and acting rationally. The brain's threat-sensing circuitry, led by an organ called the amygdala, becomes activated. This can draw resources from the brain's cognitive circuitry, often called the 'executive function', resulting in distractibility, inattention, slower processing and errors of omission, and sometimes can trigger a strong (and occasionally inappropriate) emotional response colloquially referred to as an 'amygdala hijack'.

In this context, simply giving someone breathing room, a place and space to exhale, is really helpful. Because you don't just help the situation get back to normal – you actually help improve it.

If you spot body language or words that express high stress (or distress), don't try to get through with facts or reason – that won't work. Instead, give the person plenty of time to express whatever they have to say. Listen sensitively, and periodically restate the last two or three key words that they said in order to validate and help them feel they've been heard. Avoid making any judgements. Don't get into a debate or become defensive, simply listen without interrupting. Simply saying, "Tell me more" and then listening in an open-minded manner is a powerful way to help someone overcome a stressful situation.

It's also important to be prepared to share your own vulnerabilities. Doing so doesn't make you weak – it actually makes you accessible. Vulnerability builds trust. And trust is one of your principal allies in getting through to someone who is highly stressed.

4. Asking powerful questions to increase learning and motivation

Managers and leaders who ask questions instead of giving instructions set the stage for better learning and communication, high levels of motivation and performance.

But what makes for good questions? Is it really that hard to ask a question that will open up discussions, create learning and sharing, and result in productive communications?

The truth is, most of us don't know how to ask good questions, or when we do ask a really great question, it is by accident. There are several ways to ask questions. Some people seem really good at it, others use a random, whatever-pops-into-head approach.

4.1 What powerful questions do

Powerful questions are designed to help the other person think, to learn about their way of thinking and to gather information. Truly neutral questions are rare.

Most people tend to overuse the leading style of questioning instead of asking open questions designed for learning. But people communicate much better when they start asking neutral and open questions to learn about the perspective of the other.

Here are five great reasons to ask:
- Asking creates buy-in.
- Asking improves communication.
- Asking empowers.
- Asking develops leadership capacity.
- Asking creates authenticity.

4.2 Different types of questions

There are many types of questions. Some authors define questions in terms of being empowering or disempowering; I find it a helpful criterion.

Empowering questions are positive ones, such as:
- What works best for you?
- What are you doing right?
- What would you do differently next time?

Disempowering questions are also called **judging questions.** They bring up negative feelings and focus on what is wrong. Common disempowering questions include:
- Why did you do that?
- What went wrong?
- Who caused this?

Notice that these disempowering questions can appear to be neutral; it is therefore sometimes easy to confuse them with information-gathering questions. Often, to be able to know whether it is a judging or a neutral question, you have to look at the context and notice the tone of voice. There is a fine line between information-gathering, where one is exploring causes in order to find solutions, and questions that judge and blame. It also depends on who is asking the questions, their position of authority, and their prior history of being judgemental and blaming or otherwise.

In order to frame questions in a neutral, exploratory way, it is sometime useful to qualify questions with a statements such as, "Help me to understand this situation ..."

Coaching questions are powerful because they can bring about mindset shifts. These types of questions are transformative as they enable the recipient to see things from other perspectives.

Examples of powerful coaching questions include:
- How do you need to be in order for this to be solved?
- What shifts in your thinking and being need to happen?
- What else needs to be considered?

And there are a number of asking mistakes that should be avoided:
- **Closed questions:** Asking closed questions (ones that can be replied to by yes or no) shuts people down. On the other hand, open questions have two key benefits: they let the person direct the conversation and they make the person think by eliciting longer answers.
- **Why questions:** Why questions tend to make people clam up because they challenge motives. When you ask a question like, "Why did you do that?", you are asking the person to defend or justify their actions. Replacing the 'why' with 'what' is an easy way to avoid getting the other person defensive. As an example, instead of saying, "Why can't you talk to her about that?", say "What do you need to talk to her about?"
- **Leading questions:** Leading questions are ones that subtly point the person to a certain answer – the one that the person asking the question (knowingly or unknowingly) wants. It's easy not to realise that you are leading the conversation in a certain direction. A good technique if you realise that you've asked a leading question is to add "or" and then ask the opposite question: "If you take on this new role, will it prevent you from spending enough time with your family? Or will it open doors to get the kind of family time that you really want?"
- **Interrupting:** Interrupting is a habit that many aren't aware of. Here's an exercise that you can do to break an interruptive habit: when you listen to someone, make sure that you count off two seconds after the person has stopped speaking before you say something or ask another question.
- **Solution-orientated questions:** A special type of closed question is a piece of advice with a question mark added at the end, such as, "Can you give him the benefit of the doubt on this one?" We want to tell the person the answer but we phrase it as a question – we give our solution in the form of a question. Instead, try to shape an open question with many possible solutions.

5. Giving feedback to fuel growth and performance

In its original sense, feedback is the exchange of information about how one part of a system is working, with the understanding that it affects everyone else within the system. If any part goes off course, prompt remedial action is critical.

Feedback is every organisation's lifeblood, the mechanism that lets people know whether they're doing a good job or if their efforts need to be fine-tuned, upgraded or entirely redirected.

There are two main types of feedback:

- ongoing feedback – *ad hoc* and occurring regularly; and
- formal feedback – given and received during performance reviews on an annual or semi-annual basis.

What follows will help you to provide and receive both types of feedback.

5.1 Why we avoid giving feedback

Most partners are uncomfortable when giving feedback. It's one of the most important leadership tasks to master, but most procrastinate and try to avoid it altogether.

Some of the reasons why we avoid feedback include:

- We worry that giving feedback will make the recipient dislike us, or that it will strain our relationship.
- We assume that the other person cannot handle the feedback.
- We recall or know of previous instances when the recipient resisted feedback or didn't act on it.
- We feel that the person is already too stuck in his or her ways and that the feedback won't be helpful.
- We are afraid to create an awkward or even risky situation.

5.2 Effective feedback

There are seven golden rules to providing effective feedback:

- It is given at the right time, in context and frequently (see below).
- It is based on facts, not assumptions.
- It is delivered with respect.
- It aims to achieve a specific outcome.
- It is a two-way conversation.
- It is expressed as a point of view, rather than an absolute truth.
- It provides opportunities for follow-up.

5.3 When to give feedback

Offering feedback can be most useful when:

- Good work, successful projects and resourceful behaviour deserve recognition.

- The likelihood of improving a person's skills is high.
- The person is expecting feedback (either because a feedback session was scheduled or because the person knows that their behaviour or performance was noticed).
- A problem cannot be ignored, because the person's behaviour is negatively affecting a colleague, the team or the firm.

5.4 When not to give feedback

It is counterproductive to give feedback when:

- You do not have all the information about a given situation.
- The only feedback you can offer relates to factors that the recipient cannot easily change or control.
- The person who needs the feedback appears to be highly emotional or especially vulnerable immediately after a difficult event.
- You do not have the time or the patience to deliver the feedback in a calm and thorough manner.
- The feedback is based on your personal preference, not a need for more effective behaviour or way of doing things.
- You have not yet formulated a possible solution to help the feedback recipient move forward.

5.5 Managing emotions

Although too many negative feelings can inhibit learning and communication, emotions do play a vital role in giving and receiving feedback. Emotional experiences are better remembered – they stick for longer and are easier to recall. Don't eliminate emotion from the discussion altogether as this can lead to a cycle of less effective interactions. Bringing the right dose of emotion will depend on what is being discussed and the relationship itself, and will vary from one day to the next.

It is of course difficult to calibrate what emotions we bring to a conversation and also how we react to the other person's emotion. One helpful approach is to practise giving and receiving feedback. The more we are used to doing it, the better we know how to manage our own emotions and to deal with the other person's.

5.6 The art of receiving feedback

Receiving feedback is an equally important and valuable leadership skill to possess, yet a large number of managers and leaders struggle with it. Being on the receiving end involves an entirely different set of emotional and psychological skills.

Few leaders deny feedback's benefits, but their openness to hearing and applying it often falls short. Accepting feedback is a best-practice skill that requires emotional intelligence, relational aptitude and humility. The benefits extend to everyone in the firm and beyond.

When receiving feedback, be mindful of the following:

- Recognise feedback for what it actually is: information about yourself. It almost always involves someone's assessment of you, fairly simple yet not always fair.
- Inherent tensions will affect how you feel during any feedback session (ie, your need to excel, be accepted and be seen as worthy). Each of us has these emotional survival traits, which can cloud our emotions as we listen to feedback, especially negative feedback.
- Consequently, it is natural to experience resistance to feedback. Some of us brace for it, some fear it, and others try to prevent its delivery altogether.

6.   Having difficult conversations with courage and empathy

Some conversations are so difficult that we do anything to avoid them. Then when things have really built up, we finally have no choice but to confront the issue and the person.

A difficult conversation is anything that is hard for someone to talk about. It can be asking for a pay raise or providing someone with negative feedback. These conversations are particularly tricky because there is often a gap between what people are thinking and what they say.

What is difficult for someone or not is subjective but these conversations share two common characteristics:

- There is usually *something important at stake.*
- They have an element of *identity*. The conversations that are the most difficult are the ones that threaten our *self-image.*

Conversations can be difficult because they can generate powerful emotions. Emotions have an important purpose – they signal us about things that are important to pay attention to. Certain emotions can trigger our threat-sensing circuitry and put us into what psychologists call "fight, flight or freeze mode". When our ancestors were cave-dwellers, this mechanism had a high survival value. In today's complex world, we can easily trigger fight, flight or freeze mode when it's unnecessary. It is however possible to have difficult conversations in a way that improves relationships instead of risking hurt feelings.

Untangling the complexities of difficult conversations and breaking them down to basic components makes it easier to say what needs to be said, and still preserve relationships.

All difficult conversations share a common structure. To see the structure, we need to understand *what is being said*, and also *what is not being said*. We need to see what both people are thinking and feeling but not saying to each other.

6.1 Three components of conversations[12]

There are basically three kinds of conversations, no matter what the subject. In each of these kinds of conversations, we make predictable errors that distort our thoughts and feelings.

(a) The 'What happened?' component

There is usually disagreement about what happened or what should happen. Stop arguing about who's right: explore each other's stories and try to learn something new. Don't assume meanings. Disentangle intent from impact. Abandon blaming anyone and think in terms of contributions to the solution.

(b) The 'Feelings' component

Every difficult conversation also asks and answers questions about feelings. Are they valid? Appropriate? Should I admit them or deny them? What about the other person's feelings – will I hurt them? What if they get angry? Often feelings are not addressed directly and so they interfere with the conversation even more.

(c) The 'Identity' component

This is where we examine what's at stake: What do I stand to lose or gain? Am I competent or incompetent, worthy or unlovable? What impact might this have on my career, self-esteem, our relationship? These issues determine the degree to which we feel off-centred and anxious.

Every conversation involves grappling with these three components. Engaging successfully requires learning to operate within each of these three domains. Managing all three simultaneously may seem daunting, but it's easier to do than facing the consequences of engaging in conversations blindly. When you take time to consider each of these factors before having a difficult conversation, it's a first step to better conversations.

6.2 Tips for difficult conversations

Consider these four steps when engaging in a difficult conversation:
1. Work out what happened, what the feelings are, how identity is involved.
2. Interpret the significance of what is said and what is not.
3. Identify the erroneous and deeply ingrained assumptions that keep you stuck.
4. Manage strong emotions – yours and theirs.

And try these tips:
• Always start with the other person's agenda. From a communication standpoint, you get what you want by first giving others what they need.

---

12   Douglas Stone, Bruce Patton and Sheila Heen, *Difficult Conversation: How to Discuss What Matters Most*, Penguin Random House USA, 2010.

- Listen without saying a word 70% of the time.
- Focus not only on what people are saying, but also on what they are not saying. Pay attention to others' facial expressions.
- Frequently confirm what people are thinking, feeling and believing. Don't assume you know what they mean.
- When people are trying to make their points, practice the art of saying, "Tell me more."
- Don't go into difficult conversations unprepared.
- Think about where you want to end up.
- Think about what's really going on.
- Begin the process of discovering and designing an action plan.
- At the end of every important conversation, review the commitments.

6.3 Turn the conversation around

Building on the tips in the previous section, Table 1 illustrates how a difficult conversation, with a shift in perspective, can become a learning one.

Table 1. Difficult conversations can become learning conversations

	Difficult	Learning
The What happened? conversation	The question is who's right or wrong; it's either/or.	I wonder why we see things differently? What is our respective data and reasoning?
The Feeling conversation	My feelings are their fault and I should either let them have what they want or keep quiet.	My feelings say something about me and something about their actions. I can share my feelings without blame and acknowledge theirs with empathy.
The Identity conversation	My identity is being attacked unfairly.	Realistically, some parts of what they're saying make painful sense. What am I afraid of here? How can their story have validity without negating mine, and vice versa?

Source: Created by author based on an article by Karen Christensen, featuring an interview with Douglas Stone and Elaine Lin Hering, "Mastering Difficult Conversations", Rotman Management Magazine, May 2020.

7. Conclusion

There is no doubt that what it takes to be a partner involves more diverse skills and competencies than it used to: the managing and leadership sides of the role have increased in importance. Knowing how to build trust, foster engagement, fuel performance and inspire brave behaviours have become essential skills for partners to master. Accepting vulnerability and sharing emotions openly require courage, but when partners manage and lead in this way they build great strengths inside and around them. They create firms where, at all levels, people are inspired to be their best selves for the benefit of all.

Using smart collaboration to achieve your strategic business and talent goals

Heidi K Gardner
Harvard Law School

1. Introduction

Now more than ever, lawyers with highly specialised expertise must work across silos to tackle clients' increasingly volatile, uncertain, complex and ambiguous (VUCA) problems. Take the example of the COVID-19 pandemic and resulting economic crisis: this multifaceted problem required partners to collaborate across practices, sectors and geographies to develop a robust, tailored and commercially sound response – well beyond flawless technical legal expertise. Even before the crisis, the globalisation of business meant that the clients of professional services firms (PSFs) were demanding seamless, multinational service. Going forward, counsel must frequently collaborate across geographic and cultural boundaries with far-off partners to ensure that work is aligned with the client's global strategy and takes accounts of country-specific issues. This is an example of what we call 'smart collaboration': highly specialised experts integrating their unique knowledge in order to tackle more VUCA problems than any of them could manage on their own.

Many firm leaders have recognised the importance of collaboration for enhancing client service and improving talent processes such as lateral hiring. By my estimate, more than 70% of major law firms have incorporated collaboration as a core pillar of their strategy. The problem is that most law firms have carved up their highly specialised, professional experts into narrowly defined practice areas, and collaborating across these silos is often messy, risky and costly. Unless you know why you're collaborating and how to do it effectively, it may not be smart at all. That's especially true for partners who have built their reputations and client rosters independently, not by working with peers. Many leaders therefore need hard evidence to convince their powerful partners to incorporate collaboration into their own routines and priorities.

To answer this call, I have spent more than a decade examining smart collaboration among partners in PSFs while on the faculty at Harvard Business School and now at Harvard Law School. Based on millions of data records from dozens of firms, statistical analyses, case studies, survey results and in-depth interviews, our research has uncovered robust confirmation about the effects of collaboration. When firms get collaboration right – that is, do complex work for clients that spans practices and offices – they earn higher margins, inspire greater client loyalty, gain access to more lucrative clients and attract more cutting-edge work. Section 1 of this chapter outlines these empirical research findings and demonstrates the financial and strategic business case for smart collaboration. Section 2 shows how collaboration can enhance the talent strategy across the whole employee life cycle, from hiring, through engaged and productive working, to post-firm alumni loyalty. The ability to attract, motivate and retain talent underpins a firm's ability to drive business results; in turn, commercial success enables the talent strategy not only by generating financial resources but also by creating opportunities, generating more stimulating work and boosting individual and firm-level reputations.

Section 3 focuses on two recently developed approaches for firms to implement a strategy of smart collaboration. First, our research with over 5,000 partners and functional leaders in PSFs having uncovered the typical barriers to collaboration, our in-depth work applying those findings in dozens of law firms has reinforced the need for each organisation to understand its own specific obstacles and generate buy-in from the broader partnership to make necessary changes.

Secondly, leaders need to equip their talent with better collaborative abilities. Individuals must understand their own starting point on collaborative tendencies, and learn how to leverage their strengths to make teams more effective. Likewise, group leaders need to understand how to draw out the strengths of each team member to enhance their overall functioning and outcomes. Firms that invest in these approaches stand a much stronger chance of creating distinctive competitive advantage by becoming their clients' strategic partners through smart collaboration.

2.   The business case for collaboration

For more than a decade, we have examined smart collaboration among partners in PSFs. Our quantitative and qualitative research among thousands of leaders and corporate executives reveals that firms fostering smart collaboration earn higher margins, inspire greater client loyalty and gain a competitive edge.[1]

The financial benefits of multi-practice collaboration are clear: the more practices that serve a client, the more revenue the client generates for the firm each year. Moving from one to two practices serving a client often *triples* that client's revenues, and the addition of each subsequent practice continues to

---

1   Dr Heidi K Gardner, Chapter 1, *Smart Collaboration: How Professionals and Their Firms Succeed by Breaking Down Silos*, Harvard Business Press, 2017; Dr Heidi K Gardner, "Why it Pays to Collaborate with Your Colleagues", *The American Lawyer*, March 2015.

grow fees. Clearly, if 1+1=3, then the lawyers who are involved in cross-practice service are doing more than just referring their colleagues to provide their own siloed work.

In one firm, we saw that revenues were 5.7 times higher for clients served by three practice groups than by a single one. Those clients served by five practice groups generated fees 17.6 times higher than those with just one kind of service. See Figure 1.

Figure 1. The revenue impact of smart collaboration

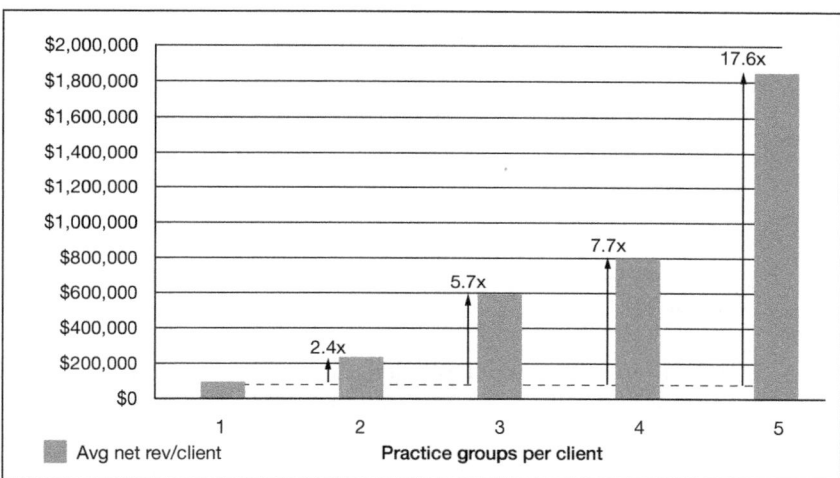

Source: Author.

The 'money on the table' analysis quantifies what your firm is currently leaving behind by not serving clients with the full range of offerings.[2] The numbers along the solid graph line in Figure 2 show the number of clients served in each category; the ones in the circles along the dotted line show the hypothetical new portfolio if 10% of clients in each category moved one step to the right. For this firm, the incremental revenue of this shift would add up to nearly $43 million. That's an 11% increase in the firm's total revenue.

This figure is typical across the firms we studied that are collaborating well – that is, doing complex work for clients that results in appropriate levels of increased revenue. In general, firms are missing out on an additional 5% to 12% of overall revenue by not figuring out how to make this shift. When you translate this into a money terms – "We could gain forty million dollars of profit by collaborating better" – it tends to catch partners' attention!

---

2   Dr Heidi K Gardner, "By Failing to Collaborate, Law Firms are Leaving Money on the Table", *The American Lawyer*, October 2018.

Figure 2. The upside of shifting portfolio by 10%

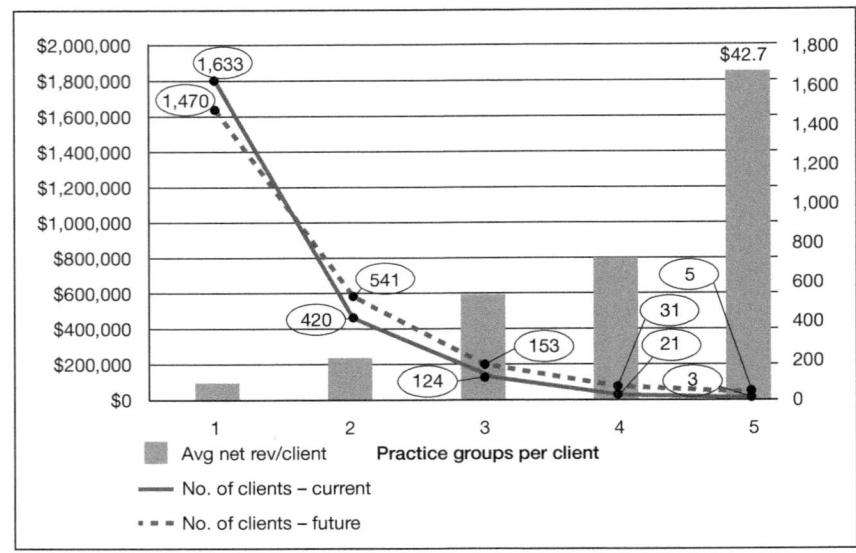

When using these findings to gain firmwide commitment to a programme to advance collaboration, leaders can learn from the work of Daniel Kahneman, for which he won the 2015 Nobel prize in the field of behavioural science. His Prospect theory shows that "losses loom larger than gains".[3] According to this theory, it is more powerful for leaders to frame the outcome of increased collaboration as avoiding loss (that is, making sure there is no "money left behind") rather than revenue gained.

Cross-practice collaboration is more valuable than mere cross-selling for several reasons. First, more involved practices means that more lawyers are developing a web of relationships and can spot more opportunities to provide service.

Furthermore, cross-practice collaboration allows lawyers to move up the food chain within their client – that is, gain access to more senior executives with broader responsibilities, larger budgets and more sophisticated needs. This complex work commands higher margins – as one partner said, "The clients are much more generous on fees because if it's so big, the deal's got to get done, and they cannot waste time negotiating or nit-picking." Overall, cross-practice work is less subject to price-based competition. Whereas clients view an engagement involving single-specialty expertise (about a basic employment or tax issue, for

---

3 See Daniel Kahneman and Amos Tversky, "Prospect Theory: An Analysis of Decision under Risk", *Econometrica*, March 1979.

instance) as a commodity that can be awarded to the lowest bidder, they know that cross-specialty work is complex and harder to accomplish effectively.

Done right, cross-practice collaboration also makes clients stickier in the long run by creating switching barriers. As the general counsel of a Fortune 100 company explained:

Despite what they think, most individual lawyers are actually quite replaceable. I mean, I could find a decent tax lawyer in most firms. But when that lawyer teamed up with colleagues from IP, regulatory, and ultimately litigation, I couldn't find a whole-team substitute in another firm.

Our empirical research shows a direct correlation between client longevity and the number of practice groups involved. While 75% of clients working with a single partner would consider switching firms if said partner left, 90% of clients served by two or more partners would remain loyal to their firm under the same circumstances. These numbers indicate that revenues don't just multiply as a result of effective collaboration: they become significantly more sustainable.

3. The talent case for collaboration

Today, we have a pretty robust understanding of the complex relationships between collaboration, partners' motivation, attitudes toward their firms and, ultimately, their retention levels.[4] In this section we examine the statistical evidence that clearly demonstrates how collaboration can make an important and unique contribution to building the people resource at law firms. We lay out the case for collaboration as a winning strategy for the entire talent life cycle: attracting and integrating new hires, helping engage talent and make them more productive, and even maintaining them as friends of the firm when they leave.

3.1 Collaboration supports the integration and success of lateral hires

Of course, a successful talent strategy is partly about recruiting the right people. But just as important, it's about helping them be productive and engaged in their positions. One of the strategic challenges in law firms today is recruiting laterals into the firm – and then finding a way to hang onto them and make them successful.[5] Unfortunately, however, firms are generally quite poor at integrating laterals in a way that makes them more productive. One researcher concluded, for example, that external hires cost a firm 18% more money in salaries than did its internally promoted colleagues.[6]

---

4   Dr Heidi Gardner and Anusia Gillespie, *Smart Collaboration for Lateral Hiring*, Globe Law and Business, 2018; Heidi Gardner, "Integrating Lateral Hires: The Key to Retention and Productivity", *The American Lawyer*, 2019; Heidi Gardner, "The Lateral Hiring Paradox", *PD Quarterly*, 2019.
5   'Laterals' can include anyone who has some successful experience in the workplace – in other words, anyone who's not fresh out of school – but I tend to use the word to describe relatively senior people.
6   Matthew Bidwell, "Paying More to Get Less: The Effects of External Hiring versus Internal Mobility", *Administrative Science Quarterly*, September 2011, vol 56 no 3, 369–407.

Our research shows that collaboration is essential to ensuring that lateral hires can become successful and productive. That said, it has to happen *quickly*: if laterally hired partners are to be successful at their new firm, they have to be sufficiently integrated with incumbent partners and clients within the first 10–12 months, and preferably sooner.

Specifically, two things need to happen in that short time:

- Laterals need to have had the opportunity to work on at least a couple of the firm's incumbent clients (on pitches, if not actual projects).
- They need to have got at least a couple of long-term partners to help on client work they generate (either with clients they imported, or brand new ones).

If either is missing, they're at a higher risk of leaving; if neither subsequently happens, they're likely to be gone by their three-year anniversary, as illustrated in Figure 3.

Figure 3. Collaboration and lateral hires – two paths

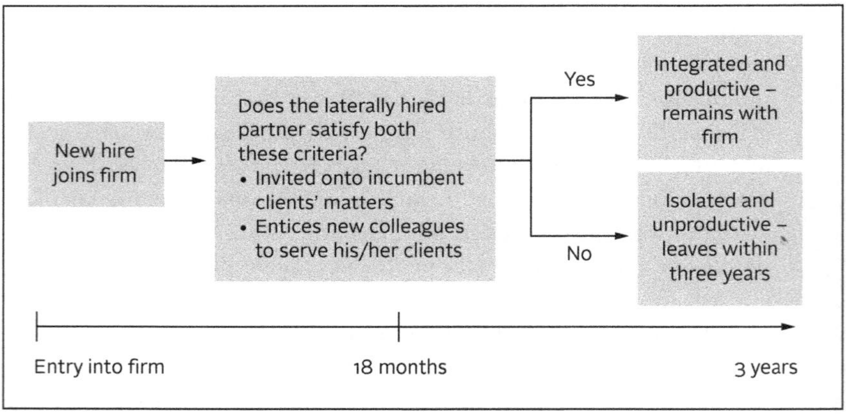

Source: Author.

How exactly does smart collaboration help laterals to thrive? Smart collaboration gives new hires the opportunity to share their valuable expertise, promote their reputation and foster their colleagues' interpersonal and competence trust early on at their new firm. Further, collaboration helps to bring lateral hires up to speed with the way the firm operates – especially the unwritten rules and cultural expectations. Through these experiences, new joiners become part of the fabric of the firm, finding not only commercial and professional success, but also more meaningful and deeper relationships. In short, smart collaboration – combined with clear planning and proper follow-through – can help lateral hires to acculturate and thrive.

The trick, of course, is making sure that your firm is set up to foster this kind of lateral–incumbent collaboration. Firms need a well-constructed plan, and a relentless focus on execution and clear accountability processes, if they expect to help laterals achieve two-way collaboration quickly and efficiently. Many law firms claim to have a plan but then rely on opportunistic approaches. As one law firm managing partner put it, "'Opportunistic' is a euphemism for no plan." Through our research, we have developed a three-stage process to help increase your success rate with lateral hires, outlined in the Special Report, *Smart Collaboration for Lateral Hiring*.[7]

3.2 Collaboration enhances engagement and productivity

Decades of psychology and sociology research show that the higher the number of formal or informal connections between individuals and their colleagues, the more those individuals are committed to both their job and their employer. The point is worth emphasising: employees who collaborate more develop a stronger psychological attachment to the organisation, with the result that they tend to see the firm as an important part of themselves.

My own survey and archival research confirms that many knowledge professionals' motivation, sense of belonging and, ultimately, retention rates increase as a result of their collaborative experiences. Many partners who had participated in collaborative client engagements reported that the most important benefit for them was the opportunity to meet new colleagues or deepen existing relationships. For example, one respondent wrote about "the camaraderie that comes with working as a group". Conversely, another welcomed collaboration because otherwise "being a partner can feel quite lonely sometimes".

Partners also mentioned how collaboration helped them feel supported in their work. For example, one wrote, "A problem shared is a problem halved – it is reassuring to have the right expertise on hand. I feel more supported and less anxious about the responsibility I carry." Still another answered, "I'm more engaged as part of a team."

That respondent was speaking to specific circumstances, but our empirical analyses show that it's fair to extrapolate a bigger picture. We have compelling statistical evidence across firms that people who collaborate more – that is, participate in substantive client work with a greater number of colleagues – not only stay longer at their firms, but are more financially productive while they're there.

And committed, collaborative partners almost certainly generate positive trickle-down effects, too. When partners are better at collaboration, they are

---

7   Dr Heidi Gardner and Anusia Gillespie, *Smart Collaboration for Lateral Hiring*, Globe Law and Business, 2018.

more likely to involve more junior partners and senior associates in substantive client work. Not just delegation of the "do this discrete task and return it when you're done" variety, but rather the engaging of smart minds to help solve complex problems. Not just taking their ideas as background for top-to-top discussions, but exposing those juniors directly to real-life clients. Juniors on those sorts of teams get not only increased opportunity to learn and demonstrate new capabilities, but also more mentoring. Each of these aspects, in turn, enhances the retention of both high-performing associates and young partners.

The more contacts a person has within an organisation – such as the kinds of relationships that emerge from working on deal teams or joint pitches – the more strongly that person will believe in and accept the organisation's values and goals. Senior leaders often bemoan their partners referring to "my" instead of "our" clients. Collaboration could be the remedy: collaborative experiences motivate people to move beyond seeing themselves as a franchise and to view themselves instead as part of an interdependent team.

Partners often volunteer this perspective when responding to my survey questions about their personal experiences of collaboration. One wrote, for example, that he valued teamwork with fellow partners because it produced "the feeling that colleagues and I are working towards a common goal, namely the success and prosperity of the firm as a whole".

Another way that collaboration among partners can increase motivation and productivity is by giving people a broader perspective on clients' problems, and a deeper understanding of how their specialty contributes to a bigger solution. Psychological research has convincingly demonstrated that when a person feels like his or her work has meaning and is important to their organisation – and by extension, to clients – then he or she exerts more effort and becomes more committed, both to the team and to the organisation.

In response to my surveys, partners frequently mentioned their ability to learn from their peers during collaborative work. Broadly, the type of learning people talk about falls into two categories: content and process. Respondents reported gaining "knowledge about what other parts of the firm are up to, as well as market opportunities", a "broader understanding of what our client's business is, and which individuals to target for a particular business proposition", and "learning more about nuances of other colleagues' business lines".

Beyond content knowledge, partners also mentioned developing their professional capabilities through collaboration, such as enhanced skills in processes such as problem solving, preparing for client pitches and communication.

These collaboration-related outcomes might be derided by cynical partners as mere feel-good effects or 'soft stuff' – the sort of nonsense valued only by people who can't handle real work. They could not be more wrong: empirical research demonstrates clear, measurable, positive financial results associated with engagement. In a study that sought to identify the key differences between high- and low-performing teams, the Gallup organisation asked 1.4 million employees from 50,000 teams questions about everything from mission and purpose to pay and career opportunities. Next they picked out the statements that high-performing teams agreed with, while others did not. At the top of the list: "At work, I have the opportunity to do what I do best every day." Teams whose employees "strongly agreed" with this statement were 44% more likely to earn high customer satisfaction scores, 50% more likely to have low employee turnover, and 38% more likely to be productive (see Figure 4).

Figure 4. Optimise engagement and motivation to perform

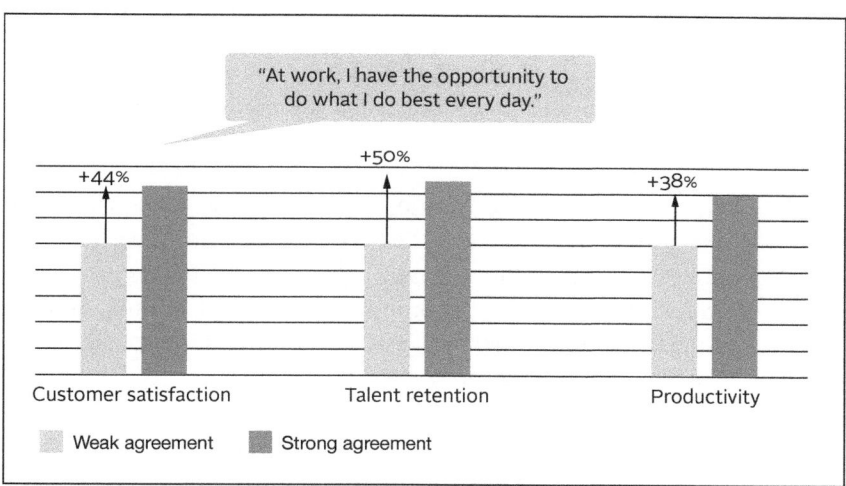

Source: Author.

3.3   Collaboration builds alumni loyalty

Your firm can't and won't retain everybody – the odds and the economics are against it. But a collaborative approach is likely to engender their ongoing loyalty even after they have moved on – and this loyalty can be of real value to your firm.

How does collaboration play a role in this? Simply stated, somebody who feels much more tightly tied into the firm is going to behave as a friend of the firm after they've left. McKinsey – my former employer – never releases its numbers, but longstanding industry lore has it that the firm derives a large majority of its revenue through its strong relationships with its alumni.[8]

---

8   McKinsey is mentioned here because it is credited with pioneering the idea of 'alumni relations' for PSFs. But many other consulting, accounting, law and financial service firms have similarly built programmes to foster mutually beneficial relations with former employees. See "Gone but not forgotten", *The Economist*, 1 March 2014.

McKinsey also touts its alumni network, including a database of more than 34,000 former consultants, as a major benefit for potential recruits.

Building loyal alumni – McKinsey case study[9]
Transparent, public communication about the firm's "up or out" model increases trust and enhances alumni pride and connectivity.

Excerpt from the McKinsey website about its alumni programme:
"As profoundly stimulating as it is at McKinsey, people do leave. We're OK with that.

In fact, we're proud of what they achieve as global leaders. Around a quarter of our alumni have started their own entrepreneurial ventures, and more than 400 are CEOs of organizations with revenues north of $1 billion.

We think it's great that there's a lot of McKinsey in places other than McKinsey. Because of the collaborative, supportive nature of the culture, people here make friends for life.

Our alumni number nearly 30,000 and work in virtually every business, public, and social sector in 120 countries. Through formal events and informal networking, former McKinsey consultants make and sustain professional relationships. For those alumni who are interested, we regularly communicate via e-mail, bi-monthly webcasts, LinkedIn, and surveys through the McKinsey alumni website. This dynamic network is a lasting benefit of a McKinsey career."

Additional steps to increase employee engagement and sense of fairness during the performance management and exit process – people leave as "friend of the firm":
1. Keep people informed with honest feedback about their progression. When it becomes evident that they're not on track, give them a choice (if possible): "Up your game to these specific standards by showing improvement in these specific ways, or start looking for another place." Feedback should never be a surprise.
2. Keep communications positive but realistic. McKinsey has a clear mantra that even people who don't succeed at the firm are still "winners", but that they need to find a place where they can leverage their skills better or thrive in a different environment.
3. Give them time to search for the next opportunity, and help them find positions that fit their skills. Firms find it mutually beneficial to place

---

9   See Heidi K Gardner, *Smart Collaboration: How Professionals and Their Firms Succeed by Breaking Down Silos*, Harvard Business Review Press, 2017. The article from which the case study was adapted is no longer available on the McKinsey website.

leavers with existing or desired clients, but the sophisticated ones know that having employees leave on good terms is the most important aspect.

4. Allow the leaver to control the messaging. At McKinsey, most people left for "an exciting new opportunity". Except for a few close friends, perhaps, it was never clear whether leaving had been their choice or whether they were managed out. And it didn't matter, because by the time they left, they really did have a great place to land.

The accounting firm PWC counts more than 100,000 former employees in its alumni network, and the firm reaps many benefits from staying connected with them. First, its 'communities of practice' – which include alumni – help the firm identify new trends and connect with potential clients. Secondly, it has created a new class of what might be called 'semi-alumni' – that is, people who no longer work full-time with the firm, but return to work for short stints during especially busy periods.

The prescriptive point here is to make sure that people feel such affinity with the firm while they're with you that after they leave, they are eager to share expertise, contacts and other resources. Collaboration helps instil this perspective: if they have been part of a strong, collaborative team, then that kind of identification can be enduring.

Chances are also good that if your firm's culture and talent management systems are robust enough to support this sort of alumni-building programme, they will also help to foster collaboration before people consider leaving.

4. Key steps for implementing a smart collaboration talent strategy

Even when partners accept that smart collaboration can produce financial, strategic and talent-related benefits, their intellectual buy-in often fails to translate into their own behavioural change. It's what researchers have identified as the 'knowing-doing gap'.[10] To help you close this gap and create lasting collaborative change, this section draws on our ongoing work with firms to focus on two of our most recent approaches. Both combine top-down and bottom-up actions and perspectives to help achieve buy-in and lasting change.

4.1 Uncover internal barriers to collaboration

Many leaders have a set of hypotheses or assumptions about what holds the firm back. When we conduct research inside firms, however, we often find that leaders' views are only partially supported by the data.

---

10   Jeffrey Pfeffer and Robert I Sutton, *The Knowing-Doing Gap: How Smart Companies Turn Knowledge into Action*, Harvard Business School Press, 2000.

Why are leaders' views disconnected from others'? One reason is that leaders' views are biased, merely because of their position; research in social psychology backs up the oft-observed situation where people's views change when they attain greater power.[11] Beyond the mere perceptions, though, leaders' experience of collaboration is often genuinely different from others in the organisation for a few reasons. First, leaders often are long-tenured in that firm, meaning that they have had ample time to build broad-reaching, productive networks of colleagues inside the firm. Secondly, they were presumably elected because people trusted them; as we see below, trust is a critical foundation for collaboration. Finally, few people say no to a leader's request for help. All in all, people at the top actually do face fewer collaboration obstacles – the distortion between their views and others' on collaboration is not merely one of perception. Nonetheless, getting a clear-eyed view of the firm's true readiness for implementing a collaboration-related strategy is crucial for getting started on the right path.

This process starts by soliciting broad-based inputs from across the entire partnership – not only to ensure that you are collecting and interpreting views from everyone, but also to build a sense of participation amongst the whole group of senior leaders. Research clearly shows that 'voice' is a critical element for helping people feel invested in a change effort.[12] The way to access wide input is to use surveys that ask simple, open-ended questions about partners' perceived barriers to collaboration. Such methodology prevents biases and invites the participants to contribute a wide range of inputs from tactical, operational vantage points to conceptual, blue sky perspectives. Ideally, a team trained in qualitative research methodology will analyse these free-text responses, separating discrete barriers that respondents had co-mingled, assigning each to a category. Multiple people should code each response to minimise interpreter bias, check that inter-rater reliability is high and discuss differences to get a clearer, unified interpretation. Although labour-intensive, this method preserves the integrity of people's own words and avoids the 'demand bias' problem associated with multiple-choice surveys.[13]

Running such analysis across 5000+ PSF partners worldwide has helped us to distil a number of common barriers to collaboration:

- **Knowledge of the firm's offerings.** Since firms can vary in size and jurisdiction, it may be difficult to know who can do what, to what extent, and with what resources. This barrier is especially prevalent in firms that have grown through mergers. It's also frequently cited as a barrier in large firms with dispersed offices, although it is remarkable

11   G Van Kleef, C Oveis, I Van der Löwe, A LuoKogan, J Goetz and D Keltner (2008), "Power, Distress, and Compassion: Turning a Blind Eye to the Suffering of Others", *Psychological Science*, 19(12), 1315–22.

12   Rune Lines (2004), "Influence of participation in strategic change: resistance, organizational commitment and change goal achievement", *Journal of Change Management*, vol 4 no 3, 193–215.

13   Demand bias occurs when responses appear to be influenced by the perceived purpose of the study – based on affiliation with the researcher or deduced from the survey structure.

how little awareness partners have of their colleagues' capabilities even in smaller firms.

- **Competence trust.** When collaborating, one needs faith in others' professionalism, skillset and capabilities – not only technical legal skills, but also client handling ability such as responsiveness. The lack of strong trust presents a clear barrier. It shows up in references to "loss of quality control" or having to "prod and then being embarrassed by poor delivery". Again, this can be an issue for firms that have merged: a partner will think, *By definition, half the partners who joined from the other firm are below average … but which ones?*
- **Incentives and key performance indicators.** Many partners report their firm's compensation and performance management structure as barriers to collaboration. And rightly so: no perfect compensation system exists because each one has known both trade-offs and unintended consequences. Some, however, are more broken than others – especially the ones that rely strictly on formulaic calculations of individual outcomes.[14]
- **Lack of time/inefficiency of collaboration.** The collaborative process can be logistically challenging due to different time zones and language or cultural barriers, for instance, or to the time required to explain the task to someone else. Every partner is undoubtedly busy: the real question is not whether they have time, but where they choose to spend it. We often see this barrier arise in firms where the structure (eg, incentives) and leaders fail to hold people accountable for delivering on collaborative goals.
- **Selling skills and confidence.** Oftentimes, it's best if partners can identify collaborative opportunities for their clients – picking up on different clues that may demonstrate additional client needs or broadening the scope of the initial pitch. This is the most under-reported barrier by partners: many do not recognise their deficiency, and even those that do are typically reluctant to admit it.
- **Interpersonal trust.** Unlike competence trust, interpersonal trust pertains almost entirely to distrust in someone's character and intentions – rooted in previous observations or simply a lack of familiarity. Typically, partners who joined as lateral hires have been vetted extensively in terms of their ability, but their new colleagues will worry about their prowess in porting client relationships from one firm to another: "Are they going to steal my client next?"
- **Preference for independent working.** Professionals in general, and lawyers in particular, have a strong desire to work independently. This tendency is typically engrained through legal education and training.

---

14   For more on this topic, see Dr Heidi K Gardner, "Collaboration for Ringmasters" in *Smart Collaboration: How Professionals and Their Firms Succeed by Breaking Down Silos*, Harvard Business Press, 2017.

Unlike an MBA programme, for example, where graduate business students work extensively in teams, many law school programmes reinforce a competitive mindset through forced-rank grading systems and solo assignments. The 'tournament' promotion system for associates, individualistic incentive system for partners, and law firm cultures that celebrate individual stars further reinforce this mentality.[15]

Our work in one law firm revealed the relative importance of these barriers in the minds of that specific firm's partners (see Figure 5).

Figure 5. Barriers to collaboration in one global law firm

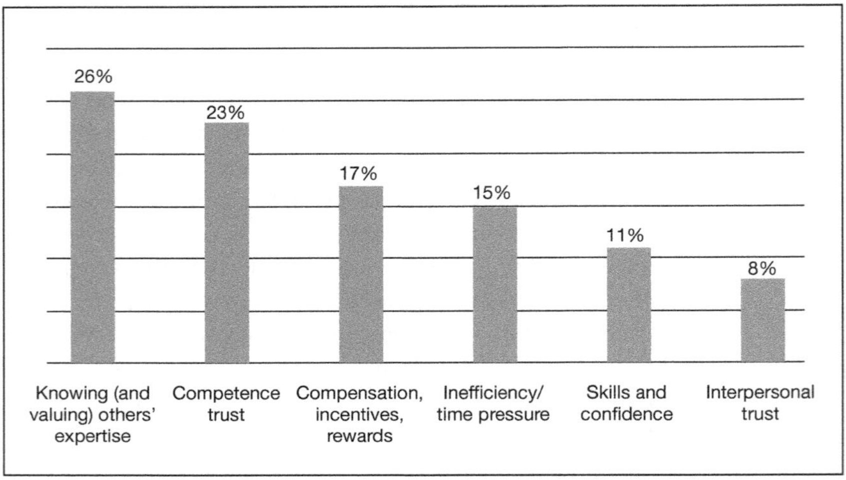

Source: Author.

Each firm needs to identify its own internal 'battles' and win them through its own uniquely tailored strategy and execution.[16]

4.2   Optimising individuals' and leaders' collaborative efforts
Leading an organisation towards enhanced collaboration requires more than top-down action. To drive towards a more collaborative firm, leaders need to equip their talent to be able to collaborate better: individuals need to understand their own starting point on collaborative skills and tendencies, and learn how to leverage those tendencies to create more effective teams. Likewise,

---

15   Marc Galanter and Thomas Palay, *Tournament of Lawyers: The Transformation of the Big Law Firm*, University of Chicago Press, 1991.
16   For a more complete description of uncovering barriers to collaboration, see Heidi Gardner & Ivan Matviak, "Implementing a Smart Collaboration Strategy" in *Law Firm Strategies for the 21st Century: Strategies for Success*, Globe Law and Business, 2020.

group leaders need to understand how to draw out the strengths of each team member to enhance their overall functioning, and outcomes.

Each person has the potential to enhance collaboration at the team and organisational level by deploying their unique combination of strengths in conjunction with the diverse strengths of others in the group. Smart collaboration at the organisational level hinges on team diversity – effectively deploying the group's broad set of behavioural tendencies and skills to maximise the benefits of collaboration. By becoming aware of your natural tendencies and making deliberate choices about how to behave in a team setting, you have the power to help the group collaborate more effectively.

For example, one behavioural tendency we have uncovered is known as 'risk spotting'. If you are strong on this tendency, you will be acutely aware of potential risks. You can use this ability to help groups avoid falling prey to group-think and ensure that a diversity of views, including dissenting opinions, is heard. In contrast, people with a 'risk-seeking' tendency are relatively quick to identify opportunities. This tendency is valuable in surfacing new and potentially bold ideas. At the same time, a watch-out for risk seekers is their potential for over-optimism, even in the face of critical challenges.

Both behavioural tendencies (risk seeking and risk spotting) can thus be valuable depending upon the context, and they will be more valuable if used intentionally and in balance with tendencies of other group members. More generally, because no single behaviour is optimal across varying situations, individuals, leaders and teams need to understand how to use those tendencies effectively and flexibly.

(a)   *Research-backed tool to identify collaborative strengths*

The ability to identify collaborative strengths starts with people understanding their own behavioural tendencies and preferences, as well as the natural tendencies of those they work with. Many people have, to some degree, an intuitive sense of their behavioural tendencies. However, this can lead to an overreliance on those strengths, emphasising them even in sub-optimal situations and blind spots. People need an unbiased view of their tendencies so that they can choose how to respond in any given situation and thereby increase their ability to create the outcomes they want. This objective view can be gained through psychometric tests.[17]

We have conducted empirical research with multiple law firms to identify specific behavioural tendencies closely aligned with smart collaboration. We measured the results of partners' actual collaborative actions, such as expanding a client relationship across practice groups, and studied the behavioural

---

17   M Ziegler and M Brunner, "Test Standards and Psychometric Modeling" in A Lipnevich, F Preckel and R Roberts (eds), *Psychosocial Skills and School Systems in the 21st Century: Theory, Research, and Practice*, Springer, 2016.

tendencies associated with those successful collaborative outcomes. We distilled these behavioural tendencies into seven dimensions of smart collaboration:[18]

- **Individual vs group:** our tendency to engage in collaborative work. In general, would you rather work on your own or in a team?
- **Close vs distant communication:** our preference for the frequency of interactions and comfort with revealing personal information. Do you talk about your outside relationships and interests with colleagues, or keep that side of your life private?
- **Wary vs trusting:** the base level of trust we are likely to feel for our colleagues. Do you inherently trust others, or wait for them to prove themselves?
- **Complex vs concrete:** the attraction to complex problems and innovation. Do you enjoy abstract concepts and new ways of working, or prefer to deal with practical ideas and applications?
- **Risk spotter vs risk seeker:** how do you balance the risk with the opportunity of working with others? Do you readily see risks and feel motivated to avoid them, or do you more readily see opportunities for success even if there is a risk of failure?
- **Responder vs initiator:** to what extent do you take the initiative and anticipate events? Do you tend to deal with situations as they arise, or do you look several steps ahead to influence the future?
- **Hands-on vs hands-off:** How much control do you need in your environment? Do you have a high desire for routine and structure, or do you prefer spontaneity and less structure in your day-to-day activity?

(b) Individuals' path to enhancing collaborative behaviours

Once people get an objective view of their own position on each dimension, they can learn how to use their tendencies as a strength. This is critical: rather than try to change an individual's preferences, the objective should be to help a person maximise their effectiveness by being mindful of when and how to use those tendencies.

Turning insights into action requires practical, personalised guidance. For example, a 'distant' communicator requires less frequent communication, minimises small talk and pleasantries and prefers to get straight to business, among other tendencies. One way he or she can leverage those preferences for higher team performance is by sharing the limelight and giving others – especially introverts – the time and space they need to contribute fully.

Research also shows that change occurs over time and requires deliberate, repetitive effort. To achieve this – especially getting time-starved lawyers and staff to focus on collaboration – people will need to get periodic prompts over

---

18   See The Smart Collaboration Accelerator website at: https://smartcollaborationaccelerator.com/.

time to help them focus on the most high-impact practical action they can take to engage in smart collaboration.

(c)   *Leaders' strength-based approach to enhanced collaboration*
With access to their team's psychometric test results (collectively – not attributed to any specific individual), leaders can better understand, manage and motivate their teams to engage in enhanced collaboration within the group, with other parts of the firm and with clients.[19]

For example, imagine that you lead a team with a high proportion of people with a 'concrete' tendency (preference for tackling pragmatic issues rather than ambiguous ones). Your team overall may struggle to understand and lean into ill-defined problems. By identifying the few team members with a preference for the 'complex', you can leverage them to help the group break problems down into comprehensible pieces to facilitate a common understanding. As the group moves towards a clearer view of the issue, the majority 'concrete' members can focus on developing execution plans.

By understanding the behavioural tendencies and skills within the team, the leader can identify potential barriers to effective collaboration and intentionally deploy the needed skills to drive the team forward.

5.   Role modelling collaborative leadership
The clear signals of how and where partners spend their energy, and how they direct others to do the same, have a strong influence on how collaboration gets engrained (or not) in the firm's culture. Through their actions, leaders must constantly reinforce that smart collaboration is a means to a much larger end: providing holistic solutions to clients' complex issues. If, instead, the partners feel that they are being asked simply to collaborate more, then they are likely either to waste time and effort, or simply to ignore the mandate. A call for unfettered collaboration is irresponsible and counterproductive. Role modelling collaboration, through both words and actions, requires ongoing and committed leadership.

To be clear: all partners in a law firm are de facto leaders, regardless of whether or not they hold a formal title.[20] Each one needs to step up to lead the firm towards a more collaborative environment – one where talent thrives and the firm provides the highest-value service to its clients. Through strong, collaboration-focused role modelling, leaders can help the firm and all of its people achieve their best possible futures.

---

19   For a technical treatment of different compositional effects of personality on group outcomes, see Lisa M Moynihan and Randall S Peterson, "A Contingent Configuration Approach To Understanding The Role Of Personality In Organizational Groups", *Research In Organizational Behavior*, vol 23, 2001, 327–378.
20   Heidi K Gardner, Rebecca Normand-Hochman and Larry Richard, "Leading Lawyers in a VUCA World" in Rebecca Normand-Hochman and Heidi K Gardner (eds), *Leadership for Lawyers: Essential Leadership Strategies for Law Firm Success*, 2nd edition, Globe Law and Business, 2019.

The role of personality in lawyer development

Larry Richard
LawyerBrain LLC

1. Introduction

Increasingly these days, lawyers are required to take on other roles besides the practice of law itself. Research at Harvard has shown that increases in complexity precipitate a greater need for management and increases in external uncertainty precipitate a greater need for leadership.[1] Both complexity and uncertainty have skyrocketed in the legal profession, and consequently nearly all lawyers today have to manage and lead.

My own research into the lawyer personality over the past 30 years has revealed that lawyers have stronger and more atypical personality traits than the general public, and these 'outlier' traits therefore play an outsized role in everything they do – as lawyers, as leaders and as managers.

In order to describe the key role that personality plays, I have organised this chapter as follows:

- a brief history of what led to my interest in measuring the personality traits of lawyers, along with a summary of the most important findings that have emerged from that research; then
- an introduction to the seven outlier personality traits that differentiate lawyers from the general public, what the traits measure and the kinds of behaviour to expect from high- or low-scoring individuals; and finally
- some insights and recommendations about how you can incorporate this information into your own development as a lawyer, leader or manager.

2. A brief history

When I earned my PhD in psychology, I focused my doctoral dissertation research on the personality traits of lawyers. I administered the Myers-Briggs Type Indicator (MBTI) to a statistically randomised national sample consisting of over 3000 lawyers in all 50 US states. What I found surprised me. The personality preferences of lawyers turned out to be dramatically different from those of the general public, and to explore this further I eventually turned to a

---

1   John P Kotter, John P Kotter on *What Leaders Really Do*, Harvard Business Review Press, 1999.

more sophisticated and accurate personality tool called the Caliper Profile. In the mid-1990s I began to test lawyers in earnest to see if this tendency for lawyers to score as outliers showed up there as well. It did. The first study I conducted, in 1998, was reported in my article "Herding Cats",[2] and it revealed that on six of the 18 traits measured by the Caliper Profile, lawyers scored as outliers – that is, their average score for each of these traits was outside the standard deviation for that trait. In plain language, that means that the average score for lawyers was either far below or far above the range in which the average member of the general public is expected to score.

There's a seventh trait, discussed below, that has always hovered near the boundary, at 41%, but never formally fell below the 40th percentile line to qualify as an outlier, so I never have reported on it in my writing till now. As I will note below, it's now solidly in outlier territory and qualifies as the seventh outlier trait.

These seven outlier traits tell a consistent story. People who become lawyers are atypical, that is, significantly different from the general public. Further, it seems self-evident that most of these traits help lawyers to be effective at practising law, which is why they show up so persistently. However, today these very same traits may impede lawyers' effectiveness in their newer roles of leader or manager.

Each of the seven outlier traits is summarised in section 3, below.

Note that most of the testing that I've done over the years has been in my role as a consultant to lawyers. Feedback from testing can play a powerful role in behaviour change, leadership effectiveness and team productivity. Here are three brief examples:

2.1 Behaviour change

I was asked to coach a high-powered partner in a small specialty law firm. He was a very significant rainmaker, but he also created a stressful environment and was considered by others to be difficult to work with. He was frequently critical and fault-finding. When I discussed the results of his personality test with him, he was curious about one score in particular – he had a 1% score on the trait of 'accommodation'. He asked me what that meant, and I explained that a high score generally denotes a person who is nurturing, helpful, and puts others' needs ahead of their own, while a low score like his may mean that he can be blunt, no-nonsense and intolerant of excuses. I asked him if he related to these adjectives and he agreed they described him. He explained that when someone made a mistake, he felt that he was doing them a favour by being blunt and not sugarcoating his feedback. In other words, his intention was

---

2   Dr Larry Richard, "Herding Cats: The Lawyer Personality Revealed". Available at: http://lawyerbrain.com/sites/default/files/caliper_herding_cats.pdf.

positive – he wanted to help them. Once he realised that the effect of his bluntness actually produced the opposite effect from that intended, he literally changed his behaviour overnight. I had calls from other partners in the ensuing weeks saying, "What happened to Fred?!" (not his real name.) This kind of dramatic and relatively instantaneous change is rare but not unheard of.

2.2 Leadership

I worked with the managing partner of a top AmLaw firm who had a 'resilience' score of 1%. This means that he was very thin-skinned. (By contrast, high-resilience individuals are thick-skinned – they let criticism roll off their backs.) It's quite natural for constituents to push back when leaders make decisions – in any business – but in a law firm, pushback is particularly common. This thin-skinned leader told me that every time he made a decision, certain partners criticised or pushed back, and every time that happened, he felt like a failure and wondered if he should quit as managing partner. He tortured himself with doubt. During our de-brief he learned, of course, that his score on resilience was 1%, and while lawyers tend to be low in resilience to begin with (we average at 30% while the general public averages at 50%), his resilience score was much lower than even the lawyer average.

At first, he felt bad – most low-resilience individuals do. However, once we talked through the strategies that he could employ to build his resilience, his tone changed and he became more comfortable with his role as a leader. As I told him, effective leadership is a function of the leader's *behaviours*.[3] High or low resilience simply influences how easy or hard it will be for an individual to consistently do those behaviours. Luckily, some groundbreaking research has identified several formidable techniques for building resilience which he found very helpful.[4]

2.3 Team productivity

The executive committee of a prominent midwestern regional law firm was composed of seven partners, including the managing partner. I asked each of them to complete the Caliper Profile. They then all voluntarily agreed to share their scores with each other. I conducted a de-brief with them as a group. When we got to the trait of 'urgency', I showed a graph that stopped the conversation. The managing partner had a score of 99%; no other partner had a score over 60% on this trait. That's actually unusual for lawyers, since lawyers typically average about 70% (compared to 50% for the public). The managing partner stared at the graph, and then asked his partners, "Do I ever rush things

---

3   Jim Kouzes and Barry Posner, *The Leadership Challenge: How to Make Extraordinary Things Happen in Organizations* (6th ed), Jossey Bass, 2017.
4   Karen Reivich and Andrew Shatté, *The Resilience Factor: 7 Keys to Finding Your Inner Strength and Overcoming Life's Hurdles*, Broadway Books/Random House, 2002.

through?" Every other partner in the room stared at their shoes. Finally, one of the partners – his closest friend in the firm, actually – said, "Joe [not his real name], you do it all the time!"

The managing partner realised in that moment for the first time the effect he was having on the rest of his leadership team. He intentionally slowed down the pace for the rest of the meeting. Several months later, I met with the committee again, and they reported significantly higher productivity which they all attributed to the more deliberative and patient way that their managing partner had been conducting their meetings.

3. The seven outlier traits

3.1 Scepticism

The personality trait of 'scepticism' measures the degree to which an individual is vigilant about information or people. A high score is typical of people who challenge the assertions of others, focus on what's wrong or could go wrong, and question the motives and possible hidden agendas of others. They tend not to give others the benefit of the doubt.

A low score is characterised by an open, accepting and trusting nature. Low-scoring individuals tend to give others the benefit of the doubt, take them at their word, and focus on what's working, what's good, what's possible.

It's no surprise that this trait is the highest-scoring outlier for lawyers. As noted above, in the original study the trait averaged at 90% for lawyers. While not unheard of, it's very uncommon to see a scepticism score for any individual lawyer that's below the 50th percentile. By contrast, half of the general public score below that percentile. Lawyers are paid to be sceptical. It's a mindset that helps them protect their clients.

The challenge for lawyers today is that in addition to wearing their lawyer hat, they are often expected to play one or more of the newer roles that I mentioned earlier in this chapter. Virtually all of those roles depend on building and sustaining effective relationships for success in the role. One of the most important ingredients for building effective relationships is trust (which is, in fact, one way to label low scepticism). Trust and scepticism are opposites.

Let's take the leadership role as an example. Constituents in any kind of organisation are much more likely to trust and therefore follow a leader who is him/herself trusting – and less likely to do so if the leader is sceptical. Scepticism is a reciprocal trait – when someone is sceptical of us, it's human nature for us to be sceptical of them. Scepticism undermines effective leadership – even in an organisation of sceptics.

3.2 Abstract reasoning

Lawyers are also outliers on a trait called 'abstract reasoning', scoring on average at the 82nd percentile (compared to the 50th for the general public). High-scoring individuals on this trait like analysing, intellectual stimulation and problem-solving. Many of them like to argue for the sake of arguing. They like using their intelligence in their work. It's no surprise that individuals who score high on this trait are disproportionately attracted to the field of law. Low-scoring individuals are more practical, and less academic. They don't generally enjoy the abstract analytical process – even if they're good at it. While there are certainly some very practical-minded lawyers in practice today, my data shows that the vast majority of lawyers are individuals who seek and are stimulated by intellectual challenge, analysis and argument.

3.3 Urgency

The personality trait of 'urgency' measures how patient or impatient one is. High-scoring individuals tend to want to get to the finish line as quickly as possible. They want to be where they're going, not where they are. They may finish the sentences of others, cut corners, roll through stop signs. Low-scoring people are patient, deliberative, reflective, and like to take their time before they act.

Lawyers in private practice tell me repeatedly that their clients want responsiveness above all else. Studies confirm that clients put this at or near the top of their list of criteria by which they evaluate the lawyers they hire. So, it makes sense that the profession would attract people who are dispositionally urgent (ie, urgency is part of their innate personality).

But once again, this same useful trait can impede success in other roles. Take, for instance, mentoring. One of the skills for success in a mentoring relationship is the ability of the mentoring lawyer to be patient and to fully listen to the mentee. Lawyers with a high urgency score may be inclined to do the opposite – to interrupt, finish others' sentences, and so on. Likewise in the role of leadership – leaders need to gain buy-in from their constituents in order to foster voluntary followership in the direction in which they are trying to lead others. But the leader who is impatient will face far greater challenges in gaining buy-in than his or her more patient colleague.

I should note at this point that the best science today suggests that all personality traits are the result of both 'nature' and 'nurture', that is, part genetic predisposition and part social learning during our formative years. Psychologists used to glibly say that personality is 50% nature and 50% nurture; but that was a more axiomatic statement made at a time when we didn't have solid empirical data. Starting in 1979, a series of remarkable studies of identical (monozygotic) twins who were separated at birth and raised apart was begun at the University of Minnesota. Other researchers followed with similar studies.

These studies have revealed that, in general, personality is more genetic than we previously believed,[5] although the nature/nurture contribution seems to vary depending on the particular trait.[6]

Given that personality is more genetic than learned, you won't be surprised to learn that changing your personality is very hard to do. We can all learn to manage our personality, that is, to regulate when and even whether we use a trait at a particular moment, but the trait remains our default or go-to response at all moments except those during which we're vigilant. In effect, your personality hasn't changed, but your behaviour has. Nevertheless, you will always feel the tug of the personality pulling you back to your comfort zone.[7]

Individuals with a high score on urgency may need to learn how to regulate their natural tendency to cut to the chase under certain situations in order to increase their likelihood of success.

3.4 Autonomy

Technically speaking, there is no trait called 'autonomy' on the Caliper Profile. There is a trait called 'external structure' – high-scoring individuals tend to look outside themselves for guidance about what their priorities should be, and how to do their job. They pay attention to the expectations of others. They may consult procedures manuals, or rely on the chain of command, or on the instructions of superiors in their organisation's hierarchy, or on rules and regulations. By contrast, low-scoring individuals don't like being told what to do. They bridle at the confinement of following rules. And they resist authority. Lawyers average around 11% on external structure – in other words, they're highly autonomous. Over the years, I have found that the label 'external structure' is off-putting and even confusing for many people, and the concept of autonomy makes much more sense. So instead of reporting this as an 11% external structure score, I reverse it and describe lawyers as having an 89% autonomy score. Same thing, different label.

3.5 Resilience

There are actually two kinds of 'resilience'. The more common version, often

---

5   If you're interested in a deeper dive into this fascinating topic, take a look at Nancy Segal's new book *Entwined Lives: Twins and What They Tell Us About Human Behavior* (Penguin, 2000). Segal was a researcher who worked with Thomas Bouchard, the leader of the Minnesota twins studies.

6   'Extroversion', which is a trait that appears on virtually every serious personality assessment tool, is widely believed to be the most genetic trait. In the Caliper Profile, this trait is labelled 'gregariousness'. Most of the 18 traits measured by the Caliper Profile are believed to be more genetic than learned (although clearly some of each always contribute), but three traits in particular appear to be more learned than genetic – resilience, 'cognitive empathy' and scepticism.

7   For example, I have a 99% score in urgency. There are situations in which being highly urgent/impatient is simply counterproductive. I have trained myself to slow down and to be more patient in many of those situations. But I always find that it requires me to concentrate really hard to carry that out, it's uncomfortable, and I can only do it for a limited period before I lose my patience once again. So I can regulate my *behaviour* but it doesn't change my *personality*.

written about in the popular press, is what I call 'Big R' resilience. This refers to the quality of bouncing back from adversity. When an individual suffers a traumatic or dislocating setback – a fire, a flood, a divorce, a tragic accident – and they nevertheless recover and resume a normal life, that process of recovering or bouncing back is correctly called resilience. The Caliper Profile does not measure this quality. Rather, it measures what I call 'Small r' resilience. Small r resilience measures how thick- or thin-skinned a person is in the face of criticism, rejection or other setbacks.

Individuals who score high on resilience on the Caliper Profile tend to be thick-skinned. When criticised, either they don't let it affect them, or they briefly feel the sting and then let it go and turn their attention to other things. Years ago, I tested a lawyer in New York City who was practising as an IP litigator. He scored 95% on resilience, which is unusual for anyone but highly unusual for a lawyer. I asked him, "What is it like for you when someone criticises you?" He thought for a moment, shrugged his shoulders, and responded, "I guess it means that someone else has a problem."

There are really two stages in how an individual responds to criticism or rejection. The first is how well they tolerate it in the first instance. The next is how well they bounce back in those situations in which they suffer a setback.

Individuals who score low on resilience tend to be more vulnerable to criticism or rejection. They are easily hurt, even wounded, by criticism. They often rely on a variety of defensive responses – they may vociferously defend themselves and spend a lot of energy explaining why they did what they did. Such defensive explanations are often misplaced. Let's say that you step on my toe, and I say, "You're stepping on my toe," and your response is, "Oh, but I didn't mean to step on your toe. I thought it was a lump in the carpet. Actually, you put your toe under my boot. You know, maybe you're just too sensitive ..." If I'm like most people, I really don't care why you stepped on my toe. I just want you to get off it!

Low-resilience individuals may also use denial, deflection or counterattack:

- *Denial:* "I don't think I actually stepped on your toe."
- *Deflection:* "Can we have this conversation some other time? I'm really busy working on a matter right now."
- *Counterattack:* "Wait, you think that my stepping on your toe is bad? Let me tell you what *you* did last week ..."

Not only are low-resilience individuals much more vulnerable to criticism/rejection in the first place, but once they experience the setback they can sulk, ruminate, and sometimes stay stuck in these unproductive emotions for hours, days and in some cases even weeks.

In fact, really low-resilience individuals can be so primed for defensive behaviour that they may get defensive even in response to a comment that others would take for a compliment. For example, let's say I'm walking down the main shopping avenue in a large city with a low-resilience individual. We pass a high-end clothing store, and I glance in the shop window and see an attractive outfit on the mannequin. I say to my low-resilience colleague, "You know, you'd look great in that outfit." A high-resilience individual would typically hear a compliment and say thank-you. But a really low-resilience individual might instead respond, "What – are you saying you don't like what I'm wearing?!"

Resilience has been the most consistent outlier trait for lawyers in the 27 years that I've been using the Caliper Profile. I consistently find that lawyers average about 30% (compared to the average for the general public of 50%). But even more significantly, the distribution of scores for lawyers does not look like the traditional symmetrical bell curve; rather, it's a skewed distribution, with nearly all lawyers bunched up in the lower half. In other words, my data consistently shows that 90% of the lawyers I test have a resilience score below the 50th percentile. (In the general public, only half of the public scores below the 50th percentile.) Lawyers are remarkably thin-skinned and defensive.

Some of the most prominent law firm leaders and some of the most significant rainmakers have resilience scores in the single digit range. I've had quite a number, in fact, who scored 1%.

Why are lawyers so low? We can't be entirely sure, but there's some evidence from research at the University of Pennsylvania and from studies done by the US Army in their Master Resilience Training programme that resilience is a function of several factors that are within our control. Two of the most important such factors are mindset and social connection.

Individuals with an optimistic,[8] glass-half-full mindset tend to be more resilient than individuals with a more pessimistic, glass-half-empty mindset. They tolerate life's bumps (criticism, rejection) better, and when they do succumb, they bounce back quicker and better than their pessimistic counterparts.

And individuals with an ongoing network of connections with others that are authentic, vulnerable and emotionally honest also tend to be more resilient

---

8   'Optimistic', in this context, refers to the scientific version of optimism, not the popular conception. In our culture, optimism is often conflated with pie-in-the-sky, unrealistic views rooted in fantasy. Optimists are seen by some as ignoring important realities. However, in scientific research optimism is seen as a more realistic mindset. The research seems to be divided into studies of optimism about the future (Will the future be bright or dark?) and studies of optimism as a way that individuals think about the future implications of *past* behaviour. The leading researchers on the future-oriented form of optimism are Charles Carver and Michael Scheier. Optimism as a way of making sense of past behaviour has come to be called 'explanatory style' – when I have a setback, do I see it as lasting forever or for just a short while? Does it ruin everything, or is it confined to a narrower set of consequences? And is it something that I could take better control of the next time, or am I a victim of circumstances? These facets of explanatory style were discovered by Martin Seligman at the University of Pennsylvania, and have been described in his book *Learned Optimism* (Alfred A Knoph, 1991), and in his more recent book, *Flourish: A Visionary New Understanding of Happiness and Well-Being* (Free Press, 2011).

than individuals whose relationships are more cerebral, superficial or even non-existent (ie, individuals suffering from loneliness). As with optimism, socially connected individuals tolerate life's bumps better, and recover quicker and better when they have a connected community for support.

Where do lawyers stand on these two qualities? Lawyers tend more towards the pessimistic side.[9] And, while pessimism is not exactly the same as scepticism, they're often found together. Highly sceptical individuals tend, more often than not, to be pessimistic. Thus, lawyers are not benefitting from a resilience-boosting optimistic mindset.

Likewise, lawyers tend to de-prioritise social connection, and thereby fail to benefit from its resilience-boosting benefits. To understand this further, consider the next outlier trait – 'sociability'.

3.6 Sociability

The Caliper Profile does not measure social connection directly, but it does include a trait called 'sociability', which measures the degree to which a person is interested in initiating new, intimate connections with others, likes people, and pays attention to and places importance on the personal lives of others, versus the low end of the scale which describes an individual as private, sometimes as avoidant of relationships or intimacy, uncomfortable focusing on or talking about relationships, and even as someone who may trivialise or altogether dismiss the importance of relationships.

My data consistently shows that lawyers are very low on the sociability trait, with average scores for most groups of lawyers falling in the bottom half of this scale. I've tested many groups of lawyers where the average sociability score was literally in the single digits, that is, below 10%. Here again, this means that at the very least, lawyers are not benefitting from the resilience-boosting potential of ongoing authentic connections.

Low sociability scores may also explain why the vast majority of partners in law firms find rainmaking uncomfortable and difficult to do. Low scores also have important implications for leadership. Research by Kouzes & Posner shows that leadership is an inherently relationship-based practice.[10] Effective leaders must gain buy-in from their constituents, and they do this mainly through establishing trusting and authentic relationships with them. Low-sociability lawyers who also serve in leadership roles may struggle to gain buy-in, compared to their less numerous high-sociability colleagues.

---

9   JM Satterfield, J Monahan and MEP Seligman (1997), "Law school performance predicted by explanatory style", *Behavioral Sciences & the Law*, 15(1), 95–105. Ironically, this same study found that pessimistic lawyers performed better in law school. This raises the possibility that the very qualities necessary for success as a lawyer at the same time may be undermining our resilience. This theme deserves further research.

10   Jim Kouzes and Barry Posner, *The Leadership Challenge, supra*.

3.7   Cognitive empathy

The preceding six traits – scepticism, abstract reasoning, urgency, autonomy, resilience and sociability – represent the six personality traits that have consistently emerged as outliers in the 27 years that I've been gathering test data with the Caliper Profile. But in the last three years, there is a seventh trait that has emerged as an outlier – 'cognitive empathy'.

Psychologists describe multiple forms of empathy. Most say there are two – cognitive and emotional.[11] Some identify three types of empathy.[12] And some posit four.[13] The Caliper Profile measures only one – cognitive empathy. This form of empathy refers to the act of intellectually understanding the experience of another, and the impact of your own or others' behaviour on that other.

Cognitive empathy is an important trait.[14] It plays a significant role in effective leadership, mentoring, teams, collaboration, rainmaking and overall collegiality. And it is indispensable in the lawyer development process from the perspective of both the lawyer who is being developed and the professional development specialist who is designing or delivering the programme.

Lawyers have always tested below average in my research, averaging for many years at 41%. (Remember, 50% is the average for all traits for the general public.) I never considered it an outlier because technically it was within the guardrails of the standard deviation (ie, above 40% but below 60%).

However, over the past three years, my data has shown a decline of about three percentage points. Today, most groups I test have lower empathy than in earlier years. The average score these days hovers around 38%. This is outlier territory.

This decline is not surprising. Several studies have presaged a decline in empathy in the general population.[15] In my experience as a coach and consultant to lawyers, I have come to believe that for most individuals, the decline is mainly due to failure to pay attention to the other person and failure to place importance on their experience, rather than to a decline in the actual skill of empathy. This is good news, because it means that the remedy is simpler – train people to pay more focused attention to the experience of others.

---

11   Sarah D Hodges and Michael W Myers, "Empathy" (on the subject of cognitive vs emotional empathy), in *Encyclopedia of Social Psychology*, Roy Baumeister and Kathleen Vohs (eds), Sage Publications Inc, 2007. See also Lesley University, "The Psychology of Emotional and Cognitive Empathy". Available from the Lesley University website at: https://lesley.edu/.
12   Daniel Goleman, *Focus: The Hidden Driver of Excellence*, Bloomsbury, 2014.
13   Theresa Wiseman (1996), "A Concept Analysis of Empathy", *Journal of Advanced Nursing*, 23, 1162–67.
14   Caliper simply calls this trait 'empathy', but it's clear from their technical manual that they are measuring cognitive empathy. In the rest of this chapter, for the sake of succinctness, I will also simply refer to it as 'empathy', but in every case in which I do so, I am referring specifically to cognitive empathy.
15   See, for example, the oft-cited article by Sarah H Konrath, Edward H O'Brien and Courtney Hsing (2011), "Changes in Dispositional Empathy in American College Students Over Time: A Meta-Analysis", *Personality and Social Psychology Review*, 15(2):180–98, reporting roughly a 40% decline in empathy from 1979 to 2011 among millennials.

4.   **Using personality to develop yourself as lawyer, leader or manager**

Taken as a group, the seven outlier traits present a complex portrait of lawyers. On the one hand, at least four of the outlier traits support them in practising high-quality law. Lawyers need to be sceptical in order to protect their clients. They feel a responsibility to be responsive to those clients, and urgency makes them naturally suited to keeping things moving. High abstract reasoning is common among lawyers because using one's intellect is a primary part of practising law. And autonomy is even written into the ABA's Model Rules of Professional Conduct – Rule 5.4 is entitled "Professional Independence of a Lawyer".

It is a bit harder to see the professional advantages conferred by low resilience, low sociability, or low empathy. It's possible that some exist, but without straining, I can't see them.

It is beyond doubt, however, that outlier scores in any of the seven traits can impede success in the roles of leader or manager, which both depend for their success on building trusting and empathic relationships.

Armed with an understanding of the seven outlier traits that characterise lawyers, let's look at some ways that you can harness this information to develop yourself and become a more effective lawyer, leader or manager.

The first step, I would suggest, is to increase your self-awareness. There are very few downside consequences, and enormous upside benefits, to self-awareness. Over the years, many clients have shared with me how useful it was to them when they got feedback from having taken a personality test of some sort. This is especially true when the test is well designed and scientifically valid and reliable like the Caliper Profile and a small handful of others.[16] Taking such a test, and getting feedback about your own personality, is a very useful first step for anyone in the professions, including the practice of law.

Once you know your own traits, you can determine if there are any particularly strong traits that you may want to either leverage to great advantage, or manage to ensure that they don't get in the way of your delivering the best outcome.

There are certain traits (among Caliper's 18) that are worth paying attention to if you want to improve your effectiveness in influencing, understanding or motivating others. Cognitive empathy (perspective-taking) leads my list. To accomplish just about any goal involving other people, it's really important to be able to step into their shoes to understand their needs, and how they're likely to react to the various things you ask them to do or learn.

Second, you should know your resilience score. Note that low-resilience individuals almost always think that a low resilience score is bad. That just goes with being low in resilience. But keep in mind that no trait is ever all good or

---

16   Other well-designed tests include Hogan Assessment, 16PF, CPI, EverythingDiSC, NEO-Pi-R, HEXACO and others.

all bad. On the contrary, every trait has advantages and disadvantages. The most important thing is to know what your strongest and weakest traits are so that you can understand what might be leveraged or what needs to be managed.

For example, one of the benefits of a low resilience score is that it can serve as a motivator for some people to self-improve. In others, it may make them more sensitive and build their acuity in interacting with others (even though the main motivation for doing so may be to avoid accidentally triggering a criticism).

That said, I suggest that if you step into the role of leader or manager, you may find yourself in situations where the lawyers you're working with give you feedback you don't want to hear, or they criticise your approach, or they disparage something that you worked hard on. If you naturally tilt toward a low-resilience response in situations like these, it may undercut your ability to get the result you want. Learning some resilience-building strategies can give you a broader palette in navigating these situations.

Below are some Caliper traits to which you may want to give special thought. Merely becoming aware of your tendency is the most important thing. You don't necessarily have to manage these traits (although doing so from time to time can benefit everybody), but by becoming aware of those traits which, for you, are strong (ie, very high or very low), you may be able to design your work life in a way that allows you to use your most comfortable (ie, strongest) personality traits more of the time and avoid having to use the ones you're least comfortable with. Note that I'm describing 'high' and 'low' scores – if you can't decide, or if you're pretty clear that you're in the middle, then you can safely ignore my advice. I'm mainly talking to individuals with strong scores one way or the other on a particular trait.

4.1 Urgency

If you're very high on this trait, recognise that the pace at which you prefer to take action, interact with others, talk, listen and set expectations of others may be much faster than other people are used to. You may want to make some adjustments accordingly. And if you're very low on this trait (which is less common in a law firm but not unheard of), you may want to rise to others' level of expectations about speed in certain key situations.

4.2 Cautiousness

This is not an outlier trait for lawyers. Lawyers' scores are distributed on the same standard bell curve as those of the general public. But it's a useful trait to understand if you're managing others, and an essential trait to understand if you're leading others. If you score high, you most likely are careful, like to have as much information as possible before you make a decision, and don't like taking most risks. If you score low, you may be more risk-taking, willing to pull the trigger more quickly ("Ready, fire, aim"), and possibly impulsive. People at both ends of this trait can do fine in a management role. It just helps to know which end you prefer. Certain tasks require operating carefully, thoughtfully and with deliberation (high cautiousness), while other tasks lend themselves to a more seat-of-the-pants, intuitive approach. The better you align your management style with your natural personality preference, the more effective and satisfied you're likely to be. But leadership is a different story – by definition, leaders must take risks since they are always guiding people into the unknown. Leaders need to understand their own tendency with respect to cautiousness – if you're high on this trait, your comfort zone may be risk aversion, which can seriously impede your ability to lead. On the other hand, if you're really low on this trait, you may lead people in a certain direction without first gathering sufficient information. In either case, the stakes can be high. Effective leaders know their level of cautiousness, and make appropriate adjustments to match the situation they're in.

4.3 Accommodation

This, too, is a standard bell curve trait for lawyers. If you score high, you may tend to put your own needs second in order to support others and help them. You may tend to be compassionate, nurturing and accepting. If you score low, you may favour tough love – being blunt, direct, eschewing any sugarcoating, telling it like it is. Again, there's room for both approaches in both leadership and management, but you'll want to know which end you favour and then try to align your work to your personality. Certain tasks naturally call for a compassionate response, while others seem perfect for the tough love approach. Every leader and manager will inevitably encounter situations in which they have to modify their behaviour – step outside of their comfort zone – in order to do the right thing.

4.4 Thoroughness

Here's another normally distributed trait for lawyers. If you score high on this trait, you may be very conscientious in dotting the i's and crossing the t's. High-scoring individuals tend to enjoy marshalling the details and take satisfaction from getting it right. They tend to like low ambiguity and appreciate precision. Low-scoring individuals are more comfortable at the 30,000-foot level, preferring to think in terms of abstractions, generalisations and intuitions, and are more comfortable with complexity and ambiguity, and with patterns and trends. They look for how things fit together (they see the forest rather than the trees), and often play it by ear. Again, in both leadership and management, there's usually something for everyone. Know your preferred style, that is, which end of the scale is your comfort zone, and try to align your work with that preference.

4.5 Scepticism

We've already discussed this quite thoroughly, but I include it here because it's really helpful to know if you're the typical high-scepticism kind of person that's so common in law firms, or if you tend to be a low-scepticism individual. If you're low on the scepticism trait, you may be more naturally trusting, accepting of others, and non-judgemental. You may give others the benefit of the doubt. And you may be more naturally optimistic, tending to see the glass half full rather than half empty. This can serve as a guide both in terms of what *kinds* of tasks you choose to do regularly, as well as how you approach doing whatever tasks you do in your job.

Note that in leadership in particular, every leader needs to learn how to be trusting in order to engender trust from their constituents. So, if you score high on scepticism, you will find it comfortable to practise law and more challenging to lead; and if you score low on scepticism, you may find the exact opposite.

I've stated earlier that most personality traits are more genetic in origin, with a smaller component of social learning contributing to the trait. However, there are three Caliper traits in particular that are clearly more learned than genetic: empathy, resilience and scepticism.

Lawyers tend to score lower than average in empathy and resilience, and higher than average in scepticism. In the practice of law, these trait ranges may work just fine. But when you shift into a leadership or management role, you will undoubtedly find that it requires higher empathy, higher resilience, and lower scepticism. The good news is that because they're all traits that have a large learned component, it's realistic and feasible to train yourself – or to train others – to become more skilled in all three. Following are my recommendations about raising empathy, building resilience and learning to selectively dial back scepticism.

(a) Empathy training

Empathy training means more perspective-taking, which is another phrase for cognitive empathy. In my experience, it's relatively easy to teach (willing) lawyers how to improve their skill at taking the perspective of others. It has more to do with teaching them how to remember to pay attention to the needs of others than it does with actually building new skills. (There are, of course, certain individuals who will also need help in building their skill at perspective-taking. And there is a small minority of individuals who are just not wired for this and who won't benefit from training. Some of these individuals may be able to learn the skills through a more concentrated course of one-on-one coaching, but the cost/benefit ratio is usually not favourable, and even if it were, in my experience the learning for these individuals is often short-lived, further reducing any justification for investing in such coaching.)

(b)   Resilience training

Because lawyers are so low in this trait, there's almost always an advantage to improving one's resilience, even slightly. As with empathy, this trait has a large learned component and thus can be readily taught. We are fortunate that in the past 20 years, the science has advanced significantly in this area, and today we have some very specific, reliable and actionable strategies for teaching individuals to raise their level of psychological resilience. There are also some excellent self-help resources available for both empathy and resilience.[17]

(c)   Scepticism-regulation training

Nearly all lawyers (especially those with high scepticism scores, which is most of them) will benefit from training in how to selectively and mindfully regulate when they employ their scepticism trait, and when they intentionally suspend it or tone it down. It should operate at full force when you are wearing your lawyer hat, and it should be dialled back when you're wearing your leader, mentor, manager, rainmaker or supervisor hats. Psychologists refer to this process of selectively dialling back a trait as 'down-regulating'.

Note that teaching sceptical lawyers to down-regulate scepticism is a little more challenging than the other two, because the scepticism itself may make the individual you're hoping to train somewhat sceptical about the value of the training. A challenging Catch-22.

5.   Conclusion

In this chapter, we have covered the background and history of my personality research in the legal profession. We have reviewed how testing can play a powerful role in behaviour change, leadership effectiveness and team productivity. We have reviewed the seven statistically significant outlier personality traits that characterise lawyers. And we have considered ways that knowledge of these traits (and others) can help you become more self-aware, align your work with your personality to enhance your effectiveness and satisfaction, and become a better leader or manager. Finally, I have explained the value of developing specific training for lawyers in the areas of increasing cognitive empathy (perspective-taking), building psychological resilience and learning to adapt, specifically by learning how to down-regulate the scepticism trait in situations where trust and rapport are essential.

---

17   For more on empathy, see Jamil Zaki, *The War for Kindness: Building Empathy in a Fractured World*, Robinson, 2020; and on resilience, Karen Reivich and Andrew Shatteé, *The Resilience Factor: 7 Keys to Finding your Inner Strength and Overcoming Life's Hurdles*, Broadway Books, 2002.

Leading lawyers through change

Robert Sharpe
Consultant psychologist

1. Introduction

Implementing change in law firms, whatever their shape or size, is guaranteed to provide a cocktail of challenge, pushback, factionalisation and mischief, as well as reasoned debate and effective changes. From my experience of law firms, from Magic Circle to high street, the phrase 'herding cats' is more applicable to only one profession – psychology. What follows is true of all of professions; and the reflections on the legal profession presented in this chapter can be doubled and more for my own, psychology. At least lawyers have managed to accommodate like-minded souls together, with varying degrees of comfort, under the umbrella of a law firm. Few psychologists have managed the same marvel of cohabitation!

I write this chapter as both a 'participant observer' (in the anthropological sense of the term) and a trusted adviser who has been invited into the thick of it to facilitate major change in unprecedented circumstances. Prior to the early 1990s, no one had ever experienced the expansion of a law firm from one office to over 40 globally. The 1990s saw several law firms achieve this through remarkable feats of human engineering. Equally, no one had experienced the tsunami of internet-delivered, commoditised legal advice that threatened to remove the bread-and-butter legal work of high street firms. Many smaller firms rose to the challenge and are flourishing today as a result of radical changes in management style, structure and legal focus.

This chapter is offered with sincere respect for the pioneers who broke the mould and rode the globalisation wave, and with admiration for the flexibility of those local firms that relaunched themselves or invited non-lawyer commercial leaders to guide them through two decades of professional change. Weaknesses addressed in this chapter are identified against a backdrop of awe-inspiring growth and development of the global legal profession, and are intended to assist with its stellar evolution.

2. Managing expectations

Change occurs within a context. This context includes tradition, ritual, promises, expectations, threats, opportunities and predictions.

The perception of change occurs within a mindset. This mindset includes motivational drivers, self-confidence and self-esteem, personal values, sense of active participation and control.

Handling change depends primarily on how the individual's mindset has evolved. This evolution includes natural predisposition, family attitudes, teaching methods, job training, leisure activities, compensation and promotion criteria.

There is no one-size-fits-all formula for leading lawyers through change. All change carries with it a degree of discomfort. That discomfort can give rise to a wide spectrum of individual responses, from exhilaration in the case of a stimulus seeker to fear in the case of a risk avoider. When this response spectrum occurs within a population of lawyers – whose purpose is to apply a sceptical mindset to any given proposition – leading them through change can be expected to be paradoxical and challenging. This chapter aims to shed light on why change is often difficult to implement within law firms, and to suggest amendments to training programmes and law firm management that can facilitate successful outcomes.

By setting out some psychological fundamentals concerning how minds work in general, and lawyers' minds work in particular, this chapter establishes a background of psychological know-how against which to discuss practical issues of change. First, however, it is important to consider the hopes, dreams and contexts experienced by today's lawyers.

3. Aspiration and the law firm context

In an increasingly complex and compliance-driven legal environment, which is simultaneously commoditising and deregulating, significant challenges face lawyers entering into and already practising in the profession.

In many parts of the world, the legal profession no longer commands the automatic respect once afforded it by clients. Accelerating commoditisation, barrack-room internet law and do-it-yourself legal document packs have all conspired to reduce the perceived gap between client and professional from the client's standpoint. This has happened similarly in other professions. Today, doctors struggle frequently against Google-assisted self-diagnosis while attempting to get the patient well, while most accountants' clients use accounting packages for all but the year-end final accounts. Of course, demystification of the professions is to be applauded, since an informed clientele usually uses its advisers more effectively. However, an unfortunate but common consequence is a reduction of the perceived value and status of professionals. Given which, who would become a lawyer?

Some study law because they come from a legal family. Others do it for the money (although not as many as might be thought, from what they tell me). Then there are those who want to help make the world a better place through their legal efforts. Still others want to find out how it all works. But whatever the deeper motivations, every postgraduate entering training with a firm knows that it is the first step in preparing for the day that the buck stops here, having entered a profession with the ultimate objective of providing the last word on legal matters. Postgraduates have not entered their professional specialisms to make decisions by committee as might, for example, the design team for a new car or washing powder. While a lawyer may seek a colleague's view, this is very different from personally signing off on an agreement or advice whose integrity may have far-reaching and expensive implications.

In short, being a lawyer is not a team sport, but rather a group activity in which individuals play out their roles on cue, according to their skillsets and regardless of the other players who make up the group. This is the basis of the self-reliance upon which, quite appropriately, any professional's status, reputation and success are built.

Lawyers get together in firms of widely varying shapes and sizes for company, economies of scale, opportunities to cross-sell to clients and a mutual understanding of each other's peculiarities. They do not gather together for homogeneity of viewpoints, values or *modus operandi*. Indeed, fighting their corner against opposing views is the stock in trade of lawyers; this makes it notoriously difficult for law firm management to implement changes which challenge colleagues' currently held views.

A law firm may appear to clients to be a brand, with team-like cross- and on-selling. To the lawyers working within it, however, it may be more like a cooperative of self-contained individual practitioners. If a law firm really were a team structure, then change by command and control might work efficiently. However, top-down edicts may face guerrilla opposition in the flat, individualistic, group cooperative structure that actually exists within most law firms, where far more individual canvassing and reassuring is likely to be needed to make change propositions acceptable.

4.   Left, right and limbic

The first component of the psychological know-how promised above is a fundamental understanding of the way in which the main parts of the brain function together, as background to a discussion on lawyers and change. That may well sound as daunting to a lawyer as completing a corporate merger would to a psychologist. For both, the truth is that it is not so hard when you know how. The following thumbnail sketch says all that we need to consider and has become the route map for thousands of lawyers, from trainees and partners to coachees and seminar attendees. Most of the rest of the discussion follows logically from the fundamental axioms it embraces.

The three brain areas that produce our thoughts and actions are the right and left cerebral hemispheres and the limbic system.

The right hemisphere is responsible for creativity, interpersonal behaviour, artistic and musical appreciation, dreams, ideas, possibilities, blue-sky thinking and innovation; it is generally the brain's playground. As such, it is where we have most of our fun and where we experience thinking outside the box – that is, insight and invention. Right-brain activity is often referred to as 'divergent thinking' – we start with the seed of an idea that explodes into many possibilities, some of which are considered for feasibility and handed across to our left hemisphere for further work. Importantly for this discussion, it is where the consideration of change takes place and especially where positive connotations of change occur.

The left hemisphere is the seat of convergent thinking. It takes those right hemisphere ideas that have made it through the strategic evaluation centre and forms them into a reality. The left brain calculates, applies logic, project manages; costs; structures; and completes the end product ready for deployment. It looks on change largely as an annoying departure from its well-honed methods, algorithms and techniques that have made it such a safe, sure calculator – unless, that is, its right-hemisphere neighbour provides it with a new possible algorithm to add to the collection.

The limbic system is the seat of emotion. While it also manages the body's homeostasis – maintaining a stable state of temperature, digestion, circulation and so on – this is of little psychological importance. The limbic system is responsible for all of our emotional expressiveness, from joy to anger to fear. This part of the brain appreciates what the other two parts have dreamt up and created and gives us the impulse to find other ideas to bring to fruition.

Essentially, this cooperation of brain areas is the entire explanation of what we call 'motivation': getting an idea, making it happen, rejoicing in the finished product and deciding to do it all over again. The more harmonious and integrated these brain areas are, the more the individual feels comfortable with consequential actions and thoughts. At its height, this harmony is the basis of what sportspeople, musicians and actors refer to as being 'in the zone': a transcendental state of flow where the performer feels completely at one with equipment or actions. This is where great performances, world records and other memorable acts occur. Virtuoso cellist Rostropovich's genius, for example, was that he was in a permanent state of simultaneous left-brain-right-brain-limbic activity. He could compose, perform and cry openly with sadness or joy – all at the same time. Most of us have to make do with doing things one by one: salutations, Maestro Rostropovich!

Parenthetically, this trilogy of brain areas also provides a framework for understanding and responding appropriately within any verbal exchange. Speech patterns can contain facts or opinions (from the left brain), desires or possibilities (from the right brain), and emotions or feelings (from the limbic system). All utterances can be analysed into one or more of these groupings and responded to appropriately. A formulaic example could be, "I can see you're [insert emotion recognised – angry, excited, worried etc] about [insert occurrence, prospect etc] and want to [insert objective, vision, possibility etc]." While this looks more like maths than psychology, it has a name – reflective listening – and works like clockwork in bonding with, enlisting and persuading colleagues or clients. So, as a prerequisite of leading lawyers through change, listening effectively to their reactions to change propositions is likely to encourage them to find new ways of looking at what could otherwise be worrying prospects. Maths, after all, has many and varied uses.

The formal – and most of the informal – training received by lawyers is exclusively left-brain dominated. The right brain is often treated as something to fit in if there is time and limbic activity is frequently considered to be an annoying distraction. Modules focusing on social skills teaching – developing self-esteem and confidence, being good fun to be around or motivating self and others – are rare or non-existent in law colleges or firms. Yet all of these are right-brain or limbic attributes and they are all characteristics that firms appear to seek keenly through popular descriptions such as emotional intelligence or thinking outside the box. "We've got any number of good technically able types," as one senior partner put it, "but few whom we feel confident to expose to clients." The inevitable conclusion is that most law firms' training and recruitment philosophies value the safe, intellectual type over the adventurous, entrepreneurial type – and that this preference will dictate the culture of future law firm generations. It is now easy to see that leading safe, intellectually calculated lawyers through change is likely to be significantly more demanding than leading adventurous, entrepreneurial lawyers who would be more likely to envision opportunistic possibilities through change via their more practised right hemispheres.

I have spent thousands of hours with trainees, associates and partners, facilitating their right-brain and limbic activities, especially in the context of mentoring and preparing partner-track associates. Invariably, working with lawyers on practical ways of involving their creative and emotional functioning leads to the qualities of fun and flexibility that are as much of a friend to change as logical analysis can be its enemy.

5.   **Rationalisation and compensation**

Rationalisation is our second fundamental psychological building block. Without it, we would cease to function. There is a basic human need to form an understanding of our environment, however individual or eccentric this understanding may be and however entropic and contrary that environment. Rationalisation works in a self-justificatory and circular fashion. On the one hand, we make sense of events by fitting them into our personal belief framework (rationale) of how things work. On the other hand, we build and strengthen our beliefs that our understanding is correct by selectively collecting a bedrock of experiences that support this rationale.

We usually rationalise after an action or event (*post hoc* rationalisation), though we can also rationalise something we are about to do (*a priori* rationalisation, often dignified with terms such as 'strategic'). Through this process, we justify our actions and proposals to ourselves and we tend to interact with others who share our rationale, justifications and views. As we age, we become progressively more certain about our viewpoint and increasingly resistant to change.

This phenomenon is closely related to the '*Einstellung* effect',[1] now more commonly referred to as 'mindset'. Mindset is the biggest enemy of change, thinking outside the box, and thought leadership. Essentially, we repeatedly resort to trusted problem-solving methods – even when shorter or more effective solutions are available – and robustly push back against change or challenges to the established ways of doing things.

As a prime example, a firm's compensation model can be as axiomatic and unquestionable as a religion. A firm might adjust its model by putting in a new bonus tweak, just as a car manufacturer might show off this season's saloon car's new fastback. But it is rare to see radical changes unless the firm, like the car manufacturer, gets sold or merged. Yet with firms adopting a wide variety of compensation schemes, from lockstep to 'eat what you kill', there is no clear winner so far as the legal industry is concerned.

Adherence to a compensation model clearly reflects the power of rationalisation. Having decided to join a certain type of compensation system, the individual will need to become comfortable that the choice is sensible. Evidence will be garnered that supports the choice; contrary evidence will be marginalised; and the individual will become a 'believer'. Once a person has moved from empiricist – or evidence gatherer – to converted believer, the serious mental commitment of rationalisation has been made.

This process strengthens important business requirements such as organisational culture, brand and unity. Problems arise, however, if a firm's top strategists wish to make radical changes to the core processes in which the culture has invested its trust. Now, the very belief that for so long had been a major ally can become a major opponent. The party line is a double-edged sword.

Beliefs are rationalisations that have become spurious axioms – personal 'truths' that are psychologically fundamental. Lawyers are, by nature and training, both analytical and rational, reaching judgements readily and strongly and becoming adherents and believers within their chosen structures. 'Party

---

1   AS Luchins, "Mechanization in problem solving – The effect of Einstellung", *Psychological Monographs*, vol 54 no 248, 1942.

line' and 'values' can become synonymous in the hands of corporate culture consultants keen to help firms engender an emotional as well as intellectual buy-in from their staff. While their techniques are often effective, later adjustments to the party line can be seen as a *volte face* and fuel for opponents' derision.

When using management buy-in techniques to embed some particular mindset, law firm leaders might therefore consider how to avoid over-tightening the nuts and bolts of organisational culture. Tight cultures can work in a pyramidal corporate structure because change can be implemented, usually quite acceptably, by fiat. The flat management structure of a professional organisation is without this luxury. To ensure that a professional workforce is amenable to change, it may be advisable not to screw its members down to a party line too tightly in the first place. Caution may be advisable to avoid carving well-intentioned sentiments of today in stone, when these may need to be revised tomorrow.

6. Drivers and the 'lawyer's mind'

All humans – and most animals – manoeuvre through life under the influence of two drivers. These are the prospect of success (winning or 'response reward') and the avoidance of failure (not losing or avoidance of 'response cost'). Carrot and stick, success and fear – these drivers can act singly or in combination, and provide our third psychological building block.

As a general psychological rule, behaviour patterns that derive from a prospect of success or reward tend to be more flexible and adaptable, especially to change. Those espousing them can usually see the opportunities that change can bring. Behaviour patterns based on a fear-of-failure model, by contrast, are generally more rigid and resistant to change, with adherents tending to see the pitfalls and problems associated with change.

All professions are based on a fear-of-failure, risk-averse model of training and an intolerance of error. Law, like medicine, accountancy and engineering, requires a specific ability to make correct binary judgements – right/wrong; in/out; good/bad – and to stand by those judgements. Such qualities are considered professional, principled and reliable, and provide the basis for the training and subsequent mindset of the professional. With successful work usually drawing little comment and errors attracting lengthy post-mortems, malpractice suits or professional exclusion, progress as a lawyer relies on observance of the rule: thou shalt not err (the stick).

Excellent sports teams and profitable corporations, by comparison, have a culture that is reward-seeking and success-focused (the carrot). The effective sports team manager holds lengthy debriefings after match wins to help the players to gain insight into how they achieved their success. After a loss, they mostly forget the match, go home to sleep and start success-hunting afresh the next day. Such a culture contrasts sharply with the almost universal absence of the celebration of professional victories and the enervating post-mortems that accompany professional mistakes.

Thought leadership and lateral thinking seem to preoccupy law firm management as desirable qualities among their lawyers. By definition, to be innovative and brilliant, a solution or process must involve doing something that is not tried and tested. Little wonder, then, that an innovation might well be seen as risky to propose or carry out, since if it works, the innovator may be mostly unsung while failure may bring severe penalties.

Firms on recruitment drives have learned to make themselves look more appealing to hire prospects by espousing appreciation of the unusual and innovative, since innovation is usually fun and attractive. If this appreciation is well grounded in reality within the firm, the prospects of talent retention and adaptability to change may increase significantly. If it is not, then a costly lateral hire may fail rapidly and expensively.

A poignant sentiment I have often heard during lawyers' exit interviews or retirement processes goes something like this: "Well, at least I can look forward to making a real contribution now …" On one such occasion, the speaker was oblivious to the irony that he had led a 20-lawyer, cross-border, bank-syndicated acquisition worth $5 billion only a year ago. Just another banal, routine matter for that law firm, then … and for the lawyer, apparently.

Law firms must walk the talk when it comes to appreciating flair, daring and innovative creativity. These qualities are unlikely to flourish if they are not trumpeted, celebrated and referred to in compensation terms at every opportunity. If encouraged, they are likely to promote thought leadership and innovative behaviour, which are close cousins of change acceptance.

7. Self-esteem and the lawyer

"But wait a minute," says our lawyer, progressing well through seven or eight years of qualification. "I've stuck to the rules and the established methods and now I'm being told I have to be a thought leader. Won't that be a risk? I have to get myself board consultancies or appointments – but boards will not want someone who is always telling them why their ideas might be hazardous. And I have to merge into a team when I've been taught that ultimately I should only rely on my professional judgement. I'm also being told that my chances of partnership and my compensation are determined not only by how good my legal skills and fees yield are, but also by how good a salesperson I am; how inclusive and facilitative I am with my colleagues; whether I can contribute to a system where my group's file is the measure of my success rather than my individual earnings; and an array of similar soft skills attributes that my law college didn't have in its curriculum. Help!"

For this lawyer and the majority of his peers, a significant element of personal development has been omitted – the building block of self-esteem. Superb training in the technical elements of law is rarely augmented with coaching aimed at gaining insight into how lawyers can blend legal competence with interpersonal skills and innovative thinking – a practice that is fundamental to a strong sense of self-esteem and confidence. Where this happens, it usually does so informally and through the luck of the draw of early work experiences with a senior role model who has mastered this blend of talents and can coach the junior similarly. Clearly, luck should not be the determinant for such an important blending process. Instead, firms might encourage appropriate role model lawyers to mentor juniors more widely on the development of a style that suits their personality and blends interpersonal skills with legal competence.

Self-esteem is closely related to, and dependent upon, rationalisation, through which we make sense of our environment. From this rationalisation stems a common belief that if we do things well, we will develop self-confidence and self-esteem. Sometimes this happens, though usually by chance. Most often, there is a gap between doing things well and self-esteem, leading to impostor syndrome.[2] While first researched as a particularly female issue, we have discovered that there are just as many men – maybe more – as women making their way through professional life thinking, *When are they going to find me out? Do they realise I'm only ... well ... me?*

Self-esteem is developed not just by doing things well, but by working out how we do the things that we do well and relying on that knowledge to feel confident that we can do similarly well on future occasions. This makes future successes more likely and we come to feel comfortable that we can replicate the use of our underlying skills and attributes in the future. Those firms, companies and organisations who swap, "Well done, now here's another task to do" for "Well done – how did you do that, then? Can you see how to apply that in the future?" foster a robust sense of self-esteem and confidence in their staff and support an innovative culture of pride in a job well – and cleverly – done. That single move from "what I did" to "how I did it" is the most important determinant of high self-esteem – and it is very inexpensive to implement.

Resilient self-esteem means retaining self-belief, self-confidence and self-worth, notwithstanding the risk or commission of errors. If a lawyer's self-esteem is based on risk avoidance and error-free performance, it will be threatened by the prospect of change, with resistance to change more likely.

So, risk aversion and fear of failure frequently produce a mindset of technical excellence within a vulnerable self-esteem framework. The more vulnerable an individual's self-esteem, with the attendant fear of failure, the

---

2   PR Clance and SA Imes, "The Impostor Phenomenon in High Achieving Women: Dynamics and Therapeutic Intervention", *Psychotherapy Theory, Research and Practice*, vol 15 no 3, 1978.

greater, typically, will be the resistance to change. For many lawyers, their individual billings are their most direct measurement of their worth and largely underpin their self-esteem. Before leaving this subject, therefore, it is worth paying a visit to the popular old chestnut of individual billings versus one-file billings. In this long-running debate, senior management strives to develop greater team playing and client development by changing from a 'Whoever opens the file claims the billable hours credit' model of individual lawyer appreciation to an 'It is immaterial who opens the file: many lawyers might work with this client and their reward lies in how facilitative they have been of each other's input', idealised model.

There are many difficulties with making this change, not least of which is that most firms will have selected their young lawyers in assessment centres where candidates perform as gladiators in points-scoring group discussions and the objective is to defeat as many of their opponents as possible to secure the job. It is unsurprising that lawyers selected by such methods will be reluctant to join a lawyerly collective where their glory is shared and diluted. Already professionally sceptical, lawyers working in a firm changing to a one-file culture will look with predictable scorn upon the de-equitising or dismissal of colleagues whose personal numbers are low and be unlikely to believe, going forward, that individual file brownie points do not matter. Lawyers are, after all, persuaded by evidence rather than rhetoric, making actions far more convincing than promises from the top.

The advice here is, first, to pay attention to the lawyer's successes, victories and problems solved. Paying attention means finding out, from them or others, how they achieved their success. What attributes, skills and talents did they discover that can be relied on in the future to ensure repeated success? "Good show, Carruthers" and a glass of champagne may suffice for a 30-minute fix at a matter completion, but long-term esteem building requires interested, focused exploration of that lawyer's core resources. Such interest will facilitate the strengthening of self-esteem and confidence and likely make the introduction of change less threatening and, consequently, less resisted.

Secondly, if major changes are proposed that affect compensation, or even the criteria upon which job security is based, then senior management would do well not to act in ways that can be interpreted by their colleagues as ambiguous. Lawyers do not react well to ambiguity at the best of times, let alone where their livelihood is concerned.

8. Change, recruitment and partner selection

Very successful lawyers – financial and professional rainmakers – are not usually successful simply because they are good lawyers. A few years ago, a study was conducted of several Magic Circle high-fee-earning partners. The objective was to produce a video, *Winners in Law*,[3] which was completed with fascinating results.

Star lawyers or rainmakers succeed because they are personable, attentive collaborators – with their clients, with their partners and with their associates. This has nothing to do with law and everything to do with collegiality. Winners in any endeavour are necessarily good at creating and sustaining *ad hoc* teams. They rapidly gain the trust and respect of those they need to work with, rolling up their sleeves with client, partner or associate on an equal footing. The law comes second, often implemented by others in the *ad hoc* team – others who may not be so fluent in these collegiality attributes.

It was put most elegantly by a senior figure:

Up until we make an associate up to partner, we have been employing them for excellent legal technique. When they become partners, we suddenly expect them to push most of that downwards to their associates and become marketers and business builders – which many find quite difficult. The partner who adapts most easily and successfully to that is the one who, as a student, realises they are actually an entrepreneur or marketing person; subordinates that for 10 years while they do a law degree and go up the ladder; gets their partnership; and then lets their underlying natural personality burst through.

What this wise senior was saying is that anyone entering the legal profession anticipating a lifetime just doing law is courting disappointment. With deregulation, commoditisation and the internet, most of the jobs that a lawyer would have settled for happily a generation ago are increasingly being done by trained clerks or computer software.

There is little doubt that a generation from now, we shall see a different kind of entrant applying to and being recruited for membership of the legal profession. This will probably require a change in traditional selection criteria for future trainee or lateral hire lawyers and should be of major concern to law firm partners. They should be in a position to justify the selection criteria that they and their HR departments use to recruit key professional personnel – criteria such as mid-adolescence exam results and the ability to handle role-played conflict with an actor in the interview process, or to out-talk other candidates around an assessment centre's group discussion table.

In the case of academic achievement, many law firms in the United Kingdom still rely on the arbitrary exclusion of candidates who have not excelled in mid-adolescence examinations, notwithstanding that they may have achieved a master's or PhD degree at postgraduate level. This takes no account of the growth and development potential of candidates and discounts those individuals who may not have flourished in a school environment but have accelerated rapidly once entering further education. Such selection criteria may thus exclude those with significant potential for personal and intellectual development, selecting arbitrarily along left-brain criteria and completely

---

3   Dr R Sharpe, *Winners in Law*, video publication, 2003.

ignoring right-brain creativity, innovativeness, fun, collegiality and limbic emotional intelligence in the initial rough grading of applicants. Many older generation star lawyers had average to dismal mid-adolescence exam showings, while others did the old-style articles in order to qualify. Neither historical landmark appears to have handicapped them en route to rainmaker status.

In the case of trainee or partner candidate assessment centre exercises, it is usually the quiet operator who listens and waits for the right moment that is most effective in real life. Yet this behaviour will almost certainly be marked down at an assessment centre group discussion exercise, while the candidate with the bombast will grab the points and doubtless get the job, even though he has failed to demonstrate collegiality, supposedly a modern-day prerequisite.

Candidate assessment measures of the type just described have as much *a priori* bearing on the real-life qualities of candidates as horoscopes, serving more to justify the existence of their creators' roles than as evidence-based future-proofing of the firm's stewardship. Since not even psychologists would be able to draw meaningful conclusions from such snapshots or parlour games, it would seem far-fetched to expect HR operatives or even senior line management to believe that they could do so.

My conclusion, based on first-hand experience of having observed many partner selection boards' processes in order to give a view on their fairness, is that, on debriefing them, few if any of the parlour games' observers have the slightest idea of what the point is, let alone how the participants should be scored. Indeed, instances of resorting to asking role-play actors for their opinions on candidates' efforts are not infrequent. This is a questionable approach to selecting the firm's most valuable assets – its future custodians and ambassadors.

As for the candidates, in such an instance there is little that could be more demeaning of their countless hours of professional advancement than being judged by a jobbing thespian. They may, however, be comforted by the plethora of blog posts that give detailed advice on how to use interpersonal techniques that will score well – ironically, regardless of how candidates behave in real life.

Raising the stakes yet higher, many of the larger law firms are beset by even more complex cultural issues surrounding partner selection assessment centre procedures. This was expressed most eloquently by an Italian international lawyer:

Anglo-Saxons think in black and white, whereas Italians think in shades of grey. We both get to our end goal most of the time, but in quite different ways. The problems come when trying to judge which approach is 'right', especially in recruitment and partner selection.

In role-plays conducted in an Anglo-Saxon-centric partnership assessment centre, points are awarded for identifying the problem, elucidating the other person's point of view, implementing a solution and facilitating the other person in retaining their dignity – all within 20 minutes. This rarely happens in real life. So the Italian candidate would simply be unable to demonstrate the value of an approach that would likely include a long lunch with the other party; discussion of many non-work interests; talk around the problem; and parting company as new friends, agreeing to talk the next day to agree on a solution, thus weaving the particular interpersonal magic that retains that client or enlists that colleague for life.

Frequently described by partners as a ridiculous way to select trainees and partners, the use of such selection criteria and procedures has a clear bearing on leading lawyers through change, especially internationally. By selecting and promoting the firm's lawyers on the basis of quasi-measurements that inevitably miss many of their personality attributes, law firm leaders may allow themselves to assume a homogeneity of views across their colleagues that simply does not exist. It is obvious from the Anglo-Saxon–Italian example above that leading British lawyers through change will be an entirely different prospect to leading Italian lawyers. Multiply this by as many nationalities as any one firm includes in its global reach and it then ceases to sound implausible to suggest considering the hiring of outside applied anthropologists to pave the way for major change proposals.

Interestingly, although these questionable selection procedures proliferate, I have never seen any personality disorder screening interviews carried out among candidates – this notwithstanding that the legal profession and judiciary have been represented by Dutton as carrying a greater than average percentage incidence of psychopathy,[4] second only to bankers (with the clergy not far behind both). Dutton's research and views have inevitably attracted criticism, though Hare, with several decades of experience in the subject, concurs.[5]

Personality disorders, of which psychopathy is one, are likely to cause disruption in the workplace – more so during periods of change. Distinguished by the common elements of insightlessness, lack of empathy and emotional flatness or inappropriateness, the estimated 10% of the general population with personality disorders (2% being the estimated incidence of psychopathy) are disproportionately attracted to professional and senior executive positions that hold obvious opportunities for control and influence. Their disruptive characteristics encounter little hindrance because the professions tend not to censure their own and senior executives tend to rise above straightforward disciplinary action.

Such personalities are unlikely to do well where interpersonal skills or collegiality are concerned: once dug in, they may become self-aggrandising,

4   Kevin Dutton, *The Wisdom of Psychopaths: What Saints, Spies, and Serial Killers Can Teach Us About Success*, Farrar, Straus and Giroux and *Scientific American*, 2012.
5   Paul Babiak and Robert D Hare, *Snakes in Suits: When Psychopaths Go to Work*, Harper Business, 2007.

tyrannical or unaccountable, and will often absorb a disproportionate amount of management and HR time. To ignore such a selection criterion is to dismiss a large body of psychological research as irrelevant. It also further calls into question the selection, from an assessment centre group discussion exercise, of the 'thought leader' impositional contestant, who will often have shown clear evidence of an absence of empathy, insight or emotional competence. To add a final layer of misdirection, an accomplished psychopath, sometimes called a complex psychopath, can demonstrate the most charming and charismatic attributes during a selection process, simply by learning to mimic the socially acceptable behaviour of genuinely collegial people. Navigating through such convolutions is challenging even for psychologists experienced in the subject; expecting lay assessors, even other professionals, to detect these personality attributes is probably unrealistic.

Law firm seniors should consider carrying out audits of the quasi-measurements captured in parlour-game-based assessment centres to examine exactly what they think they are measuring. Psychologically, assessment centre processes are sufficiently obscure as to be worthless as predictors of suitability (though they may well reveal characteristics of undesirability) and demeaning of the candidates who still bewilderingly submit themselves to the ordeal. Of course, the games and snapshots are far easier to employ than psychological rigour and the evaluation of post-hire evolving intellectual patterns, which are likely to cost law firms in partner time and professional advice. Time thus spent, however, brings partners into first-hand contact with this fundamental process and is much more likely to result in staffing up with flexibly minded, inspirational and effective lawyers, rather than technically efficient lawyers of indeterminate collegiality.

In addition, international law firm leaders should ensure that their firms' selection processes and assessors have sufficient cultural intelligence to encompass the rich diversity of alternatives by which interpersonal challenges can be addressed. If respected, such diversity can be of significant assistance in change implementation, but can equally be costly if ignored.

9.   The change paradox

Two frameworks currently co-exist – uneasily at best, clashing at worst. On the one hand, the lawyer has been trained and developed to be reliable, planned, unsurprising and unsurprised, conservative in respect of tried methods, risk averse, stable and left-brained. On the other hand, just like other organisations, law firms are finding that they must compete for market share; demonstrate daring and creative innovation; experiment with management styles; and generally behave in a more extrovert, right-brained fashion than they used to.

For many lawyers, the firm that they joined a decade ago has altered dramatically. It is little surprise that many talented lawyers leave the profession when they see shifting goal posts, narrowing bottlenecks to partnership and little by way of celebration of their successes and excellence. And little wonder that change engenders such personal strain and resistance (albeit mostly unconscious) among lawyers at all levels.

Here, in a nutshell, is the paradox: the discipline that has made for a good technical lawyer is premised on a fear of failure. Failure is minimised by adhering to old ways of doing things. Adhering to old ways of doing things is facilitated by resisting change. But resisting change also means missing opportunities for growth and risking being surpassed by agile competitors.

The components that make up the professional experience of lawyers can thus be summarised as follows:

- They are trained to know and remember the due processes and precedents by which previous lawyers have succeeded in addressing their clients' matters (*Einstellung* effect).
- Their method of training has been based on low tolerance of error and the corollary that errors are anathema to a career (response cost effect).
- Little is ever made of intellectual or interpersonal triumphs on the way through a matter or deal, by either colleagues or the individuals themselves ('banality of brilliance' phenomenon).
- The focus is always on the What, When, Who of the matter's completion and rarely on the How (self-esteem factor).

This results in efficient problem-processing technicians who function well unless confronted by either an intellectual accident (error) or the prospect of a change that could heighten the risk of such an accident (change aversion).

10. Conclusion

This chapter has addressed the challenge of leading lawyers through change by considering those elements of the lawyer's professional journey that conspire to produce change resistance. The implications are that if lawyers of the future are to embrace change – in respect of innovation, business needs, team file assessment, boardroom consultancy, and trusted advisory and thought leadership – then law college curricula and law firm induction, training, appraisal and compensation need to adjust significantly so as to include professional training, as distinct from cursory reference, in these areas.

From student to practising lawyer, legal professionals can be encouraged to undertake activities that are likely to facilitate right-brain and limbic thinking, including:

- collegiality skills-building at law college;
- regular internal teach-ins by those displaying excellence;
- "How did you do it?" debriefings after all completions;
- at least one funny story garnered from every matter;

- innovation break-out lunches;
- stand-up comedy training days (yes, really);
- solution-focus workshops (rather than problem-seeking meetings); and
- training in handling difficult people.

As a final piece of advice, there is a golden rule in psychological intervention, whether in treatment, mentoring or training. Before attempting to implement change, first break existing ritual moulds and barriers. Ideas such as those above are designed to do just that and, by loosening up the thinking culture, provide a better chance of successfully implementing change.

'What got you to here won't necessarily get you to there' is a useful axiom for those about to lead lawyers through change – applicable as much to themselves as to those they are leading.

The publisher acknowledges Amber Sharpe for her contribution to this chapter in the previous edition.

The importance of emotional intelligence

Sarah Martin
Martin & Levin
University of Oxford, Saïd Business School
Faculty of Meyler Campbell

1. Introduction

A successful lawyer, today more than ever, needs to be talented at developing strong professional relationships. Whatever kind of lawyer you are and whatever position you hold in a firm, forging good sustainable relationships with clients and colleagues is fundamental to driving the success of your practice and your career.

Like other professionals, lawyers are trained to use their intelligence to become technical experts and to deliver a technical service. As many know to their benefit, developing and succeeding with clients and leading or managing others require a different kind of intelligence: the intelligence to understand and manage emotions, which lies at the core of good relationships.

Many senior lawyers have spent their careers honing this intelligence, and in the rapidly changing landscape of legal practice it is one of the most important skills that they can develop and manage in younger lawyers within their firms.

We know that our ability to adapt to change depends on the assistance we receive from trusting, supportive relationships with others.[1] Establishing networks of enablers early in our careers underpins our ability to develop, grow and successfully tackle new challenges. Young lawyers would be well advised to start creating their own 'personal board of directors' to give them the encouragement, support and accountability necessary for a successful career.

In most parts of the world, legal professional training and development is still largely focused on the law and technical legal requirements, particularly at entry level. In the United Kingdom, legal professional training as a whole is changing in 2021, but despite the strong lobby for inclusion of a broader skillset, the focus will remain firmly on legal knowledge and skills. What a missed opportunity – now, more than ever, good lawyers can no longer afford to rest on their technical laurels.

---

[1] Richard Boyatzis, Melvin L Smith and Ellen Van Oosten, *Helping People Change: Coaching with Compassion for Lifelong Learning and Growth*, Harvard Business Review Press, 2019.

While formal professional training maintains its narrow focus, it is all the more important for law firm leaders to recognise the value of:

- using their own emotional intelligence to inspire, develop and manage the talent in their firms;
- helping to develop the emotional intelligence of their colleagues; and
- creating an emotionally intelligent culture generating confidence, strong bonds and motivation.

2.   Emotional intelligence

In essence, emotional intelligence refers to our abilities to recognise and understand emotions in ourselves and others, and to use this awareness to make better decisions and manage our behaviour and relationships. In other words, it is about developing a good sense of how our actions are perceived and experienced by others and how we respond to their behaviour.

Recent developments in neuroscience have shown that in many situations our brains are wired to give emotions precedence. The limbic system where emotions are processed is the root from which our brain developed. Messages entering our brains via our senses come through the limbic system. Emotional areas are interwoven into the neural circuits connected to the rational neocortex, so the brain's first reaction to an event – particularly in high-stress situations – is going to be emotional.

Scientific research is now showing just how contagious our emotions can be, both positive and negative, in particular through our social bonding hormones, oxytocin and our stress hormones, cortisol. It is becoming all the more important for us to be able to manage our emotions, so we can set the intended emotional tone in our relationships and, in particular, our leadership.

Although we all have emotional set points, it is possible to learn how to manage the reactions and thoughts that follow so that they do not become hijacked by emotional responses.

3.   The importance of emotional intelligence

Studies suggest that there is a higher correlation between emotional intelligence and success than between intelligence quotient (IQ) and success. It seems that people who develop their emotional intelligence tend to be the highest performers and earners.[2]

The good news for talent management is that, unlike IQ, which changes little from childhood, emotional intelligence can be learned over time and at any age. It takes time, effort and practice, but the investment can reap huge rewards for individuals and those who interact with them, including colleagues and clients.

---

2   Daniel Goleman, *Emotional Intelligence and Working with Emotional Intelligence, ibid*; Travis Bradberry and Jean Greaves, *Leadership 2.0*, TalentSmart, 2012.

Why is developing emotional intelligence particularly important for managing legal talent now?

3.1 The economic context

As the social, political and economic effects of the global pandemic take hold and the economic squeeze gets tighter, clients of law firms are becoming more demanding and competition for legal jobs is tougher. More than ever, lawyers in many jurisdictions are suffering from exhaustion, broken relationships and depression, and are turning to alcohol and drugs. Despite the financial rewards, the costs to health and happiness can be high. As a result, many talented lawyers are leaving the profession. Developing emotional intelligence is a foundation for the understanding and support required to manage and counter the effects of these demanding conditions. It underpins both individual and organisational resilience.

3.2 The changing nature of the lawyer's role

Studies reveal that intrinsic motivation levels are significantly increased if individuals understand and buy in to the purpose of what they are doing and have a reasonable degree of autonomy in their work.[3] Lawyers, in particular, tend to like autonomy and having a sense of the big picture.

Yet an overall sense of purpose and a fair degree of autonomy are increasingly rare experiences in legal practice, as it has become more specialised and commoditised in many jurisdictions. Individuals can end up having limited knowledge of the big picture and little scope to make decisions. In this environment, frustrations and tensions can simmer and build to a point where they boil over and create resentment and disengagement. Senior lawyers can bring their emotional intelligence to this problem, explaining the overall purpose of the work to their more junior colleagues, so that they have an appreciation of how they are contributing. They can also try to give junior lawyers more opportunities to participate in client interactions and face-to-face meetings.

As many observers of legal markets have commented,[4] the legal profession is subject to unprecedented change from rapid developments in artificial intelligence and technology, political volatility, globalisation, protectionism, the global economic downturn and liberalisation of law firm structures. We can now add to that list the effects of the global COVID-19 crisis. Change on such scale creates greater complexity, uncertainty, ambiguity and anxiety. The shift to short-term performance and higher monetary rewards risks making

---

3   RM Ryan and EL Deci, "Self Determination Theory and the Facilitation of Intrinsic Motivation, Self Development and Well-Being", *American Psychologist*, vol 55 no 1, January 2000.

4   See, for example, Richard Susskind, *Tomorrow's Lawyers: An Introduction to Your Future*, Oxford University Press, 2013.

relationships within firms more transactional and losing the give and take of strong, long-term bonds. If this continues, firms may become reluctant to invest in and develop people over the longer term, and there will be more uncertainty for individuals over their legal careers. Firms may also find that they do not have the buy-in for implementing necessary changes. In these circumstances, it is all the more important to build mutual support and reduce uncertainties within the firm as much as possible.

3.3 Limitations of current legal training

Legal training continues to be narrow – some would say that it is even worse than this.

Martin Seligman put it like this:

Lawyers are trained to be aggressive, judgemental, intellectual, analytical and emotionally detached. This produces predictable emotional consequences for the legal practitioner: he or she will become depressed, anxious and angry a lot of the time.[5]

It may be an extreme view, but there is some truth in it.

3.4 The legal character

Like any group of professionals, lawyers have differing characters and personality traits. While not wishing to make generalisations about the character of lawyers, some similarities are worth exploring to appreciate the impact on developing emotional intelligence.

(a) Being challenging

As highly intelligent people, lawyers have an inbuilt talent for challenging, questioning and making clever points. Some may also feel the need to prove that they are right. Although this gives the immediate satisfaction of winning the argument, it can also destroy respect and trust, eroding the quality of the relationship. Legal talent management can help individuals to appreciate the impact of this approach on their clients, colleagues and leaders, and to understand how undermining trust with any of these groups will ultimately be counterproductive.

(b) Quest for feedback

Like many high achievers, lawyers often need the approbation of their clients and colleagues to maintain their self-esteem. In such a demanding environment, they need to know how they are performing and to feel supported by their leaders, knowing that if something goes well it will be

---

5   Martin Seligman, *Authentic Happiness: Using the New Positive Psychology to Realise Your Potential for Lasting Fulfilment,* Nicholas Brearley Publishing, 2013.

recognised, and in circumstances where they need support, they will be sure to get it. They need specific, timely and actionable feedback from people they respect. Good emotional antennae are needed to find the fine balance between promoting confidence and giving the necessary support, so that individuals develop and do not crumble under pressure. Encouraging them to adopt a learning and open approach – described as a 'growth mindset'[6] – can help them to see new or difficult things as opportunities to grow and develop, rather than as threats.

(c) **Need for challenge**
Lawyers, like other professionals, have a strong appetite for challenging work.[7] One of my clients has spent his professional life working on international transactions and travelling constantly. In his spare time, he runs marathons and has climbed to Everest base camp. He has a constant need for new challenges in and out of work. If you are challenge-driven, developing your emotional intelligence is particularly helpful for appreciating the impact that you have on others when you focus solely on achieving the task in hand. Developing self-awareness can also help you to work out how to stay motivated between the adrenaline-driven peaks.

(d) **Fairness**
Lawyers, unsurprisingly, have a strong sense of the importance of fairness. In any important firm decision, they will want to have their say. Significant emotional intelligence is required to create 'decision justice' – taking time and care to explain things well, to listen and understand the different points of view and to communicate why the decision does or does not reflect the input. This emotionally intelligent approach allows you to build the long-term trust and mutual support required for future decisions.

(e) **Tendency to search for the negative**
One of the reasons that lawyers are in the high-risk category for demoralisation, according to a leading psychologist, is that many have a natural tendency to look for the negatives. The legal mind that looks for problems and imagines the worst in order to protect against it is a wonderful talent – as far as the client is concerned. As one major client said: "It's terrific working with Jim, because he does all my worrying for me." Emotional intelligence can help to prevent that mindset becoming pervasive in all aspects of life, as explained in research into motivation and learned flexible optimism.[8]

---

6   Dr Carol S Dweck, *Mindset: Changing the Way You Think to Fulfil Your Potential*, Robinson, 2017.
7   Thomas J Delong, John J Gabarro and Robert J Lees, *When Professionals Have to Lead: A New Model for High Performance*, Harvard Business Review Press, 2007.
8   Martin Seligman, *Learned Optimism: How to Change Your Mind and Your Life*, Vintage Books, 2006.

(f) Caution and perfectionism

Psychometric studies of lawyers' personalities show, unsurprisingly, some strong tendencies toward high caution and perfectionism. These natural tendencies often inhibit our desire or ability to show any of our vulnerabilities. Sharing vulnerability is a proven way to create strong connections and bonds. Brené Brown's research into human connection led her to deep insights about vulnerability. Her TED talk,[9] watched by over 47 million people, amusingly explains how having the courage to be imperfect and the compassion to be kind to ourselves, warts and all, enables us to build the strongest relationships. In the field of consulting, Patrick Lencioni's amusing fable, *Getting Naked*,[10] shares stories of having the courage to be vulnerable with clients, admitting ignorance and asking dumb questions. To build trust, he advocates shedding the three common fears that sabotage client loyalty:

- fear of losing the business;
- feeling embarrassed; and
- feeling inferior.

All of these will be familiar fears to most lawyers and can hold them back in their quest to be trusted advisers.

4. Developing emotional intelligence: the five components

According to Daniel Goleman, the American psychologist who popularised the concept of emotional intelligence, "Great leaders use their emotions to unleash the energy of others."[11]

Goleman identified five components of emotional intelligence:

- self-awareness;
- self-regulation;
- motivation;
- empathy; and
- relationship management/social skills.

4.1 Self-awareness

The starting point for understanding the impact that we have is to develop a good level of self-awareness. It takes time, honesty and courage – inevitably, we discover things that are unsettling – yet the benefits can be long term and widespread. First, we should focus on improving our own performance and

---

9   Brené Brown, *The Power of Vulnerability: Teachings on Authenticity, Connection and Courage* (audiobook of TED talk), Sounds True Inc, 2013.
10   Patrick Lencioni, *Getting Naked: A business fable about shedding the three fears that sabotage client loyalty*, John Wiley & Sons, 2010.
11   Daniel Goleman, *Emotional Intelligence: Why it can matter more than IQ*, Bloomsbury Publishing, 1996; and *Working with Emotional Intelligence*, Bantam Books, 1999.

interactions. Then, having experimented on ourselves, we can use this knowledge to enhance our skills of managing, developing and leading others.

Over several years, I have been asked by firms and individual lawyers to help them with different aspects of their professional relationships. The case studies in this section are drawn from this work and illustrate the development of different components of emotional intelligence. Names and other facts have been changed.

a) *Case study*

In the *The Nicomachean Ethics*, Aristotle wrote:

> *Anyone can become angry – that is easy. But to be angry with the right person, to the right degree, at the right time, for the right purpose, and in the right way – that is not easy.*

Caroline was a partner in a major firm. The quality of her relationships with her team had plummeted. She had worked in M&A for years and was successful, but she was burnt out by the highs and lows, did not enjoy going to work and felt under-appreciated and angry.

The benefits of increasing her self-awareness are set out as a starting point using the Johari window model in Figure 1.

Figure 1. Self-awareness

Solicit feedback —————————————————————————➤

Self-disclosure	Known to self	Not known to self
Known to others	Public self The arena: I see the pluses and minuses about myself and so do others.	Hidden to self My blind spots: I don't see these pluses and minuses about myself, but others do.
Not known to others	Private self The façade: I see these things about myself, but keep them hidden.	Subconscious self The unknown: buried to both myself and others.

Source: Adapted from J Luft, Group Processes: An Introduction to Group Dynamics, *Mayfield Publishing Co, 1970.*

The aim was to increase the size of the upper-left-hand box, 'The arena', by seeking feedback and being as transparent as possible. In this way, we are operating with fewer blind spots and without wasting energy hiding behind a façade, making us more effective in building our relationships over the long term.

I collected anonymous 360-degree feedback from some of Caroline's colleagues. There were strong themes. They sang her praises for conscientiousness, loyalty, authenticity and passion, but also mentioned volatility, mood swings and a propensity to wear her heart on her sleeve.

As part of the exercise Caroline shared her feedback from two psychometrics: the Myers-Briggs Type Indicator (MBTI) and the Fundamental Interpersonal Relations Orientation-Behavior (FIRO-B) instrument.

Of the many psychometric instruments designed to help increase self-awareness, the MBTI is the most popular for raising awareness of overall personality, with over two million users each year. Based on the work of Jung and developed by Briggs Myers and Meyers,[12] it looks at four dimensions of how people manage their energy, take in information, make decisions and explore or seek closure. It has its critics, but it works very well to show and develop appreciation of differences in personal preferences and approach. One of its major strengths is that it is non-judgemental and therefore amenable to the sharing of results in order to appreciate differences.

FIRO-B was developed by Schutz in the 1950s from research on interpersonal relations and conflict, to help submarine crews work together for long periods. It identifies how we tend to behave towards others and how we want them to behave towards us. It provides information about three fundamental dimensions of interpersonal needs – inclusion, control and affection – and the extent to which we differ in how much we want and how much we signal we want. It is particularly good for raising self-awareness when working with teams.

Caroline's MBTI feedback showed that she had a 'feeling preference' in taking decisions. Her FIRO-B showed that she wanted and expressed a high level of affection.

After discussing the combined feedback, Caroline appreciated that she had a blind spot about the overt intensity of her emotions. She began to see what a destabilising effect her behaviour was having on her colleagues by creating volatility, uncertainty and emotional exhaustion. This made them more anxious, guarded and unlikely to appreciate her positive behaviour. It seriously affected her gravitas. With this in mind, she became strongly motivated to work on a plan to channel her emotions for the benefit of herself and her team, enabling them to flourish in a more predictable environment.

---

12   See Isabel Briggs Meyers and Peter B Meyers, *Gifts Differing: Understanding Personality Type*, Davies-Black Publishing, 1995.

(b)   Improving self-awareness

As obvious as it may sound, simply asking people to think about self-awareness is a good starting place. They can note strong reactions and triggers, try to work out what is happening and why and look for patterns. Recognising feelings as they happen can reduce the chance of them reappearing uninvited.

As we have seen, objective constructive feedback is powerful. It is usually difficult to get, particularly for those higher up in the firm. Asking a trusted colleague for open and honest feedback can work. In practice, anonymous 360-degree feedback from several colleagues is more helpful and will include a mix of positive and negative comments.

I always encourage lawyers to concentrate on the positive feedback first, but this is not always straightforward. We are all programmed to seek out the negative or problematic and work on it. Lawyers excel at this through a natural disposition enhanced by years of training and practice. So, seeing the positive comments first, resisting the urge to flip the page and taking the time to digest them is an essential part of setting the context for the areas that need work.

Psychometric instruments are widely used and helpful if they are employed with a purpose and the feedback is fully discussed. Other useful tests are the highly regarded Neuroticism–Extraversion–Openness (NEO) personality instrument, which includes a dimension on emotional stability, and the Hogan Development Survey, which highlights aspects of our personality that are usually strengths but that under stress can derail our progress and leadership capabilities.

The critical thing to remember on developing self-awareness is that it is far from a linear process and many 'mistakes' can give us useful information about what to do differently. It is difficult to start noticing things of which we were previously unaware and which we do not particularly like.

4.2   Self-regulation

Self-regulation is more than managing emotional outbursts. It involves regulating our responses and tendencies over time into desired reactions and behaviour. To achieve this, the individual has to put his or her immediate needs on hold and think of the impact on others and of longer-term, more important goals. It is also about achieving balance and reducing volatility and over the long term it builds resilience.

The developing interest in mindfulness reflects the hard, scientific evidence that it can literally change our brains and help us to develop the ability to purposefully direct attention and behaviour, suppress knee-jerk reactions and become more adaptive.[13]

---

13   Christina Congleton, Britta Hölzel and Sara Lazar, "Mindfulness Can Literally Change Your Brain", *Harvard Business Review*, 8 January 2015.

(a) **Case study**

Nicola was a lawyer with an international firm. A highly intelligent woman in her mid-forties who rose rapidly through the firm, she was known for her ability to win business with her solutions-based approach. Nicola also had a reputation for intimidating others intellectually.

The senior partner was concerned that this attitude was limiting both a very talented lawyer and the rest of her colleagues, who were afraid to venture their views. It was my role to help Nicola to improve her relationships with her colleagues and develop her team.

I began by seeking feedback with an anonymous 360-degree process. Hearing different viewpoints was essential to gain Nicola's attention, to help her understand how others experienced her and to recognise blind spots. She found some of the feedback difficult to accept. Her peers at times experienced her as scary, dismissive, often interrupting, not listening and dogmatic, with a strong need to be right. She recognised the comments from her partners and knew that she had to improve if she were to advance in the firm. She saw how her need to demonstrate her intellectual capacity was destroying trust with her colleagues. This realisation was critical for developing the motivation to change, the humility to recognise that her current ways were counterproductive and the determination to practise on the job in the coming months.

Nicola developed a practical plan focused on areas for change, and created a safe practice zone with feedback from a trusted colleague. She started with the perceived lack of listening and managing her need to be right. She practised trying to wait until the other person had finished their point, avoiding interruptions and listening carefully to gain a deeper understanding. She started with one colleague and explained to him what she was doing and why. She then asked others to remind her if she interrupted. She knew that giving full attention and listening would show respect and build trust, her underlying goal.

She focused on how to recognise, acknowledge and use the valuable contributions of others. She put aside her embarrassment about praising people for their ideas and was genuine and specific in recognising their value. She resisted the temptation to try to trump them. If she had things to add, she found positive ways to do so. Her aim now was not to show them she was smart (which they knew), but to encourage the smartest bits of them and build their trust. She saw that focusing on flaws in the ideas of others invokes self-doubt, is intimidating and destroys trust.

I asked her to make notes about how this felt, what she noticed, heard and learned and the impact she saw on others, emphasising the importance of recognising her emotions about these changes.

After six months, we took additional feedback from her peers. They reported that Nicola was no longer belittling people with her intellect, but listening more carefully and interrupting less. She had learned to value their contributions and no longer felt a need to outplay them. She became more relaxed, continued to build trust and was seen as a much more effective and successful partner in the business.

What is happening here and why does it take so long? Recent developments in neuroscience have helped us to understand this a little better. The neocortex, which learns technical skills and cognitive abilities, gains knowledge quickly. The development of emotional intelligence involves the emotional centres of the brain as well as the neocortex. These seem to need to unlearn old habits and learn new ones through repetition and practice over time, in order to develop new neural pathways that become ingrained habits. During this time, numerous relapses into the original default behaviour are likely to occur, until the new one takes over as the default option.

(b)   Improving self-regulation
Through self-awareness, we start to identify what we are trying to manage. In practice, it is best to choose one or two things to focus on at a time. The aim is to recognise trigger signs and then practise remaining objective, taking control of our inner voice and modelling the behaviour we would like to see in our colleagues. Sharing goals with a trusted colleague, as Nicola did, helps to hold us to account and improves our chances of success.

Increased self-awareness also helps us to assess our energy levels and take time to recharge physically and emotionally, exercising self-regulation to avoid falling prey to burn-out. It can help to shake off anxiety and irritability and to build resilience.

Self-regulation applies to positive as well as negative emotions. Being over-exuberant and over-enthusiastic can overwhelm colleagues, while overconfidence and excessive optimism can impair sound decision making.

4.3   Motivation
We hear so much about how lawyers are suffering from disillusionment, fatigue and lack of motivation.

Having a passion for what you do and are trying to achieve is an important part of the emotional skillset for any partner in a law firm in order to win clients and do a good job for them. Equally, it inspires younger lawyers and helps them in turn to develop their own passion for their work.[14]

Part of developing emotional intelligence is to become aware of your own strengths and those of colleagues. Law firms make sound investments when they take the time to discover the particular strengths and passions of their individual lawyers. This is not just about technical expertise, but natural talents

---

14   Susie Cranston and Scott Keller, "Increasing the 'meaning quotient' of work", *McKinsey Quarterly*, January 2013.

as diverse as networking, courage and creativity. A whole body of research demonstrates the increased motivation, energy and performance levels that occur when people are playing to their strengths.[15] Looking at individual roles and, where possible, reshaping these to facilitate tapping these strengths will lead to greater satisfaction and lessen the unhappy and disillusioned exodus of young talent.

4.4 Empathy

Empathy is at the centre of social awareness – it is the ability to pick up what is happening for another person and put ourselves in his or her shoes. It is the capacity to understand what they are feeling, even if we do not feel it ourselves, and to resist the tendency to project our own emotions onto others. It involves developing highly attuned antennae to gather critical information.

(a) Case study

George was, in the words of his senior partner, "a fantastic lawyer". The main challenge for George was how to manage himself and his people. He headed up a significant department in the firm and I worked with him to develop his management and leadership of the group.

We started with self-awareness. George already knew that he needed to manage his time better, have more structure in his department, delegate more effectively, relinquish some control and run a more organised office. These were some of the goals he set for the coaching. He had tried to achieve some of these before, but to no avail. People thought that he had lost his motivation, but in reality he was frustrated.

It was here that I saw the full power of 360-degree feedback to invoke natural empathy. His colleagues' comments fell into clear themes: praise for the creation of a successful department, his innovative legal and client-facing skills, passion and high standards. As he anticipated, the challenges arose in management of himself and the department: taking on too much work, perfectionism, lack of willingness to delegate, cancelling meetings at the last minute, a fire-fighting approach and a lack of respect for procedures. The chaos made it difficult for others to become involved.

George's motivation to change was rooted in his empathy and deep respect for his team. His reaction to the honest and open comments that they had made was, "I see that some people suffer more than I had realised; it needs sorting out."

This set him on the road to practical solutions, including recruiting an

---

15   Martin EP Seligman, *Flourish: A Visionary New Understanding of Happiness and Well-being*, Free Press, 2011; Christopher Peterson and Martin EP Seligman, *Character Strengths and Virtues: A Handbook and Classification*, Oxford University Press and American Psychological Association, 2004.

excellent personal assistant, ruthless tidying of his office, setting up regular meetings and asking others to take him to task if he tried to cancel them, delegating routine and administrative tasks and developing techniques for delegation of more complex matters. George was able to free up more time to spend on his award-winning legal work and start mentoring junior lawyers to explore creative solutions that met clients' changing needs. His team had less ambiguity to manage and felt more respected.

(b) *Developing empathy*
Learning to appreciate others' differences requires listening and observation to tune into how they may be seeing things. Research shows that in appreciation of a message, words account for only about 7%, tone of voice for about 38% and body language for about 55%.[16] So, while lawyers are experts of the written word, they must also develop keen powers of listening and observation – the foundation skills for empathy. Experience and intuition then help to build the ability to recognise the different emotions that everyone brings to the workplace.

Careful listening inevitably means to stop talking, anticipating, interrupting. It requires practice, as seen in section 4.2(a). Practising empathy also involves developing objective observation, trying to see others' emotions while staying neutral and picking up on different moods and energy levels. The more time invested in getting to know clients or colleagues, the easier it becomes to appreciate how they see things and to adjust your responses and behaviour accordingly. MBTI is an excellent psychometric for appreciating how people see, approach and respond to things differently.

4.5 **Relationship management**
Clients often state that they consider technical expertise as a basic requirement and that they select their lawyers on the basis of personal qualities and relationships. As one private equity client puts it, "You may as well choose someone you get on with, as you have got to spend a lot of time with them." Remember too that it helps to strengthen those relationships if you are able to 'get naked' and show some vulnerability.

Lawyers who are willing to invest time listening carefully and understanding their clients' challenges, standing in their clients' shoes and owning their legal issues with passion have a much better chance of winning and retaining business. This means making time for face-to-face meetings regardless of location, maintaining regular contact and alerting clients to interesting trends and developments. It involves a fundamentally curious approach, building a deep knowledge of and interest in clients and their worlds.

---

16   Albert Mehrabian, *Silent Messages*, Wadsworth Pub Co, 1971.

(a)   Developing relationship management with clients

Talent management has an important role to play in encouraging a change of mindset from the transactional, chargeable-hour, short-term approach, to one of long-term relationships. This involves a renewed focus on developing empathy with clients, understanding the environment that they operate in internally and externally, thinking about the drivers of their profitability and growth, listening to what is concerning them, and thinking about their organisational structures and decision making. This is the world of the in-house lawyer, with a talent set that should be of fundamental interest to the independent lawyer who wants to create enduring client relationships. At the heart of this talent lie the fundamentals of emotional intelligence: self-awareness, listening skills, awareness of others, motivation and empathy.

These skills are best learned from an experienced lawyer and law firms can enhance their talent by treating this as an essential element of on-the-job training, with senior lawyers acting as role models and mentors. There are stories of young lawyers who have not yet met a client, despite being in their second or third year of work. They need to see and hear first hand what it takes to understand and engage in a client's issues and develop a passion to take on their work. Likewise, they should be able to understand how experienced lawyers develop and maintain networks and how to put their energies into forging their own.

(b)   Developing relationship management with colleagues

Engaging our awareness to manage interactions successfully and build positive long-term relationships applies equally outside and inside the firm. Investing time to find common ground and build rapport will help to sustain relationships through trickier times.

Whether we are working with individuals or leading teams, most relationships are built on reciprocity and collaboration. Empathy includes understanding what is important to others and what you have that they may value. Thanks, recognition, praise and challenging work are all often underestimated in this context. Lawyers place a high value on genuine praise from someone they respect. Celebrating successes even in tough times reinforces the effect.

Listening skills are central to effective relationships – concentrating on hearing everything that is being communicated before responding, noticing silences and looking for the important non-verbal signals. Listening with full attention and genuine interest in what the other person is saying demonstrates respect. It will help you to identify your colleagues' strengths and harness them to increase motivation.

As we have seen, feedback is vital and has most impact when it is concise, clear and given as soon as possible. Constructive and balanced feedback meets a strong desire in lawyers to develop. It is most effective when it is as factual as possible and the intention is to benefit the learning of the recipient, rather than to be critical or demonstrate superior knowledge. Feedback along the lines of, "It would be even better if …" can be more readily accepted. Most firms are thankfully now encouraging a more day-to-day approach to seeking and giving feedback rather than storing it all up for the annual appraisal. Research suggests that we may need as much as 5:1 positive/negative feedback to be able to process the positive feedback effectively, our brains being so wired for seeking the negative.[17]

Relationship management inevitably includes handling difficult conversations. Many lawyers shy away from these, and conflicts at work tend to fester. Tackling tough conversations is a separate topic, but if an interaction is going to be tough, it is best to start with self-awareness and a good understanding of the other person's position.

Finally, it is important for leaders to model – as consistently as possible – the skills and behaviour that they wish to see in others. Remembering that only about 7% of communication is through words, it is best to have face-to-face interaction whenever possible.

---

17   Jack Zenger and Joseph Folkman, "The Ideal Praise-to-Criticism Ratio", *Harvard Business Review*, 15 March 2013.

Coaching for lawyers

Jonathan Middleburgh
Edge Consulting
Simon Pizzey
Business coach

1. Introduction

Ruth is a 35-year-old senior associate in a medium-sized law firm. A first-class graduate in history, she specialised in tax early in her career. An acknowledged technical specialist, Ruth has struggled to build an independent client base. Having recently failed to make partner, she has been offered coaching with an external consultant.

Stephen is managing partner of a leading international law firm and is two years away from an agreed date for retirement. His senior colleagues have urged him to plan for the future. Stephen has admitted to a couple of close colleagues that the future terrifies him. At the suggestion of the firm's senior partner, the HR director has set up coaching for him.

Jason has six years' post-qualification experience in a 10-partner firm. He has excellent client-handling skills, but recent appraisals have flagged issues with delegation and people management. Jason's manager, Heather, has tried to help him address these, but without any real success.

The above situations are doubtless familiar to anyone who has worked in a law firm. Perennial problems present themselves – how does a technical specialist redefine him- or herself as a winner of work? How does a successful lawyer transition towards retirement? How best to help someone who struggles with delegation and people management?

Coaching claims to provide a solution to these problems. But does it? Does it offer a panacea or is it just an expensive placebo? How do coaches measure their impact? At a more fundamental level, what is coaching and how does it claim to shift entrenched behaviours?

This chapter provides an overview of coaching principles for those new to the field, as well as a discussion of issues of interest to those more familiar with coaching but perhaps unconvinced as to its efficacy.

Starting with a working definition of 'coaching', the chapter sets coaching in its context among other approaches to professional development, such as technical skills development, training courses, postgraduate qualifications such as MBAs and reading management books.

The chapter goes on to discuss how to get started: setting up a coaching

159

contract, agreeing on the number of sessions and ensuring that the relationship does not end up with the the coaching client (or 'coachee') being dependent on the coach.

Using three case studies (adapted to preserve confidentiality), the chapter illustrates how coaching actually works and how it drives outcomes. The chapter describes how the coach works with the coachee to set goals, typical topics covered during coaching and what common outcomes look like. Coaching is distinguished from other approaches, in particular from mentoring.

The chapter further highlights key elements of the coaching approach that make it particularly suitable for lawyers.

The difference between external and internal coaching is also addressed. For example, if a law firm hires an external coach for one of its lawyers, how will that relationship work? The chapter explains how internal coaching relationships work best and how using a coaching approach when managing others can be more effective than traditional hands-on management.

Coaching is a developing field; like any relatively young field, it continues to define and redefine itself and will doubtless do so for many years to come. Alongside some excellent, skilled practitioners there are inevitably people who claim to have coaching skills, but who in reality fail to deliver a proper coaching experience. This is likely to persist until coaching becomes globally regulated and routes to accreditation are more widely understood. With this is mind, the chapter considers how to find a coach, what to look for, what questions to ask and what accreditations to seek out.

2. What is coaching?

There is no widely accepted definition of 'coaching'. Nonetheless, many definitions contain similar elements.

Tim Gallwey, author of the best-selling *Inner Game* series of books which he began writing in the 1970s, defines coaching as "the art of creating an environment, through conversation and a way of being, that facilitates the process by which a person can move toward desired goals in a fulfilling manner".[1]

Philippe Rosinski similarly defines coaching as "the art of facilitating the unleashing of people's potential to reach meaningful, important objectives".[2] Anne Scoular, co-founder of the well-known Meyler Campbell coaching programme, aptly describes coaching as concerned with "pulling out the capacity people have within".[3]

For practical purposes, most definitions encompass the following elements:

---

1   W Timothy Gallwey, *The Inner Game of Work*, Thomson, 2000, p177.
2   P Rosinski, *Coaching Across Cultures*, Nicholas Brealey Publishing, 2003, p4.
3   A Scoular, *The Financial Times Guide to Business Coaching*, FT Prentice Hall, 2011, p7.

- Coaching is a learning activity.
- The coach does not teach the coachee.
- The coach facilitates a learning process.
- This process typically involves the coachee acquiring additional understanding or insight into his or her actions or behaviours.
- The learning process is frequently goal oriented – that is, successful coaching will help the coachee to get closer to the attainment of his or her stated goals.

Of these elements, the second is one of the most important to grasp. The coach does not teach the coachee. Coaching can be more or less directive or non-directive, but all coaching starts from the premise that:

- the coachee has to take responsibility for the outcomes of the coaching process; and
- the focus is on the coachee acquiring insight and learning, rather than the coach dispensing knowledge to the coachee.

Take the example of Stephen, the managing partner approaching retirement. A coach will not tell Stephen how to plan for his retirement or provide him with financial advice or strategies for how to spend his newfound leisure time. What the coach will do is help Stephen to think through his goals for the next stage of his life, acknowledge and address his anxieties, and then plan for the future.

Or take the example of Ruth, who is struggling to build her own client base. A good coach will not advise her where to look for clients or tell her how to network. Good coaching will help Ruth to reflect on any obvious blockers to her obtaining new clients – for example, lack of confidence or reluctance to sell herself. A good coach will use a variety of tools and techniques to help Ruth overcome her confidence issues and develop strategies for networking and building her own brand.

Coaching creates a safe environment where the coachee can reflect on the goals that he or she brings to the coaching. It is a space for reflective learning, where the coachee can receive and process feedback from both the coach and colleagues. But coaching is a purposive, goal-based activity and a good coach will not have done their job if they do not help the coachee to move towards the attainment of those goals.

Contrast coaching with more traditional forms of learning and the differences stand in sharp relief. Traditional skills training for lawyers is usually aimed at the acquisition of technical skills. The prevailing teaching technique is 'chalk and talk', and the teaching method is the transmission of 'knowledge' from teacher to learner. Chalk and talk has its place, of course, especially where the learner needs to acquire some defined knowledge. Even in that case, however, research into effective learning suggests that we remember only around 20% of what we see or hear, 50% of what we both see and hear and 70% of what we see, hear and discuss. By contrast, we remember 90% of what we see, hear, discuss and practise. Coaching is active learning, in the sense that coaching always involves practice, both within and outside the coaching sessions.

Above and beyond this last point, chalk and talk cannot help where the goal is the acquisition of insight, the development of understanding or the need to make behavioural change. Consider the example of Jason, whose delegation and managerial skills are poor. Does Jason have a granular understanding of where his skills are lacking? His performance appraisal might have flagged a broad area for improvement, but he may need to get more detailed feedback from relevant colleagues. Having received that feedback, what is he to do with it? Does he have the tools or insight to become a better delegator or manager? Chalk and talk might cover the basics of delegation and provide some useful frameworks for becoming a better manager, but it will not address or meet Jason's individual needs. It cannot help Jason to obtain clarity as to his own development needs, still less to practise a changed mode of behaviour. Coaching can help to do all of this, and more.

The same points can be made about all conventional training courses and MBA-type courses. They all have their place and some are highly interactive and provide plenty of opportunities for skills practice and development. But few, if any, provide an individualised learning experience akin to coaching, unless an element of one-to-one coaching is built into the learning process.

Coaching shares some similarities with the concept of mentoring. Mentoring, like coaching, has grown in application in the business setting over recent years. The International Bar Association (IBA) has recently promoted a mentoring scheme as part of its service to members. The programme is designed to provide small and medium-sized law firms, especially those in developing countries, with the opportunity to access advice on various management issues in their practice from mentors who are experienced law firm managers, such as former managing partners.

3. How to get started

A relationship with an external coach typically starts either when an individual feels that he has a need for coaching or when an organisation recommends coaching for an employee.

An individual does not always know what they need. They may know that they need help, but not what that help looks like; they might have heard about coaching from a colleague or friend, but not know the full extent of what it might involve. An organisation recommending coaching may be a sophisticated purchaser of coaching services and the coach may be known for it. The potential coachee, by contrast, might have little or no prior experience of coaching. In either case, it is the coach's professional responsibility to explain what the potential coachee can expect from the coaching process.

Very early in the coaching engagement, preferably before starting work, the coach needs to discuss the ground rules. Who is paying? Who owns the information coming out of the coaching? Is all that information confidential – that is, to go no further than coach and coachee? If there is to be feedback to a third party – for example, a line manager or someone within HR/learning and development of a sponsoring law firm – what are the rules around feedback? It may be important for the coachee to know that anything personal will stay in the room. This is vital if the coach is to develop a relationship of trust and confidence with the coachee. Most paying organisations will want some feedback – to know what the coaching is achieving – and it is therefore important to set rules around specificity of feedback.

The nature of what is agreed will vary from case to case. For example, in a situation where the coaching has been set up to assist a partner approach the prospect of retirement, one would expect there to be complete confidentiality, unless that partner should choose to share the outcomes. On the other hand, where the coaching has been set up to assist development of, say, a group of department heads, the full value of the coaching will become apparent only if there is a degree of sharing what has been learned. In a more general situation, such as coaching for performance development with the use of psychometric tests, it might be agreed that the data will remain confidential to the coachee, but that a report on the coaching outcomes will be produced.

As long as the ground rules are discussed and agreed at an early stage, problems rarely arise in practice. Most coachees understand that if a law firm is paying for expensive coaching, it will require some high-level feedback. Problems typically arise only if there has not been a clear conversation about ground rules. It is essential that these ground rules be recorded in writing and signed by all parties involved.

Personal chemistry is paramount in choosing a coach. In theory, the coach might decide that the chemistry is not right or that the coachee is not ready for coaching. Sometimes the coach will discern that the paying organisation is foisting coaching on an unwilling individual. In that situation a sensible coach will decline to proceed, as an unwilling coachee will not engage constructively with the coaching process.

Assuming that coach and coachee both decide to proceed, they will need to agree on the number and frequency of coaching sessions. These will depend on the presenting issues. If the issues are complex, there may need to be at least four to six sessions. If the issues involve a need to make behavioural change – as they often do – it is important to recognise that changing behaviours takes time. It takes a long time to form habits and behaviours, and sometimes longer to unpick them.

Equally, however, a good coach will want to avoid allowing the coachee to develop a dependency on the coaching relationship. Stereotypes about dependent therapeutic relationships abound (viz Woody Allen and his years in therapy). Coaching itself can develop into a dependency and it is incumbent on the coach to avoid this happening. Any coach who suggests a long-term coaching relationship may not have the coachee's best interests at heart.

4.   How does coaching actually work?

Once all preliminaries have been dealt with, the coaching itself can begin. It is important to stress that every coach has a distinctive style and approach. That said, there are certain typical ways to coach. The approach described here is the well-known GROW model of coaching.[4] 'GROW' is a mnemonic for the stages of the coaching process:

- **G**oal setting;
- **R**eality checking;
- reviewing **O**ptions; and
- identifying **W**hat will be done.

In the first stage of this process, the coach explores what the coachee wants to get from the process and helps the coachee to formulate goals. Typically, the coach will ask the coachee a range of questions aimed at defining these goals. A skilful coach will use a combination of insightful questioning (usually starting with open questions, then probing as needed) and active listening.

Take the example of Stephen, the partner who is two years away from an agreed retirement date. Stephen might initially formulate quite limited goals around planning for his leisure time in retirement. Insightful questioning from the coach might elicit that Stephen is feeling anxious about retirement and frightened about his future; that he is not sure whether he actually wants to retire; that he is worried about his financial future or about atrophying in retirement. The coach might suggest that Stephen should frame some wider goals for the coaching. Very different goals might emerge – for example, identifying what Stephen ideally would like to get out of his life over the next five to 10 years and determining whether, in fact, he wants to retire or would rather explore the possibility of some alternative role within the firm.

In the second stage of the process, the coach explores reality with the coachee. In Stephen's case, this might cover a number of areas:

- What motivates him? Where do his core interests and values lie? Is work a fundamental motivator for Stephen? Could he envisage a lifestyle where he is no longer working? Is he putting off retirement because of fear?

---

4   Sir J Whitmore, *Coaching for Performance* (4th Ed), Nicholas Brealey, 2009, p55.

- What is the financial reality for Stephen? Can he afford to retire? Are fears about the cost of retirement simply a proxy for some deeper anxieties about the future?
- How much of Stephen's view of himself is invested in his work and current status? Lawyers often underestimate how much of their sense of self-worth is invested in their professional status. Relinquishing this status can be challenging, not just from a financial perspective.

Often, the coachee will want to move swiftly from reality checking into reviewing options. Lawyers tend to prefer action planning rather than reflection, but coaching is a reflective process and it is often the reflection that underpins a breakthrough. How can someone really plan for retirement if they do not yet know what they want to get out of their retirement? Reflecting on values, motivators and interests is an essential precursor to action planning and many coachees find unfacilitated self-reflection difficult or impossible.

Coaching is not just about reflection – it is about shifting from reflection to action. The skilful coach will stimulate reflection but, at the right moment, shift towards action. This third stage of the process – reviewing options – typically involves the coach working with the coachee to generate a range of options which are then explored.

In stage two of the coaching process, for example, Stephen might recognise that he is not ready to give up work entirely. He may have seen retirement in black-and-white terms, but might now move towards viewing it as a mix of work (some paid, some voluntary or less well remunerated) and leisure.

Stage three might then initially involve generating a range of possibilities for Stephen:

- finding a new role within his existing firm, such as a business development or ambassadorial position;
- finding a similar role within a different firm;
- doing consultancy work on a part-time basis;
- seeking a non-executive role within a client or another company;
- deepening existing leisure interests;
- trying out a new leisure activity;
- taking on voluntary work; and
- spending more time with his grandchildren.

Quite often, the coachee initially finds it difficult to generate options. Sometimes it takes a while to get going, but then the options flow. It is key at this stage for the coach to open up the coachee's thinking (the coach will use various techniques to do this). Once a range of options have been generated, these can be examined and whittled down. Some will be unrealistic – not working at all may not be an option because of family commitments or insufficient pension provision. Some will be fanciful – travelling might seem attractive, but when interests are discussed in more detail, Stephen might conclude that he would prefer to take one long and two shorter trips each year. A skilful coach will help the coachee to review the options and test them out. This might take more than one session – the coach might suggest, for example, that the coachee research the practicability of certain options for further discussion in the next session.

The fourth stage involves action planning – identifying what will be done and when, and committing to a plan of action.

It is important to correct any impression that the process is simple or linear. It can sometimes be circular and often iterative. For example, Stephen might have formulated limited goals at the beginning of the process, focused purely on planning for a non-working future. Once he starts looking into options, he might realise that he wants to broaden his goals – for example, by considering whether he really wants to stop working or whether he might contemplate a part-time position. Our other coachee, Ruth, might focus on business development outcomes at the start of the coaching process, but gradually realise that she needs to make behavioural changes in order to build a reputation as a trusted strategic adviser, rather than a back-room technical specialist.

5.   What makes coaching so suitable for lawyers?
Traditional training can be a challenge in areas of development apart from the acquisition of technical legal knowledge, because of the characteristics that many lawyers share. Lawyers tend to be fiercely independent and highly autonomous. They often have strongly held views and generally think that their own ways are best. This manifests itself in a desire to be in control and to have freedom in decision making.

Lawyers are trained to be critical and to look for potential problems in any matter or transaction. Indeed, the well-known US psychologist Martin Seligman builds a powerful case that negative thinking or pessimism is a strong predictor of success when it comes to technical lawyering skills.[5] However, the personality characteristics that serve lawyers so well in their early careers come back to bite when the lawyers advance into managerial or leadership roles. A lawyer's immediate response to any situation, whether it involves potential legal issues or not, is often to point out what is wrong with it, a reaction that is not always productive when leading others.

Moreover, lawyers are busy people, often facing significant pressure to meet client demands. They tend to prioritise client work and will quickly object if they feel that their time is being wasted on something of limited perceived value or relevance.

---

5   Martin Seligman, *Authentic Happiness: Using the new positive psychology to realize your potential for lasting fulfilment*, Free Press, 2002, p178.

A combination of key ingredients within the coaching approach make it an ideal solution to address these challenges. Arguably the most important of these factors is that the lawyer remains in control of the agenda, sets direction and spends time on his or her own priorities. The process is focused on the uniqueness of the coachee and their situation, rather than on the intentions of the coach. One can therefore expect that objectives will be different for each person, even if they are part of the same firm, department or work team. For example, in coaching two associates within the same firm on the topic of partner promotion, each may come to the sessions with completely different approaches and ideas. A standardised, structured partner development training programme – without a one-to-one coaching component – would not meet the needs that they can articulate within the confidential setting of a coaching environment.

The classic GROW model provides a disciplined means of ensuring that the coachee directs the agenda. The starting point of a coaching conversation is to invite the coachee to articulate his or her goals. This emphasis on setting clearly defined goals works particularly well with lawyers. Lawyers are used to the need for precision and tend to focus on outcomes. They often have no difficulty in framing goals (in contrast to other clients, for whom articulating goals can be an enormous hurdle). The risk is that lawyers might jump straight to a conclusion without giving sufficient time for reflection and testing. In this respect, the second element of the GROW model has a significant role to play, requiring the coach to test the reality of the proposition.

Interestingly, some of the associates whom we have coached found the freedom to set their own agenda to be unsettling. This seemed to reflect the fact that the opportunity to do so was uncommon. However, having overcome these feelings, they ultimately found coaching to be a profoundly rewarding experience.

The second key factor that so readily marks out coaching as suitable for lawyers is the emphasis on the coachee finding their own solution. Fundamental in this endeavour is that coaching is about listening, not telling. This is grounded in the belief that "clients are naturally creative, resourceful, and whole and are capable of making the best choices".[6] The coach does not take responsibility for the outcome and is not there to advise. Rather, "the coach's role is to develop the client's resourcefulness through skillful questioning, challenge and support".[7] Advice giving is believed to create dependency – the very opposite of the coachee staying in control and maintaining responsibility for the outcome.

The third key factor that makes coaching so suited to lawyers is the action-

---

6   L Whitworth, K Kimsey-House, H Kimsey-House and P Sandahl, (2009), *Co-active Coaching*, (2nd Edn), Davies-Black, 2009, p19.
7   J Rogers, *Coaching Skills*, Open University/McGraw-Hill, 2008, p7.

based approach. Lawyers, perhaps like others, are generally averse to commitments, but equally are often pragmatic, goal-focused and competitive. Lawyers frequently find the fourth stage, action planning, the easiest as it comes naturally to many of them. They like the certainty that comes from having an agreed set of actions.

Lawyers often become reflective more readily than coaching clients in other organisations. They tend to grasp the concept of coaching very rapidly. For example, they often quickly understand the intellectual ideas about emotional intelligence – however, they then want to move on to other topics, sometimes at breakneck speed, without necessarily reflecting fully and applying the learning. Clients in other organisations can be slower to grasp the intellectual content, but can be more reflective and may spend more time on practising and making the necessary behavioural changes.

A stumbling block within some legal organisations has been the tendency to perceive coaching as a response to a need for some identified remedial improvement. However, attitudes on this have shifted significantly over recent years. For example, many leading law firms in the United Kingdom now offer coaching to senior partners as a matter of course. Heads of HR and learning speak of a new view of coaching as a positive opportunity. A helpful analogy is that of leading sports players using coaching to continually make small improvements in performance.

6.   Is coaching an expensive placebo?

Prospective clients often question whether coaching is anything more than expensive conversation. How can one measure the impact of coaching and does the outcome justify the cost?

These questions are entirely understandable. Coaching is a 'soft' process and outcomes are typically intangible. However, a growing body of science demonstrates the efficacy of coaching outcomes, and lawyers can be shown hard data providing evidence that it is not just a placebo.[8]

Nevertheless, the reality is that one cannot 'prove' the efficacy of coaching in the same way as that of a medicine or vaccine. The nature of the coaching process means that it is impossible to conduct blind trials with control groups or to conduct rigorous experiments. For example, other variables may impact on the coachee's development – the coachee might receive helpful input from a line manager during the coaching process or read a useful book that causes a breakthrough.

---

8   See for examples: KP De Meuse, G Dai and RJ Lee, "Evaluating the effectiveness of executive coaching: Beyond ROI?", *Coaching: An International Journal of Theory, Research and Practice*, 2, 2009, 117–134; WJG Evers, A Brouwers and W Tomic, "A quasi-experimental study on management coaching effectiveness", *Consulting Psychology Journal: Practice and Research*, 58, 2006, 174–182; A Grant, L Curtayne and G Burton, "Executive coaching enhances goal attainment, resilience and workplace well-being: A randomised controlled study", *The Journal of Positive Psychology*, 4, 2009, 396–407.

That said, the growing body of scientific research is complemented by other softer data. Coaching has grown exponentially within the corporate world over the past 10 to 20 years. Companies are not known for spending money without weighing carefully the return on investment. Their willingness to invest hundreds of millions – if not billions – of dollars on coaching is a powerful indicator that they are satisfied that good coaching drives good outcomes.

Anecdotal data, moreover, is not to be discounted or disregarded. Many business leaders have written or spoken about the benefits of coaching and their comments also provide helpful evidence as to its efficacy.[9]

In practice, it is relatively easy to track whether coaching is making a difference. One straightforward way to measure impact is to obtain 360-degree feedback data on the areas to be addressed in the coaching process before starting in earnest, then to repeat this during or at the end of the process.[10] For example, Ruth's firm could obtain 360-degree feedback on her impact and influence before starting coaching. This could include rating her on a one to 10 scale on various dimensions related to her impact, influence, gravitas and so on. The firm could then obtain ratings on these same dimensions during or at the end of the coaching process.

If the coaching is helping Ruth, one would expect to see a significant improvement in these ratings. If the ratings are relatively unchanged, it is reasonable to conclude that the coaching is not helping her. This might be due to a range of factors: Ruth's failure to engage with the coaching process, her inability to change or the inefficacy of the coach. Whatever the reasons, one could say that the coaching is not making a significant difference. Conversely, if the ratings show a significant improvement, it is reasonable to assume that the coaching is having the desired impact.

7. Internal versus external coaching

This chapter largely focuses on external coaching, primarily reflecting the fact that the authors provide coaching as external consultants to their clients. What, though, of internal coaching? Does it offer similar benefits to external coaching?

First, it is important to define who will provide internal coaching. It can be provided internally by an experienced, qualified coach – for example, someone in the law firm's learning and development department or an HR professional – or, less frequently, by a line manager (ie, a lawyer) who is qualified as a coach. Often, when law firms talk about internal coaching, they are describing less formal 'coaching' provided by a line manager who has acquired some coaching skills through internal or external training.

---

9   See, for example, www.abetterperspective.com/Quotes.html.
10   See M Goldsmith, *What got you here won't get you there: How successful people become even more successful*, Hyperion, 2007, p111.

In theory, if internal coaching is provided by an experienced, qualified coach, outcomes should be broadly similar to those outlined above. However, internal coaches rarely have the range of experience of an external coach, who will typically have worked with a wide variety of clients and may well have coached lawyers in a range of law firms. Moreover, even if the internal coach is highly experienced and well qualified, an additional difficulty presents itself. Lawyers often feel reluctant to open up to internal coaches in the same way as they will to external coaches, regardless of assurances as to confidentiality. Lawyers are typically concerned that personal information may leak or that data gleaned during the coaching process might influence other internal processes, such as performance management reviews. These concerns are usually misplaced, but they are a reality. Lawyers typically feel more comfortable undergoing coaching from someone external.

When coaching is provided by a line manager, the term 'coaching' often denotes a style of supervision or management, rather than the provision of a series of coaching sessions as described above. Sometimes, line managers say that they are coaching more junior lawyers, but have at best a limited understanding of what coaching actually entails. Indeed, some will say that they are coaching more junior lawyers when they are in fact micromanaging them.

Certainly, adopting a coaching style of supervision or management can be extremely helpful to both supervisor and supervisee. A coaching style of supervision embodies the elements summarised at the start of this chapter and sees the supervisor ask many questions, alongside giving advice. Rather than teaching what needs to be done, he or she endeavours to help the supervisee to learn.

Take the example of Heather, Jason's manager. She has, to date, failed to achieve any real success in helping Jason to improve his delegation and managerial skills. She may have attempted to help him previously by telling him what to do or by giving him hints and tips regarding better delegation. By contrast, a coaching style of supervision might involve Heather exploring with Jason how he has gone about delegating in the recent past, asking him to consider instances when delegation has succeeded, prompting him to reflect on why delegation has failed previously and so on. Heather is likely to share some of her own insights based on the answers that Jason provides. This alternative approach is centred on helping Jason to develop his own insight, rather than on teaching him what to do.

It takes time and practice to develop these skills. Many lawyers think that they are very good at asking questions. The reality is that they are often very good at asking closed or leading questions. This means they tend to be looking for particular answers and therefore are not truly listening to what the coachee is trying to communicate. The development of an effective coaching style requires training, practice and feedback. But the dividends, in our experience, justify the effort.

8. Finding and selecting a coach

Having identified coaching as an appropriate solution for a specific development need, the first step is to find someone suitable. This can be a daunting task, raising questions such as: "Where do I look?", "How do I know that those claiming to be business coaches are properly trained or adequately experienced?" or "Are there particular skills that would be useful for the coach to possess?"

The internet will provide an overwhelming number of hits, even if searches are limited to a particular city or region. It may be insightful in terms of seeing the extent of what is available, but is unlikely to assist in selecting a trusted coach.

Undoubtedly, the best approach is to seek out personal recommendations. People within the legal community are generally willing to share experiences and make introductions. Professional networks and groups such as the IBA should be good sources of contacts.

However, a coach who works well with one group of people in a particular situation may not necessarily be the best fit with another group, who may have different personalities and issues. It is therefore important to use recommendations only as a helpful starting point.

There are a number of professional associations for coaches. The difficulty is that because there are so many, there are no commonly accepted standards. Nevertheless, professional associations may be a useful starting point and their websites can be informative. Perhaps the best known is the Worldwide Association of Business Coaches, which accredits training organisations such as Meyler Campbell and certifies their graduates. Other bodies include the Association for Coaching, the International Association of Coaching and the International Coach Federation. There are also many good and experienced coaches who are not accredited by one of these associations but hold other professional qualifications – for example, in occupational psychology.

As with any other procurement, it makes sense to be clear about the desired outcomes and to invite a number of prospective coaches to explain how they would approach the assignment. Inquire also about their level of experience in dealing with similar situations. Depending on the number of coachees, there may be benefits in working with a specialist organisation, rather than with just one individual. It is unlikely that one person will be the best match for all of the firm's coachees; an organisation should be able to provide a number of alternatives. One benefit of working with an organisation is that its coaches should share core coaching values, so that all coachees receive a broadly similar experience.

It will be important to be clear how the coach or organisation addresses issues such as confidentiality, initial chemistry meetings with potential coaches (are they free of charge?) and reporting. Cost is an obvious factor in the procurement process. This can vary considerably, depending on the number of sessions per coachee and the time allowed for each session. It may be sensible to try a pilot project first. Certainly, if the investment of time and money is likely to be significant, an early review will ensure that the coaching is progressing as planned.

9.   Conclusion

This chapter has articulated some of the benefits of coaching for lawyers. It has explained how the coaching process typically works and why it therefore meets the particular development needs of legal practitioners.

A growing body of research supports the scientific efficacy of coaching. It is difficult to argue credibly that coaching is a mere placebo – a body of evidence buttresses the experience of seasoned coaches that coaching can achieve transformational outcomes. That said, the practice of coaching is as much art as science, and finding a suitable coach involves both research into his or her pedigree and qualifications and a feeling that the chemistry between coach and coachee is right.

Looking for the right coach can be a voyage into the unknown. Our concluding hope is that this chapter has provided some helpful guidance to the uninitiated as to where to go and what to look for, so that firms can see their lawyers develop into successful partners with enhanced aptitudes for leadership and management.

This chapter remains the same as published in the previous edition.

Mentoring in the law firm

Stuart J Barnett
Thought partner & executive coach

1. Introduction

Historically, the apprenticeship model formed the heart of talent development in law firms, capturing some elements of a mentoring relationship. Mentoring has evolved much since then, as has talent development. The modern large law firm has a sophisticated array of development programmes incorporating in-house academies, face-to-face and online learning programmes, seminars, workshops, e-learning and off-site retreats. Yet mentoring still plays an important part in the development of talent, as the nature of the mentoring relationship and the individualised nature of the learning cannot be readily replicated by other programmes.

It is well recognised that senior lawyers have a wealth of experience and knowledge that can be passed on to more junior lawyers, and mentoring is an effective way to achieve this. And yet, it is not always easy to capture the full benefits of mentoring. Informal mentoring is fantastic when it happens – arguably the best form of mentoring, built on a natural and organic relationship between a junior and more senior lawyer – but it leaves much to serendipity; whereas formal programmes provide the organisational structure and impetus for mentoring but can fail due to being overly formal and bureaucratic.

The challenge for the law firm is to create a programme that captures the informal and organic aspects of a mentoring relationship via a more formal programme that increases participation and develops a broader culture of mentoring. This chapter provides an overview of mentoring and how a law firm can implement a best practice mentoring programme.

2. What is mentoring?

In its traditional sense, mentoring in the law firm is the process by which a more experienced lawyer will transfer their valuable information and insights in the practice of law to a less experienced lawyer via a relationship built on rapport, trust and confidentiality.[1] But this doesn't capture the full depth and spectrum of what mentoring can be. Take, for instance, the mentor (the more

---

1   Tod Aronovitz, "Mentoring is for you!", 77 *Florida Bar Journal* 4, 2003.

experienced partner in the relationship) who sponsors or champions the mentee (the less experienced partner seeking guidance) opening up career opportunities or a pathway to promotion. Or what of the mentor who supports the mentee through a particularly difficult and challenging work issue – like a strong personality or style clash with a supervising partner – to strengthen the mentee's resilience? Or, the mentor who finds more purpose in his or her career as a result of being of value to the mentee? Mentoring in this context is so much more than simply the transfer of knowledge and wisdom.

2.1   Defining mentoring

David Clutterbuck highlights some of the challenges of defining mentoring in his well-respected book *Everyone Needs A Mentor*, arguing that the academic literature often fails to define mentoring; that what mentoring means is influenced by culture – both organisational and national; and that other forms of one-to-one development have impacted upon how mentoring is viewed.[2] Taken to the extreme, mentoring can mean what you want it to mean, from coaching to consulting, friendship to sponsorship, teacher to supervisor – wherever a one-to-one relationship exists and guidance or help is given. To best capture the benefits of mentoring it is important to understand what mentoring can offer and to compare it to the talent development need. It is useful, then, to see mentoring as separate from other relationships, not as a semantic exercise but to help provide clarity as to what to use mentoring for. What's in a name? That which we call mentoring by any other name would still provide great benefit.[3]

2.2   Sponsorship vs developmental

There are two contrasting models of mentoring: sponsorship and developmental. The former tends to be stronger in the US and the latter is a more European/UK approach (also adopted in APAC).[4]

Developmental mentoring focuses on aiding the mentee to discover and find ways to do things for themselves; it sees the mentor as more of a facilitator of the mentee's development. It is likely that the mentor will have more experience than the mentee, but the focus is on the mentee co-learning through guidance rather than through the direct transfer of skills and wisdom. It is this form of mentoring that most overlaps with coaching, where the emphasis is on the mentee and their self-discovery. This can be contrasted with the sponsorship model, which is more directive, whereby the mentor takes an active role in the career of the mentee (sometimes referred to as the protégé) and

---

2   David Clutterbuck, *Everyone Needs a Mentor*, Kogan Page Publishers, 2014, p5.
3   Shakespeare may have put it closer to this: "What's in a name? That which we call a rose by any other name would smell as sweet" (from *Romeo and Juliet*).
4   Clutterbuck, *Everyone Needs a Mentor*, *supra* fn 2.

the mentor's position of influence and power within both the mentoring relationship and the firm is of importance to the mentee.

Whereas a developmental mentor may only have an indirect influence on a mentee's career, guiding the mentee to make good career and developmental decisions, the sponsorship mentor may champion the mentee, exposing them to a network, finding work for them and sponsoring their promotion. A mentor may be chosen specifically for their ability to sponsor – and the mentee chosen very carefully by the mentor – as there is much more at stake than simply guidance and support.

The importance of the distinction in the model of mentoring is in the desired outcome. In a formal mentoring programme forming part of career promotion to senior lawyer, some law firms require a sponsor to put a mentee forward with a supporting business case. This then sets the tone of the mentoring relationship and sets out how mentors and mentees are chosen and the requisite skills of each. The mentor will desire a mentee who they think has the potential for promotion and will direct the mentee towards filling any deficiencies; the mentee will seek a mentor who has the necessary insight, influence and understanding of the business to put forward a business case that will be well received. This will also impact on other aspects of the mentoring relationship, like confidentiality (discussed below) and providing a psychologically safe environment – the mentee wanting a mentor to sponsor or champion them will likely waive confidentiality about those things they would like others to know about their work and achievements. Likewise, the mentee might not feel comfortable discussing with the mentor some of their own insecurities, doubts or areas for development, wanting only to reveal the positive side and not wanting to hamper the chances of a successful promotion.

Conversely, where a mentee is looking for more general career guidance or development, the opportunity to be in a completely confidential and psychologically safe relationship allows them to obtain the full benefit of unfettered reflection on their work and goals, unconcerned about having to always show the positive side. The mentee can explore more existential concerns, or the vagaries of politics and culture, knowing that the information and conversation will go no further.[5] In this situation a developmental approach to mentoring may be more appropriate and effective.

Arguably, to capture the full benefits of a mentoring relationship the developmental style is best practice, notwithstanding the importance of sponsoring in the right circumstances, because sponsorship by its very nature detracts from the benefits of the developmental approach.

---

5   See the discussion of confidentiality below: it may be that both actual and perceived levels of confidentiality can be impacted by the nature of the relationship with a mentor both employed and actively engaged in the firm as opposed to an external coach.

A workable model might be to set up developmental mentoring first and then, after the relationship has ceased, move to sponsorship. Alternatively, simply have different mentors to achieve different aims or use a coach to deal with the more developmental aspects of mentoring and have a sponsor as a champion.

A combination of the two models may work without detracting too much from the more developmental aspects of the developmental style, provided the approach is carefully thought out and the limitations are considered. For instance, one international law firm has successfully implemented a supervising/mentoring programme for graduates who are paired with a partner on a particular deal, where the partner acts as mentor and supervisor – supervisor of the work, and mentor for broader aspects of career development and acclimatisation to the firm's values and culture.

The developmental model may work best when:
- confidentiality is important;
- personal and professional development is key;
- the mentee is to take responsibility for their learning;
- the mentor acts as facilitator of co-learning;
- the relationship is co-directional; and
- a psychologically safe relationship is important.

The sponsorship model may work best when:
- the mentee is looking for sponsorship or to be championed;
- the mentor is seeking to advocate for the mentee;
- it is clear to both parties that more than just development is required;
- a direct and advice-driven approach is desired;
- culturally this is what is expected of a mentor;
- confidentiality is not such a pressing issue;
- developmental mentoring has ended;
- psychological safety is not so important; and
- the relationship fosters diversity or inclusion.

2.3 Coaching

The International Coaching Federation defines coaching as "partnering with clients in a thought-provoking and creative process that inspires them to maximise their personal and professional potential".[6] While coaching styles and approaches vary greatly, coaching is largely seen today as non-directive and inquiry-based, often distinguished from mentoring on the basis that the coach need not have experience or background directly relevant to the coachee. The coach relies heavily on coaching skills and personal facilitation, rather than his

---

6   See: https://coachfederation.org/about.

or her experience as a lawyer, to be of value to the coachee; and where a coachee may benefit from more directive mentoring input, then the coach could explore with the coachee if a mentor would be of value.

There is much overlap, however, between developmental mentoring and coaching; arguably a great mentor will deploy good coaching techniques, and increasingly, given the rise of coaches with relevant experience with law firms, a coach may be more directive on occasions and pass on some of their experience. The blurred lines between coaching and mentoring are particularly evident in the law firm where there is an internal coach who was previously a lawyer (particularly a partner). In this instance, what may start out as coaching can quickly become mentoring – indeed this may well be why the internal coach is sought after.

Whether using a coach or a mentor, the key is aligning the method with the developmental goal. In some instances, both a coach and a mentor are needed, the coach providing the specific personal development and the mentor the different aspects of career guidance and legal experience. For instance, a newly appointed partner might find a senior partner can provide the mentoring aspect, while an external coach can help them personally as they wade through the difficult first years of partnership, honing their skillset. This can also impact whether a formal or informal mentoring programme would be best. For the junior partner, part of the process of finding a mentor can be developmental and important to building relationships and collaborations with more senior partners, so a more organic informal mentoring programme may suit the situation better.

The danger with merging the role of coach with mentor is that you don't get the best out of either – you get a coach too quickly willing to jump in with their own knowledge and thus not providing the best environment for personal growth and discovery (this is very much the danger for coaches who are still practising lawyers and skilled at advice giving); or a mentor who has the depth of knowledge or experience but is too directive and has insufficient coaching skills and tools to really provide the full depth of coaching.

2.4 Coach vs mentor

Despite the overlap between coaching and developmental mentoring there are some general factors to consider as to when to use either a coach or a mentor. Use a coach:

- where the focus is on personal growth and strategy;
- where more specific skill development is required (eg, communication and presentation skills);
- where perceptions of confidentiality and impartiality are important; and
- for achieving specific short-term goals.

Use a mentor:

- where experience and legal expertise and skills are the focus;
- to negotiate firm politics and culture;
- where seniority of lawyer is particularly relevant;
- where a broad perspective on the legal profession is required; and
- for achieving more organically developed goals.

2.5 Leading/supervising/managing

Definitions of the developmental mentor often include the fact that the relationship is 'offline'; that is, outside the usual management hierarchy. So, a strict application of the developmental mentoring approach would not have a partner mentoring a junior lawyer in his or her own team – that would fall more into the category of supervisor or manager. Sponsorship mentoring, however, may overlap more with a supervisory role. For promotion to partner many law firms require sponsorship by the supervising partner so there will be a natural overlap.

Leadership, which arguably is not position-dependent, may include aspects of mentoring, because a good leader will be focused on developing both staff and the team. In law firms, however, leaders tend to have formal titles and therefore may straddle roles of supervisor, leader and mentor, and as a result may become well known and popular as mentors, which can create a mentoring bottleneck – a well-known leader can only mentor so many mentees. While leadership will incorporate a degree of mentoring, in practical terms the leader's capacity to mentor may be limited, and this needs to be factored into any mentoring programme.[7]

2.6 Reverse mentoring

Traditionally a mentor is the older, wiser, and more experienced partner in the mentoring relationship. The senior partner mentoring a junior lawyer, for instance. More recently, reverse mentoring has become increasingly popular in law firms, where the traditional roles are reversed but many of the aspects of mentoring retained.

The idea behind reverse mentoring is that it enables a senior lawyer to tap into the unique experience of junior lawyers, for a variety of reasons including generational difference, and diversity and inclusion. Here, the junior lawyer plays the role of mentor and the more senior lawyer, the mentee.

Initially much of the benefit of this relationship was seen to be around technology and generational difference, but reverse mentoring is particularly valuable in diversity and inclusion, giving senior partners in the firm insight into what it might be like for junior lawyers who fall into minority categories.

---

7   See Heidi Gardner and Rebecca Normand-Hochman, "Make the Most of Your Partners' Potential: Foster a Culture to Support Senior-level Mentoring", *PD Quarterly*, February 2015, 31.

While there have been some inroads towards a more diverse partnership in recent years, the decision makers in law firms have traditionally been white males. Reverse mentoring enables the decision makers not only to have firsthand information, breaking down the barriers of hierarchy, but also to be plugged into the impact of decisions they make on those directly impacted by diversity and inclusion policy.

One of the twists of a reverse mentoring relationship is that unlike traditional mentoring, it may be that the mentee could become the sponsor of the mentor, or at least a champion for the particular experience the mentor brings – use of technology, diversity and so on.

3. Benefits of mentoring for talent development

It is the mentee that is the focus of talent development in mentoring, but the benefits flow much wider than that, to both the mentor and the firm more broadly. It is useful to highlight some of the benefits here and how they impact upon the mentor, the mentee and the firm.

3.1 Individualised support

The major benefit of mentoring over other forms of talent development is the individualised nature of the mentoring. Mentoring is inherently bespoke, or should be if done properly, from the pairing of mentor and mentee, to the goals and aims of the mentoring relationship, to the knowledge and skills passed on. All are individualised for the mentee and largely based on, or partnered with, the individual skills and experience of the mentor.

The mentee is regularly able to have the undivided attention of the mentor for the sole purpose of his or her development, and to tap into the experience and wisdom of someone who has previously trod a similar career path. If not a luxury, it is certainly an opportunity not easily afforded by other forms of development which, while factoring in different learning styles and needs, cannot practically provide the same individualised attention.

3.2 Developmental learning

Numerous relationships are built in a law firm career, and while many of these may have an aspect of development to them, this is often ancillary to the relationship or limited to a specific set of circumstances. For example, in the case of the partner who delegates work to the junior lawyer, part of the approach will be to ensure the junior lawyer provides the partner with what is required, and this involves teaching and learning so that the junior can develop and improve. However, time pressures often result in such interactions being very directive. A directive approach to learning has its place, but developmental learning, which is inquiry-based and focused more on the learner, takes more time and can have a longer-term impact.

3.3 Knowledge sharing and collaboration

There is a wealth of knowledge and experience held within the law firm that mentoring can tap into and share throughout the firm, through individual relationships that go beyond the normal hierarchical structures. Mentoring helps break down knowledge silos and fosters relationships that can be invaluable for collaboration.

3.4 Sponsorship

Sponsorship is of great benefit to the firm and the mentoring participants, even if it does not tend to involve the more developmental aspects of mentoring. Sponsorship can provide a valuable addition to the more formal structures of promotion within the firm.

A sponsor can introduce a mentee to the right people, help them get the right work and create career opportunities which support talent advancement and ensure the firm is promoting the right people to the right positions. Sponsors focus more intently on who might be the best candidate for promotion and help the mentee tap into the informal aspects of promotion and advancement that may not be visible to the mentee. This is particularly important for diversity and inclusion.

To obtain the benefits of developmental mentoring as well as sponsorship, law firms will on occasion run both programmes separately, or provide the launch pad of a developmental mentoring relationship that will later turn into sponsorship. Where there is overlap, where a mentor is playing the role of both mentor and sponsor, the limitations that this may place on the developmental aspects of the relationship need to be considered.

3.5 Career guidance

Despite the formal processes available, and the courses used by law firms to provide career development and pathways for lawyers, there is not often an opportunity for more generalised career guidance and discussion. It may be that information is readily available as to the options for promotion and the process by which promotion is achieved through the formal structures, or even by tapping into HR, but there is no avenue to explore the more subjective elements of career guidance. This is where mentoring is of such benefit, providing a more holistic and longer-term view of a career and the opportunity to ask those questions that cannot easily be asked or answered. Is promotion for me? Is that what I want?

3.6 Resilience and stress

One of the key factors in becoming more resilient is perspective. In the context of mentoring in law firms, perspective is about having access to a broader viewpoint on current circumstances. One of the challenges in any career is being able to see the wood from the trees, avoiding becoming so bogged down in the day-to-day work that it is hard to see the bigger picture. Arguably, this is particularly the case for the billable hours business model which has the propensity to drive short-term thinking and behaviour – it is too easy to get stuck in the weeds. Perspective is often elusive, and as such can result in lack of motivation and suboptimal decision making, increasing both stress and poor performance. Mentoring provides a wonderful opportunity for the mentee to see their circumstances in a different light, having their thoughts and views challenged constructively and seeing things more objectively with the support of a mentor.[8]

3.7 Values, culture and norms (and possibly a little politics)

It may not be difficult to establish what the values of a law firm are – they can be found on websites or on reception walls – but the culture and norms can be a little more elusive. They are found not so much in the telling, or in training, but by observing the way things are done: the behaviours, the standards and actions of leaders. They often take experience to fully understand and are something that a mentor can pass on to a mentee, guiding him or her on how things are normally done, or at least how things should be done, in the firm.

Navigating politics, which is not something training can prepare lawyers for, is another aspect in which mentoring can be of great value. This may be of more significance to the senior lawyer, where the machinations of politics can have a more visible impact. For instance, the lateral partner hire who hasn't worked out where the politics lie and inadvertently steps on toes can cause ructions which could be avoided with a little guidance.

3.8 Recruitment and retention

Having an impactful mentoring programme can be very attractive to graduates and junior lawyers, and while it may not be a priority for more senior lawyers when deciding on a prospective employer, the research shows that mentoring can have a positive impact on employee retention.[9]

Mentoring helps provide perspective and mindset shifts. It encourages courageous conversations, which can help lawyers resolve challenges that might otherwise cause them to become disgruntled and leave.

---

[8] Good mentoring can reduce mentee job-related stress. See John J Sosik and Veronica M Godshalk, "Leadership styles, mentoring functions received, and job-related stress: A conceptual model and preliminary study", *Journal of Organizational Behavior*, June 2000, vol 21 no 4, 365.

[9] Clutterbuck, *Everyone Needs a Mentor, supra* fn 2; and David Laband and Bernard Lentz, "Workplace Mentoring in the Legal Profession", *Southern Economic Journal*, January 1995, vol 61 no 3, 783. Also, mentoring aids lawyer retention as part of a larger constellation of networks: see Monica Hoiggins and David Thomas, "Constellations and Careers: Towards Understanding the Effects of Multiple Developmental Relationships", *Journal of Organizational Behavior*, May 2001, vol 22 no 3, 223.

3.9 Space for reflection

One of the challenges facing lawyers is finding the time to pause and reflect. The best lawyers are busy, hectic even, and time taken to reflect is time that could be spent on client work. This, combined with the numerous distractions of the modern world, can drive reactive behaviour and short-term thinking. Mentoring can provide a wonderful opportunity to take a break from the daily hassles and delve into some deeper reflective thinking, breaking the cycle of reactivity.

3.10 Feedback

Feedback is generally not done well in law firms. It is often seen as something negative, something to be avoided – at both ends, the giving and receiving – and when it is given it is regularly ill-timed, overly critical or overly generous. The result is a paucity of good feedback that can be used developmentally. As the author often explains to clients: feedback is information that already exists – it is just new to you. Once you have that information, you can choose what you do with it. Mentoring, then, can provide a safe place for a mentee to explore feedback, both from the mentor directly, but also more broadly, discussing with the mentor feedback received from elsewhere or how to go about getting feedback that would be useful.

3.11 Improved leadership capability

Lawyers are often promoted to leadership positions based on their technical legal ability; consequently there is often a gap in their leadership skills and ability that needs to be bridged by formal training, coaching and mentoring. Mentoring offers a safe space for new leaders to explore and discuss developmental behaviours and approaches as a mentee. But being a mentor also improves leadership skills, as it encourages mentors to regularly practice more inquiry-based leadership skills to aid the mentoring relationship – a contrast to the more directive styles often exhibited in day-to-day interactions with staff in a time-pressured reactive environment. Improving mentoring skills can have a flow-on impact on leadership and team management skills.

3.12 Specific benefits to mentor

The focus of mentoring tends to be the development and support of the mentee. What are easily overlooked are the benefits to the mentor, which go beyond simply imparting knowledge and wisdom, or a sense of wellbeing from developing a less experienced lawyer.

Good mentoring can be a mutual learning experience. Not only does a mentor get access to a different perspective from the mentee; he or she also has the opportunity to learn how to be a better mentor, enhancing listening and questioning skills, becoming more adept at knowing when to pursue inquiry-based methods and when to be more directive. Importantly, mentors also have the opportunity to reflect on their own development, to see firsthand what impact they are having on the mentee, and to test and try methods to make that impact more powerful.[10]

4. Implementing a mentoring programme

It is generally accepted that the best mentoring relationships are the informal ones that develop naturally, and yet where there is only informal mentoring some people can miss out as they may not have the necessary relationships or network to find a mentor. On the other hand, a more formal mentoring programme runs the risk of forcing relationships or becoming overly bureaucratic and systemised, failing to fully engage participants. The art, then, of an effective mentoring programme is to capture the organic aspects of informal mentoring and place around them enough structure to ensure that mentoring becomes part of the culture.

Mentoring is not an exact science. Its success depends on many factors but those programmes that work the best tend to share a number of attributes:

- They are clear in their aims.
- They have a level of organisational support.
- They are clear on the roles of mentor and mentee.
- They provide an appropriate level of training to both mentor and mentee.
- They incorporate feedback and measurement.

4.1 What is the aim of the mentoring programme?

Having a clear sense of what the mentoring programme is trying to achieve will help decide how to structure and implement the programme. Generally, law firm mentoring aims to support lawyers in their personal, professional and career development, and the focus on each will change depending on what stage a lawyer is at in their career. Diversity and inclusion are also important factors which require support through a more formal structure.

While a generalised programme for mentoring can have a positive impact, greater focus can improve outcomes. If the aim is to help graduates newly started at the firm to adjust to life as junior lawyers, the requirement for support and structure will be different than for a newly appointed partner mentored by more senior partners, or a reverse mentoring relationship pairing a managing partner with a junior lawyer. The number of participants, the nature of the support and the level of training required will all be different.

Mentoring arrangements with a targeted impact include the following:

10   For further discussion of benefits to mentors see Kirsten M Poulsen, "A New Way of Seeing Mentoring! Benefits for the Mentors", *The International Journal of Mentoring and Coaching*, vol II issue 1, July 2004.

- graduate/junior lawyer mentored by senior associate/counsel;
- high potential talent mentored around promotion to senior lawyer, counsel and partner;
- new partners mentored by senior partners;
- mentoring aimed at diversity and inclusion, providing support for promotion diversity; and
- reverse mentoring, where senior lawyers pair up with junior lawyers.

The aim, ultimately, is that mentoring becomes part of the culture, so while a more formal programme may target specific lawyers or specific transitioning stages in a career, the overriding goal should be to foster mentoring relationships, however they appear, and to encourage mentoring conversations throughout the firm.

4.2 Organisational support

Mentoring is only as good as the quality of the mentoring relationship. The purpose of organising a mentoring programme is to have enough structure and support in place to foster good quality mentoring relationships.

The administration of the mentoring programme is often taken on by HR or learning and development departments, but it is the partners and senior management of a law firm who need to champion mentoring, not only supporting a programme but being actively involved and highlighting its importance.

(a) Championing and promotion

There are a number of ways to better champion mentoring programmes:
- Mentoring can be incorporated as part of the definition of good leadership.
- Senior management can actively encourage participation.
- Managing partner/senior partners can talk about the impact of mentoring on their careers.
- Good mentors can be shown to be valued and recognised.
- Mentoring can be tied to performance metrics as part of others' development.
- Participants and others can clearly publicise and report on mentoring.

(b) Who decides pairing?

Lack of chemistry is often cited as a factor as to why mentoring fails[11] and careful attention needs to be given to how mentors and mentees are paired.

---

11 Rebecca Normand-Hochman, "Mentoring, coaching and the practice of law" in *Mentoring and Coaching for Lawyers: Building Partnerships for Success*, Globe Law and Business, 2014.

There is a balance to be found between arbitrarily assigning pairs and allowing participants to choose their mentor or mentee themselves. It is not logistically feasible for mentees to have full freedom to choose their mentors as some partners will inevitably be extremely popular and unable to mentor everyone. In fact, there is a natural bottleneck of senior lawyers – there being less of them than juniors – which needs to be managed without overloading particular partners with extra mentees.

The aim in deciding pairing is having just enough intervention to facilitate the process without making it feel forced. If it is forced, or pairs do not have the right fit or chemistry, it is unlikely that the full benefits of mentoring will be achieved, or the relationship may even break down completely.

There are a number of things to consider when deciding on mentoring pairs:

- Some method will be required by which to narrow down pairs. This can be done by discussion with the prospective mentor and mentee, by filling out a questionnaire or form, or by using an algorithm. Artificial intelligence (AI) may in fact be the most efficient method.
- Mentor and mentee will need to have the opportunity to meet and have a chat to see if they are the right fit for each other.
- Alternative options, without negative ramifications, must be available where the fit is not right or the chemistry doesn't quite work.
- Where possible allowance should be made for pairs who have already partly connected outside the formal programme.
- A hands-on approach to finding the right partners will be required where there are specific needs like diversity and inclusion.
- Part of the training should include rapport-building and what to look for in a mentor and mentee. The right match is more than simply someone you like.
- Where sponsorship-style mentoring is required, chemistry will focus on the view of the sponsor.
- Cultural differences need to be factored in for international firms where mentors and mentees may be paired from different regions and countries.

4.3 The mentoring relationship

For a mentoring relationship to prosper it needs the right ingredients. In addition to the right chemistry, both parties need to have a clear sense of what is expected of them in the relationship, what the boundaries are, and when the relationship will reach its conclusion.

Alignment as to the purpose of the mentoring relationship is vital, and this can be something – along with frequency and length of meetings – that is discussed in the chemistry or fit meeting. It is also aided greatly by the training provided to both the mentor and mentee (see below).

While mentoring relationships can take many forms, it is the author's view that there are four aspects that form the basis of a good a mentoring relationship:

- rapport;
- psychological safety;
- confidentiality; and
- goal setting.

(a) Rapport and psychological safety

Rapport can be built quickly and established in the initial chemistry meeting. Trust, however, can take a little time and will develop as the relationship moves forward. This is important to both parties, but possibly more significant to the mentee, who needs to feel he or she is in a psychologically safe environment.

A mentee needs to feel comfortable talking about things that may expose vulnerability, or issues they are not comfortable talking about in the workplace, to fully benefit from the developmental opportunity.

A good mentor, then:

- is someone absolutely credible whose integrity transcends the message, be it positive or negative;
- tells you things you may not want to hear but leaves you feeling you have been heard;
- interacts with you in a way that makes you want to become better;
- makes you feel secure enough to take risks;
- gives you the confidence to rise above your inner doubts and fears;
- supports your attempts to set stretch goals for yourself; and
- presents opportunities and highlights challenges you might not have seen on your own.[12]

A good mentee:

- shows up and takes responsibility for their own learning;
- has the courage to talk openly;
- respects the mentor's perspective and experience; and
- takes action.

(b) Confidentiality

For a mentoring relationship to form an open and psychologically safe environment it is essential that there is confidentiality. It goes to the very heart of mentoring that conversations need to stay between the mentor and mentee. A breach of confidentiality will lead to a lack of trust and will kill the mentoring relationship.

---

12   Thomas Delong, John Gabarro and Robert Lees, "Why Mentoring Matters in a Hypercompetitive World", *Harvard Business Review*, January 2008.

Guidelines around confidentiality can be given as part of the mentoring training, but it is generally best for the pairs themselves to agree on where and when information may be passed on to a third party. While lawyers are familiar with lawyer–client confidentiality, it cannot be assumed that everyone shares the same understanding of confidentiality in this context.

There are clear instances where confidentiality will need to be waived or breached. For instance, where sponsorship is involved it is to the advantage of the mentee that the mentor pass on to relevant parties some of the knowledge gained through the mentoring – for example, a particular outcome or piece of work, or experience the mentee may have that is not well known.

Other times, breaching confidentiality may be something that needs to be discussed with the parties during the engagement. For instance, if a mentee is really stressed, it might be something the mentor can discuss with the mentee and help them work through, but if it gets more serious the mentor may suggest that the mentee could do with more support, and explore ways this could be achieved, including the involvement of third parties like HR. The key here is to respect the mentoring relationship but to understand its place in the context of a mentee's wider wellbeing.

There may also be circumstances where a mentor needs to call on their ethical and moral judgement to breach confidentiality unilaterally – where, for instance, there is a serious mental health issue (eg, a mentee is at risk of harming themselves or others).

(c)   *Goal setting*
Setting goals for the mentoring relationship as well as for each session can help ensure the relationship is productive. These can be as broad or narrow as necessary to suit the mentorship, and how strictly they are adhered to will depend on the nature of the mentoring relationship and the personalities and learning styles of the pair in question.

While good mentoring can adapt much from good coaching in the area of setting clear goals at the outset of the engagement, and then goals for each session or meeting, the key is for the mentor and mentee to work out what will work best for them. An overly prescriptive approach can crush the natural or organic nature of the relationship and goal setting should be one aspect of the relationship, not necessarily the focus. Most importantly, the goals should be agreed upon by both mentor and mentee, and not forced on either party.

It is important that goals also be reviewed regularly and adapted to changing circumstances. To this end it can be useful to have both parties pause after a set number of sessions and reflect on what is and what isn't working, and how things might work better. At this point a check-in with organisers/ambassadors of the programme might be useful, or even access to a coach for the clear purpose of discussing and refining the mentoring relationship.

4.4   Mentoring training

Both mentor and mentee will benefit from mentoring training. It should not be assumed that because a lawyer has years of experience in legal practice at a law firm, this provides a sufficient foundation to be a good mentor. In fact, the advice-driven nature of being a lawyer can provide an impediment to good mentoring – it can lead to being too quick to give advice and taking a directive rather than developmental role. Similarly, mentees can be better prepared for mentoring and encouraged to be active participants and to take responsibility for their development via targeted training.

The aim here is a light touch that provides knowledge and skill development without being overly structured and regimented. It needs to be sensitive to the time limitations of participants, but it should be compulsory. As mentoring becomes entrenched as part of the culture, the standards and practices of good mentoring are role-modelled by mentors; mentees will pick up on this and reciprocate when they become mentors.

Effective training should be engaging, target the needs of both mentors and mentees and involve a variety of channels to access information, including:

- live face-to-face training (online in light of COVID-19);
- self-paced e-learning;
- an AI app if used to match pairs;
- written guides;
- input from previous mentors/mentees; and
- coaching or personalised briefing.

Ideally, mentors and mentees should have different training focused on their different roles; however, having them complete the same training can help each to better understand the role of the other. Where time and cost constraints play a significant role, arguably it is the mentors who might be best served by specific training.

Topics covered by training include the following:

- what mentoring is and the aim of the programme;
- logistics and administration;
- the support available to participants;
- confidentiality;
- goal setting;
- building rapport;
- questioning and listening skills;
- feedback skills; and
- what to do if the mentoring relationship isn't working.

Questioning and listening skills are particularly relevant to the developmental aspect of mentoring and can require a mindset shift for senior lawyers used to a more directive approach when supervising junior lawyers.

4.5 Ending the engagement

While some mentoring relationships will reach their natural conclusion, others will drift and will need to be brought to a deliberate end. Having a set date does not mean that the relationship cannot continue to exist, but it provides a natural point for reflection on the engagement and an opportunity to provide feedback.

4.6 Feedback and measurement

There are a variety of ways to measure the impact of a mentoring programme.

It is essential to seek feedback from the participants; this can take the form of a survey but can also include focus groups where an open discussion can provide useful insights for improvements.

The wider firm impacts of a mentoring programme may take some time to establish, but other outcomes are readily measurable, including:

- participation rates in the programme;
- whether participants achieved their goals;
- employee retention rates;
- increased diversity and inclusion; and
- improved employee engagement scores.

5. Conclusion

Done well, mentoring can have a significant impact on talent development in law firms. The best programmes engage lawyers at all levels, fostering a mentoring culture. Mentees are provided with invaluable access to more experienced lawyers who guide, challenge and help develop them into better lawyers. And mentors get to share their experience and knowledge in a bi-directional learning environment, honing their mentoring, coaching and leadership skills.

The personalised nature of the mentoring relationship cannot easily be replicated and relies heavily on the rapport of the mentor and mentee to make it work. The best programmes aim to provide just enough structure and organisation to provide the right ingredients to allow the mentoring relationship to flourish naturally. An overly prescriptive or bureaucratic programme will turn lawyers off, causing them to not fully engage.

It would be remiss not to mention the impacts of COVID-19 on mentoring, as indeed it is impacting every aspect of our lives. This chapter is largely written in lockdown, where the physical world has shrunk to the home or the local suburb with very restricted outings, and yet in a virtual sense the pandemic has opened the world up, breaking down geographical boundaries in ways we could only have imagined in the pre-COVID world. For mentoring, this means that many of the relationships – and the engagement process – will be conducted online, via video conferencing platforms. And interestingly, despite not being together in person there is something quite intimate about being on video with a mentor or mentee, when you are both talking from your home office, bedroom or kitchen table.

Arguably, the benefits of mentoring are even more salient in disruptive times, and social/physical distancing need not impede good mentoring despite the different modes of communication.[13] Mentoring is not, and never has been, an exact science and the best programmes adapt and evolve with the times, participants always keeping in mind the aim of the programme and seeking feedback and ways to improve.

---

13   David Smith and W Brad Johnson, "Social Distancing Doesn't Have to Disrupt Mentorship", *Harvard Business Review*, 6 April 2020.

Building sustainable client relationships without selling

Kevin Doolan
Møller Institute
Moray McLaren
Lexington Consultants

1. Introduction

When asking a room full of senior lawyers, as we regularly do in our consultancy work, "How do you feel when you are selling your services?", the sense of discomfort is almost palpable. Some will find that their left shoe or the clock on the far wall has suddenly become of great interest. And if groups of successful lawyers – people whom we can congratulate for already building the profitable client relations required to sustain their legal career – find this so difficult to answer, it is even worse for those junior lawyers who are now expected to develop clients at an earlier stage of their careers. The times when young lawyers could transition into partnership on the basis of their technical skills alone are long gone. During a decade of economic uncertainty, the ability to grow existing clients and win new ones is often the number one criterion for partnership. But why is this often challenging for our best lawyers?

Let us start by considering the case of Jane.

1.1 The challenge

Jane has been among the high achievers at her law firm since the day she joined. Not only was she the leading student of her graduation year, but since joining the firm she has flown through every challenge, becoming first an associate and then senior associate on schedule. After eight years with the firm, it was assumed that she would now progress to the top of her career via an invitation to join the partnership.

Today, however, her career expectations have been frustrated and Jane is struggling to understand why. The managing partner has explained that, despite exceeding expectations throughout her time at the firm, she will not be making partner as expected.

This scenario is increasingly playing out in law firms of all types, shapes and sizes. Jane is hugely disappointed and would be forgiven for feeling that the rules of the game have changed – and they have.

Working long hours and delivering a good legal service to existing clients is important, but not enough to lead automatically to progression to partner. It is only when facing this new reality that the need for all partners (not just some select rainmakers) to achieve real growth becomes so clear.

When making the case for partnership, existing partners are bound to ask, "If you are such a great lawyer, why can't you give us a list of the new clients that you have brought in? Don't great lawyers attract new clients? And if you aren't going to do that, or create real growth from your existing clients, why should we make you partner? Aren't we then just sharing the same-sized cake between more people?"

Even in countries where there is still market growth for legal services, existing partners would rather promote someone to partner who has demonstrated real business-building skills, rather than one who just 'does the legal work'.

1.2   New requirements

For all of the reasons explored in this book, Jane's career has hit an unexpected bump in the road. Against the backdrop of changing market conditions, law firms are reviewing the current skills requirements of their most senior lawyers – especially as they approach the gateway to partnership.

Lawyers now need to be more than good legal technicians: they need to be better managers, lead junior lawyers more effectively and get closer to clients and understand their needs better.

Building an effective book of business – once perhaps seen as a consequence of partnership – has now become a prerequisite. And while senior associates were previously expected to focus primarily on work output, they are now required to go out and develop client relationships.

Like a growing number of bright young lawyers globally, Jane now has a serious bridge to cross. She has to prove her ability to attract clients and build a profitable book of business before – not after – she makes partner. After almost a decade of studying and working in the law with a strong focus on chargeable hours, Jane might well be justified in thinking she is unprepared for the next stage of her career.

1.3   Market changes

In our work with law firms over the last two decades, we have seen a universal and significant change in the legal market. At the risk of both oversimplifying and stating the obvious, the pendulum is swinging in favour of clients and away from law firms. The client is increasingly now in control.

While the shocks caused by the financial crisis of 2008 and the coronavirus pandemic have accelerated this change – as supply of legal services has outstripped demand in many markets – they were not the cause. The new client mindset – the 'procurement' approach to legal services – is having a knock-on effect for all law firms. This new approach is trickling down from general counsel in international businesses to even the most traditional domestic companies. Even areas of the world that were previously unaffected by this change are now starting to see the effects.

Like many of the extreme challenges facing lawyers, this will not simply disappear with the rising tide of an improving economy. This particular train has now left the station.

2. Sales without selling

At its simplest, sales or cross-selling may be the requirements outlined by Jane's managing partner, but she is not overly excited about this new prospect. There are two good reasons for the aversion that most lawyers feel towards selling. First, they became lawyers to practise law – if they had wanted a career in sales, they would be pretty unlikely to have chosen law. Selling is not something that they actually want to do – for the majority of lawyers, satisfaction comes from delivering a great legal service, meeting the challenges that the work throws up and feeling a sense of achievement from a job well done.

Secondly, selling is about risk. Increasing the level of sales activity inevitably means increasing the risk of rejections, which can lead to a personal sense of failure.

2.1 Stop selling

During our sessions, we say to lawyers at all stages of their careers, "Remember a time that you were sold to by someone else. How did you feel?" Almost all of them can remember a salesperson trying to push some unwanted offer onto them. They recall the unpleasant feelings that they experienced – at a deep, instinctive level, people do not like being sold to. The seller seemed to be pushing something because it was in their interests. Equally, when we ask general counsel it should come as no surprise that they too dislike being sold to.

It is an interesting place to pause and reflect. Lawyers do not like selling and clients do not like being sold to. So why not stop selling?

How does this help Jane? While many law firms have invested in sales training programmes for their lawyers – at all stages of their careers – we strongly believe that selling is not the answer. The magic that will help all lawyers, including Jane, is at the same time both simpler and more complex than the average Selling for Lawyers programme would suggest.

We believe that the answer for the vast majority of lawyers (excluding the natural-born rainmakers who develop their own successful and comfortable style) is to approach the problem from the opposite direction and to ask, not "How can I improve my selling skills?" but rather, "What would make this client want to buy more from me?" and (for a potential new client), "What would make this target client switch from their existing law firm to mine?" Our experience has shown that in both cases the answer will not be that the client has been sold to.

Our approach – let's call it 'sales without selling' – requires a deeper understanding of individual clients' needs and has the fortunate foundation that it actually plays to the lawyer's core skills of investigation and analysis, and their desire to help their clients to be more successful, rather than trying to train them in a new and alien skill of 'selling'. We think that this has been the real secret behind its success – rather than trying to change lawyers in some fundamental way, our process asks lawyers to use their core skills in ways that win more work.

For this to be effective, lawyers need to understand that they are looking at two separate scenarios. Building more work from an existing client is very different from gaining the first piece of work from a new client, and a different thought process is needed to navigate each successfully.

2.2 Why would an existing client give Jane more work?

The key to unlocking more work from a current client is appreciating what inspires client loyalty. What makes them come back again and again? What might make them give Jane a whole new area of work by their own 'cross-buying' rather than by Jane's cross-selling?

The clues can be found in our own behaviour when buying services from providers such as airlines, hotels and restaurants.

Any decent provider will offer the basic service. In fact, the overall standards for legal services are continually rising – clients (particularly the most valuable international clients) have high expectations. To hold onto them, lawyers need to provide a really good standard of service.

This is exactly what Jane may have been doing – and using up almost every available hour to do so. The problem for Jane in seeking to grow an existing client is that her competitors will also be providing that high level of service.

Think about it. If talking to any client, could Jane honestly claim that her key competitors (those whom she comes across repeatedly) could not do a good job on their legal work? The reality is that clients typically have a wide choice of firms for each type of advice that they need (only in the most specialised areas of work could anyone claim real rarity of skills), and other firms should all be able to provide a good level of service.

A client will want to buy more from Jane only if she differentiates herself and becomes more valuable to the client than her competitors. It will not be about giving the client a hard sell (or even a soft sell) if her service is just the same as her competitors'.

2.3 Success factors

Our research with clients shows that success requires the following to be present:

- The client must feel that their lawyer understands their business.

- The lawyer must deliver value outside of the core service.
- The lawyer must spent time 'off the clock' and in person, in order to better understand the client's needs.

This last point is particularly important. Jane cannot succeed unless she invests time in understanding the client better (not in marketing to them), and she cannot do this via email, no matter how good a lawyer she is – phone calls, video meetings and meetings in person are essential.

3. Building personal relationships

Face-to-face time with clients (even on video) is crucial for Jane, as she will be building relationships. Doing a great job but failing to invest time in this way will leave her in the second league – and will not inspire client loyalty.

One general counsel expressed it this way:

I have eight law firms on my panel and only one of them has ever tried to build any relationship with me and my team: coming over to have coffee, asking us great questions, spending time with us in our offices. The others seem to think that we are an anonymous, remote organisation – I'm really surprised. That one firm is continually growing its share of work because they actually seem interested.

It is important to think about this statement. The winning firm was not selling. It had not asked its lawyers to sell, but rather to talk to clients about their businesses, to show interest and to learn 'off the clock'. As a result, this particular client was buying more from that law firm without anyone doing any selling.

In-house lawyers speak of the vulnerability that they feel when bringing external lawyers into their business and placing them in front of close colleagues. Building trust – on both sides – is key, and we know from the wave of current research on neuroscience that this is primarily an emotional response built around subconscious behaviours. We often do not even realise it is happening.

At its simplest, this means knowing the client better – both the business and the individual personalities involved – at the heart of which is having a better conversation with them. This is about their agenda, not Jane's – understanding their personal and business aims and how to help achieve them.

More than one general counsel has told us about those painful pitches, beauty parades where even the most senior of lawyers feels the need to explain what sounds like the history and structure of their law firm. One general counsel explained how he would have to say, "Excuse me for interrupting, but we have selected you to come here today, alongside the other firms, as we already know you are all excellent lawyers and well qualified to help us on this assignment. But if you don't mind, we would just like to explain our needs on this particular project."

3.1 Listening, but not hearing

Effective listening is the starting point, but is perhaps the antithesis of what many see as being a professional, that is, giving an opinion on what is right and wrong in a no-nonsense way. Indeed, we all know excellent lawyers who are poor listeners.

For most lawyers, building relationships requires being a good listener and having enough confidence to let the client lead the way. Jane needs to show that she is confident, but not pushy. Jane should not try to use these regular contacts to sell. In fact, she does not need to – if she is helping a client by delivering a much more tailored service and better understanding the client's business, then she will differentiate herself and more work will flow.

The secret is about building a differentiated service – an enhanced legal service that goes beyond simply doing the job. Get in professional help, if needed, in order to produce a business growth model for key clients. Or brainstorm both with clients and with fellow partners. The important outcome is to produce 10 to 20 ideas for working differently with key clients in ways that they value. Start thinking about how to make clients' daily lives easier, help them in their careers, make valuable introductions to others; show that it is not just about doing the work they have sent. Be a trusted friend, coach and adviser – not just another lawyer. One partner expressed it like this: "How can I add more value to this client in the next 12 months?"

4. Winning work from new clients

So, why should a new client, who may not yet have met Jane, start giving her legal work? This whole area of finding new clients is one of the most troubling for many young lawyers. By comparison, it is relatively easy to understand that impressing existing clients with a better level of service, understanding their business and adding value is a good route to growth. Jane's search for potential new clients raises a number of questions:

- Why should a target client move their legal work to Jane? What is the benefit of changing?
- What type of target client is most likely to use Jane's services? What are the best targets?
- How does Jane actually meet target clients and get face to face?
- Once Jane meets them, what would persuade the target client to give her legal work (given that usually the client will already be using other law firms)?

Also, what if Jane, like so many other lawyers, tells you that she has a general practice and isn't clear where to focus her attention? An increasingly large part of our work is assisting lawyers like Jane match their skills with their passion for more specific areas of law and industry groups. What from the outside looks like the simple step of Jane discovering which area she wants to specialise in is both liberating and empowering. Deciding who she needs to know and how best to approach them has now become so much clearer. Of course, building the skills, knowledge and profile this requires does not happen overnight. Unless it is an area of law and industry she finds interesting – ideally, is passionate about – the journey is likely to be too tough to complete.

.1 The benefit of change

The secret with meeting target clients is to have a distinctive value proposition to offer. If Jane's service is the same as other lawyers, then it is hard to think of a reason why it is of value for the target client to meet her. Jane's position is the same as that of any commercial business, and it is worth revisiting the 'generic competitive strategies' put forward by Professor Michael Porter at Harvard Business School in his 1980 classic, *Competitive Strategy: Techniques for Analyzing Industries and Competitors*.[1]

The three strategies that Professor Porter describes are cost leadership, differentiation and segmentation (market focus). In law firm terms, this means being:

- cheaper (offering the same service as the client's current law firm, but charging less);
- better (giving the client a more valuable service than the current law firm – for example, by better understanding their business or having subject experts that their current law firm does not have and charging more); or
- more focused (specialising in the client's business area, for example, advising only on intellectual property or acting only for energy companies; in larger firms, this can be achieved by having a clear sector-based structure).

This is an important starting point that is often missed by lawyers, who tend to focus on their own expertise rather than on the realities of a client that already has lawyers and is being expected to move work away from them.

Unless the target client happens to be particularly unhappy with their existing legal advisers, they will not give work to a new firm without a real belief that the new firm offers a more attractive service than their current lawyers. Here, it is useful to think along the lines of Porter's strategies – is Jane's message to the target client that she is cheaper, better or more focused? She needs to have this clear in her mind, because it will influence the way that she approaches and talks to that target client. If Jane is not clear about this, she cannot expect the target client to understand why they should change lawyers.

Michael E Porter, *Competitive Strategy: Techniques for Analyzing Industries and Competitors*, Free Press (export ed), 2004.

4.2   Best targets

Given that any lawyer can devote only so much time to seeking out new clients, it becomes crucially important to pursue the best targets – those that are most likely to say yes.

There is a simple way that Jane can establish this. The best targets are those that are most similar to existing clients. The expression 'most similar' needs to be defined in terms of the legal service that is being offered.

For a labour lawyer, it might mean clients with over 5,000 employees, because this is his or her area of specialisation. For one M&A lawyer, it might mean owner-managers who are looking to sell out at the end of their career; for another, it might mean clean energy companies looking for major venture capital investments.

Without doubt, the best targets look very like an individual lawyer's existing client base. Of course, it is possible to gradually move upmarket – but this must be gradual. Too often, a lawyer can become excited about acting for a Fortune 500/FTSE 100/Ibex 35 multinational corporation because it is seen as a trophy client that can help the lawyer's personal brand. But such companies may be aggressive on price, use tough procurement techniques and be demanding clients. If they are similar to that lawyer's other clients, then fine – but if not, they are unlikely to be the best targets.

In general, it is worthwhile to create a simple scoring sheet for target clients, based on the characteristics of the existing client base. A lawyer can then test target clients against this scoring sheet to help focus on the best targets. Experience has shown that a small number of current targets – perhaps two or three – is the most effective. As a first step, it is useful to set up Google alerts on these target clients. Google will then generate email updates of news stories affecting the chosen targets.

4.3   Getting face to face

Unless Jane is providing the most routine of legal services, she will not win a new client without meeting them. But how can she get in front of busy people who do not know her yet?

One of the best sources of target clients will be Jane's existing clients – she should start by asking them. If they are happy with her work, they should be happy to make introductions to others (if they are not happy, then Jane's time will be better spent in remedying this rather than chasing new clients). For example, her existing clients may be able to directly introduce her to others and set up a coffee or lunch with them – they may even be happy to come along.

This type of warm introduction is valuable and should be seen as the best route to new clients, because it comes with an implied recommendation by the current client that is reassuring to the target client. Several general counsel have told us that they are surprised at how rarely they are asked to make these types of introduction by their law firm advisers.

The next best route is for Jane to network through other non-client connections, or to use a special focus to meet potential new clients. For instance, if Jane has a particular focus on the laws relating to food labelling, she can offer to give talks on this topic at relevant food industry events or write articles for relevant journals. She will certainly want to join all the food law groups on LinkedIn and join in conversations or pass on valuable hints and tips.

In parallel, she has to position herself as a go-to person for her particular practice and industry – be that through writing articles, client alerts or other activity such as conference presentations.

If she does not feel comfortable in networking situations, it is worth taking a colleague – even better if she can go to a relevant event with a client who can introduce her to other people. She should also consider having professional training in networking – it will make a big difference to her success and is not something that comes naturally to many lawyers.

The key point for Jane is never to sell when she meets a potential client. It comes over very badly and will rarely be of benefit or interest to them. Jane just needs to let them talk about themselves and their business, asking good questions, showing interest and using follow-up questions so that the conversation does not become an interrogation. For example, she could say, "That's interesting – tell me more about how that affected your business."

If Jane asks relevant supplementary questions and empathises from her own experiences in the potential client's area of business, this will be a good first meeting. Jane wants them to gain a favourable impression, and this will not come about if she is talking endlessly about herself and her law firm. Jane needs to be interested in them rather than trying to be interesting about herself.

Jane's goal from a first meeting may be that the target client is prepared to stay in touch and perhaps come to group meetings (a roundtable that she is organising or an industry event) so that she can spend more time getting to know them.

It is essentially a courtship – the target client needs to feel safe that Jane is not going to switch into sell mode, that she has something of value and that she is showing genuine interest in them and their business. She cannot move too quickly.

During the period after the initial meeting, Jane should be in 'help' mode. Are there any articles that she can send to them relating to matters that they talked to her about? Does she have any guides or tips that she could email to them? Looking through her contacts on LinkedIn, is there anyone whom they might like to meet? If so, she should suggest arranging this. Keeping in contact and being helpful is all that Jane needs to do as she builds up to the stage where she can have a one-on-one, face-to-face meeting or video call with the target client.

Jane needs to earn the right to this meeting by being helpful, adding value and giving the client insights that they might not have thought about. That is effectively all that is needed for the sell.

4.4 The compelling case

So why should this target client give Jane legal work? In practice, we have found that the principle of reciprocity gives the best chance of generating work from a new client. It is worth examining this in detail, as many lawyers have told us that they find this final stage – actually getting work – the most difficult part. Many have ended up in a friendly circuit of meetings and conversations that never seem to get anywhere. Certainly, there will be some cases where it is time to give up, but only after these fundamental approaches have been tried. Beware of endless conversations about sport, families or other non-work topics. These can be mutually enjoyable, but can push out conversations about business.

The subject of reciprocity has been well researched by Professor Robert B Cialdini and is described in his book *Influence*.[2] It plays well with the core skill of lawyers – that of helping their clients. Cialdini's research demonstrates that if someone wants something from someone else, he or she must first give that person something.

If Jane gives, this creates an obligation of reciprocity – "Jane introduced me to an important contact; she gave me free advice on a matter that I was concerned about; she gave me some great ideas about how I might approach an issue that I was facing in my sector – so I owe her." Lawyers in highly specialised areas, or those who focus tightly on a business sector, can create this reciprocity by delivering thought leadership, insights and examples of how other clients are tackling an industry-wide issue.

Lawyers tend to feel comfortable with this concept – they feel happy about offering free help (while it has to be free at this early stage, this does not mean devoting whole days to delivering some substantial legal project for free, but rather providing small pieces of free help).

Cialdini's research shows that if Jane builds a new relationship based upon giving help, the typical businessperson will want to find some work to give her in return – something that might give them an opportunity to see her in action on a paid matter, so that they can judge whether they want to pass on more work in future.

4.5 The final step

If a target client is thinking of instructing Jane, it is important that she can minimise the risk that they feel in taking this step. At this stage, Jane is untested and the potential client might worry that she may not be as good as they thought – and this is on a paid matter. Every target client sending out instructions to a new adviser feels somewhat vulnerable.

Jane can reduce this worry in two ways. First, she should have some happy existing clients that a new prospective client can talk to, in order to find out

---

2   Robert B Cialdini, *Influence: The Psychology of Persuasion*, Harper Business, 2007.

what she is really like. This makes a significant difference, and if she does not currently have existing clients who would be happy to do this, she should focus entirely on current clients and leave new clients for later!

Secondly, Jane should try to ensure that the new client takes small steps before they think about taking a large step. If at all possible, they should try her out on something relatively small or straightforward before committing to transfer a whole area of work to her or giving her a 'bet the farm' matter. A good way to start off would be for her to be attentive for relatively small pieces of advice.

This is just as important if Jane has only major pieces of advice to sell – for example, if she is an M&A lawyer specialising in end-of-career sales by founders or managers, she needs to develop a smaller piece of advice as her entry point (eg, a workshop on preparing for sale: "Ten things you need to do in the year before you sell") to give the target client something small on which she can be tested.

This approach is supported by research. A specialist team which handled major pieces of litigation wanted to know what the main factors were when a client was deciding which firm to instruct on a large piece of work. The number one answer (for all but the most specialist areas) was, "The firm which has handled a mid-range piece of litigation for us really well." Rather than marketing 'bet the farm' litigation services to target clients, the team could make more progress by winning instructions on a mid-range piece of work (with a lower risk for the client in instructing a new law firm) and then performing on that work exceptionally well.

5. Making it happen

All of these ideas regarding selling without sales are easy to use, but they are of value only if Jane makes time for them and repeats them regularly. To some extent, they need to become habits. How is this to be achieved?

Jane will need to come up with a plan or system that works for her. For example, she may set regular time aside to run through key clients and targets and think about what she has been doing that will create a differentiated service. At the start, she may benefit from specialist training, mentoring or coaching.

Time invested in winning new work needs to be aligned with the firm's remuneration system and performance management. Jane will inevitably sacrifice some time that could have been spent doing billable work in favour of time invested in building long-term profitability for the firm. Remember that in building enough work to become a partner, the aim is to maintain the leverage (ie, profitability) of the firm, developing sufficient work – of the right quality – for her own new team of associates.

A balance must be struck between time spent on business development and time spent on work for clients. Jane will be expected to maintain high levels of utilisation on chargeable time. This makes it all the more important to ensure that time spent on business development is efficient and aimed at the best targets. However, there also needs to be an acceptance that doing a good legal job and focusing entirely on this is unlikely to create sufficient growth in existing or new clients to build a practice and a case for partnership.

The starting point is developing a powerful relationship with the client, being there for them, helping them out when they need it and acting as a support and sounding board.

In parallel, Jane also needs to find her passion. By this we mean that lawyers who have found a sector or a specialist area of advice that fascinates and energises them come across positively to clients. Enthusiasm is infectious, and it is worth Jane spending some time on finding the work type or area of business that really excites her. In order to build a successful career, we all need to find an area of work about which we are passionate and clients with whom we enjoy working.

If a young lawyer can tap into their passion and spend time learning how to provide an enhanced level of service, then growing existing clients and attracting new clients is achievable without having to change into selling mode. In our experience, this is not only the best news that any young lawyer like Jane can have; it will also enable her to develop both a successful and enjoyable career.

6.   Business development in a crisis

Writing this chapter in the depths of the COVID-19 crisis means that we are spending time working with law firms on what they need to do differently at the present time. This is not just about the radically different business conditions prevailing, but also the inability to travel and meet clients in person. Approaching clients to try to sell to them in present circumstances is likely to give entirely the wrong impression. So what can you do? From our work so far, the following key messages have come through:

- It is really important to focus on existing clients and to make contact with them, checking in on what is happening for them in particular.
- Video calling is much preferable to a voice call if the client is open to it (and the vast majority are getting used to days full of video calls).
- Having the shared experience of working from home is a great starting point – if you have pets or family with you get them to say hello on the call. Many partners told us they felt that they had really advanced their relationship with the client.
- Start on a positive note – what was the upside of working from home?
- Look for opportunities to offer help. Clients really remember those people who offered (free) help during a tough time. For example, one

client complained of feeling isolated and out of touch so the lawyer set up Friday group video calls with three similar clients so that they could share experiences.

- Start thinking longer term. If working from home is going to become much more common, how will you change your behaviours (more video calls, fewer emails) to put yourself in better standing with the client.

While the crisis may make lawyers worried for the future, there will always be new opportunities from the changes – opportunities to seek clients from farther afield and to build relationships on video calls in a similar way to the way they had previously been built face to face.

7. Conclusion

Winston Churchill was fond of saying, "Never let a good crisis go to waste."

As law firms come to terms with the ongoing economic uncertainty, some lawyers are feeling more optimistic about the consequences than others. While it is clear that many business sectors are suffering, others are adapting and continuing to grow. Clients are seeking to cut their legal spend even though their need for legal services is increasing sharply.

In response, some law firms are in marketing overdrive, while others are being more cautious. As we have seen, none of us like to be sold to, the more so when we are firefighting and trying to ensure the future of our businesses.

So how to get the balance right? The risks are high, as in times of crisis any interaction can trigger a lasting effect on our sense of trust and loyalty. In our experience, clients are more open than before to new thinking and new relationships. Communication is subtly changing, however, becoming more personal and authentic – the importance of trust has never been greater.

As we have illustrated using the example of Jane, it is the ability to develop powerful and mutually satisfying client relations that remains at the heart of a successful career. The quality of relationships is more important than the quantity.

Lateral partner onboarding and integration

Rebecca Normand-Hochman
Institute of Legal Talent & Leadership
Tom Spence
Donoma Advisors

Introduction

The battle for lateral partner talent within law firms is as fierce as ever, and this will likely continue for years to come as firms the world over continually look to adapt and shape their businesses to gain competitive edge and win market share. In this chapter we address the topic of how law firms onboard and integrate their lateral partner investments and offer some guidance as to how the legal industry can change to improve the return on these investments. While this is not a comprehensive guide, it does offer alternative ways of thinking and approaching the topic to improve the processes and their outcomes. These guidelines represent, for the most part, a clear change of mindset from the prevailing practices used today. They may take some time to assimilate and incorporate and for some firms and their leaders they will require a significant change in thinking and focus, but for others it may validate the journey they have already begun.

This chapter is based on collectively over 40 years' experience of consulting and coaching on talent within the legal industry internationally. Added to our own experience we have conducted 30 interviews with law firm leaders, heads of talent and partners who have moved themselves. We also conducted market questionnaires to provide current and focused data to develop our thinking.

It is estimated that 70% of law firms' total expenses go on talent.[1] Despite law firms' main asset being their people, the market norm of a 40% failure rate for lateral partners highlights a gap in their talent management processes. Indeed, our research has shown that in their first year at a new firm only 25%–50% of partners achieve their stated financial targets. So we wonder why, when a law firm's capital is its people, the failure rate is so high and seemingly so consistent across the industry. More importantly, how can we help firms improve these numbers?

Ultimately our findings were diverse, with firms approaching how to hire and integrate lateral partners in completely different ways with completely

---

Dr Heidi Gardner and Anusia Gillespie, *Smart Collaboration, Successful strategies to recruit and integrate laterals in law firms*, Globe Law and Business, 2018.

different results. However, the key, consistent finding from our research was that most firms view lateral recruitment and integration as separate processes when actually they are intrinsically linked.

There has been much focus in the industry recently on innovation, flexibility and change, but this focus has yet to be directed at the hiring and integration of partners. In this chapter we identify current themes and issues and provide ways law firms can innovate and fundamentally improve the way they onboard and integrate their lateral partners.

2.   The current statistics

Unfortunately, the statistics around lateral partner hiring do not make for good reading. A recent Am Law 200 study found that 40%–50% of lateral hires do not last five years at their new firm and 62% of lateral partners underperform in delivering their stated book of business.[2]

Our own research found that in their first year between 25% and 50% of laterals achieved their stated financial targets. These statistics did improve to 50%–75% by year three, but what is clear is that focusing on financial portability in the business planning stage is no longer a sustainable approach for partner integration.

Generally speaking, the view is that it takes a lateral partner three to five years to hit their business plan objectives,[3] so why firms continue to focus on immediate portability is open to question. Law firms could begin looking longer term when it comes to their investment decisions and financial planning to enable lateral partners to stand a better chance of proper integration and, ultimately, success.

Given the costs are so high, why so many disappointments? Lack of long-term planning, inadequate due diligence, lame execution and poor integration are the usual suspects. David Morley, "Comment: A triumph of hope over experience – Lateral hiring needs an upgrade for the post-Covid era", *Legal Business* blog, June 2020.

So very rarely do people hit their Y1 figures – Y2 and Y3 become more accurate. Law firms struggle with the level of honesty around entry level and transferable business as it is all linked to earnings. Firms are too short term in their thinking. Y1 should be an integration year to ensure Y2 onwards are successful. There is far too much focus on how that partner has failed and more often than not it's the firm that has not delivered. Senior partner, US law firm.

---

2   "Risky Business: Rethinking Lateral Hiring", ALM Intelligence/Decipher survey, February 2019.
3   Boris Groysberg, Ashish Nanda and Nitin Nohria, "The Risky Business of Hiring Stars", *Harvard Business Review*, May 2004.

The success rate for retention in the lateral market has been less than stellar with recent market data showing this rate at around 60%. Toby Brown, "Trends in the Lateral Partner Recruitment Market", Thomson Reuters, 15 January 2020.

From our conversations with law firm leaders the main reasons for lateral success are twofold:

- integration into existing firm clients; and
- collaboration with colleagues.

Amongst partners who themselves moved as laterals, the key reasons for success are stated as:

- personal client support; and
- increased visibility with firm clients.

And hired partners felt there were two main areas where firms could improve:

- cultural integration; and
- collegiality.

This disconnect over what contributes to success and the lack of appreciation for the emotional challenge faced by partners in adapting to a new environment show the challenging dynamic facing law firms when it comes to onboarding and integrating partners properly. Ultimately the majority of laterals being hired by law firms feel it is their personal business that will make them a success at their new firm. Firms might promote culture and collegiality but fundamentally their lateral recruits feel something different.

Not all firms fall into this group, however, with the most successful firms focusing more on skillset and fit than portability. A partner who joined one of the global elite commented that during their interview process, "The firm made it very clear that they were not interested in portable business; they wanted my skillset to build into their client and internal infrastructure. For them the message within the interview process was about integration and collaboration, not portability. That was powerful and has made integration easy." While admittedly few firms have the luxury of hiring laterals purely to integrate them into their own clients, altering the focus on portability and claiming some responsibility for revenues and business development is a good way to help laterals actually believe the promotional words of collegiality and collaboration many firms promote.

On a data feedback level, a standout area where lateral partners feel firms could improve their integration process – and indeed one of the main challenges identified by laterals – was the hiring firm's understanding of their business. This point ties into so many facets of the hiring and onboarding process but comes down to due diligence: having a desire to know more than just numbers looking good on a spreadsheet, and identifying where and how a firm can actually help a partner succeed, create more opportunities and give the process the respect it deserves by making the right and most informed decision. When law firms promote innovation and future thinking, it is surely unacceptable that their greatest assets should highlight a lack of understanding of their business as a key issue. As Heidi Gardner and Anusia Gillespie have stated, when it comes to lateral hiring, "The status quo is not a winning strategy",[4] nor is it sustainable. Law firms need to accept that change is necessary.

3. Three critical factors for success

There is a trend whereby lateral partners carry more risk in a move than firms. They account for most of the business planning input, they have to move their clients across and integrate into a new environment, and if there is any hint of not achieving what they anticipated, they are the ones to answer for it.

To understand more about what lies behind the status quo and how change can be effected, we need to address key themes to have come out of our research. Importantly, these themes were identified unanimously by law firm leadership, talent and lateral partners. Our research revealed that to increase the rate of success in lateral partner hiring, law firms needed consistency, accountability and leadership in their processes, culture and messaging.

3.1 Consistency

Surprisingly, many large international firms have no real onboarding and integration process, which makes consistency impossible. While some firms can articulate recruitment, onboarding and integration processes well enough, most of the time there is little to no consistency when it comes to their implementation and execution. This leads to the unchallenged system we see today, where firms spend far too much time and money on recruitment activities that offer them a relatively poor return. This lack of consistency comes from a paucity of clarity and understanding of, and ultimately a lack of accountability for, the processes. Law firms need to have a clear focus on consistency in their execution of onboarding and integration of laterals; by improving consistency, they will improve success.

There is also little to no consistency when it comes to onboarding and integration, as partners themselves play the roles they want to play and due to lack of accountability this varies substantially. Global practice group head, international firm.

---

4   Dr Heidi Gardner and Anusia Gillespie, *Smart Collaboration for Lateral Hiring: Successful Strategies to Recruit and Integrate Laterals in Law Firms*, Globe Law and Business, 2018.

3.2 Accountability

Our research highlighted the important role that individual accountability plays in successful partner onboardings and integrations. One chief of talent acquisition said of accountability in the case of a failed lateral, "Where does it sit in the firm? It doesn't, it floats." Generally, the lack of true accountability within the lateral hiring process means there is little to no direct internal accountability for failed lateral hires, with most of the blame being put on the laterals themselves.

Implementing clear accountability structures at every stage and every level of the onboarding and integration process improves not only the chances of success, but the business and cultural opportunities afforded the firm by getting more out of their people than they currently demand. Firms need to set objectives, hold people accountable, monitor progress and reward the right behaviours.

Accountability sits with the nearest and easiest scapegoat, which is the lateral partner... ultimately, nobody wants to accept responsibility so no one looks for failures. Head of lateral talent, international law firm.

3.3 Leadership

There is little point trying to implement consistency and accountability if the leadership of the firm is not fully engaged and doesn't model the way. As in all change initiatives, leadership plays a vital role in steering the new direction and showing commitment to embed new and more strategic approaches.

Leadership involvement and commitment to creating and promoting alignment throughout the process are therefore critical factors for success.

Law firms who look to implement change and innovate with their talent in mind will almost certainly move ahead of those who don't, and in the coming years we expect to see the gap increase significantly between leadership teams who commit to driving change in how they onboard and integrate lateral partners, and those who don't.

Management is responsible, but the responsibility needs to cascade down to different levels of partners who need to be held accountable for the success of the integration. Former senior partner, international law firm.

Law firm leaders should be accountable for failed lateral hires and investments. Too much emphasis is on the partner but it is the firm making the investment decisions and they need to be accountable. Global practice group head.

Figure 1. The roles of consistency, accountability and leadership

Leadership
Leadership sets the
whole tone for the
organisation. Without a clear
message and leadership from
the top, any improvements will be
ad hoc and advancement will take
longer than needed.

Accountability
Integrating clear levels of accountability will help drive
consistency of behaviour into the process.

Consistency
Developing a consistency in how processes are implemented and
approached builds in greater levels of execution. Without consistency of
execution any process improvements will be diluted.

Source: Authors.

4.   Best practice for recruiting and integrating lateral partners

4.1   Mindset change: linking recruitment with integration

Currently law firms generally view the recruitment and integration processes as separate, with integration being considered towards the end of the recruitment process and only beginning once the lateral joins the firm. However, our research has identified key areas where the recruitment and integration processes are directly linked and it is important to appreciate that the recruitment process should be the foundation for integration. A mindset change is needed in order to gain from the often rich information obtained during the recruitment process in order to positively impact the integration stage.

Integration should begin early in the recruitment process; indeed, the recruitment process is an important integration tool.

Table 1. Interaction between recruitment and integration

Stage of recruitment process	Opportunity to improve integration
Preparation to hire	Develop a clear internal plan and stakeholder buy-in to a recruitment process to create support for the lateral.
Interviews	• Substantive feedback to be circulated between all the parties involved in the recruitment to further develop the understanding of the individual. Using all relevant business support teams to add value to client and business elements can help improve integration and raise further valid questions as the interview process continues. • Use interviews to start potentially integrating the prospective hire into the firm's culture, be it through tone and message or through meetings with relevant network groups core to the firm's culture. • Utilise a greater diversity of perspectives in the interview and feedback loop processes to develop a wider view and understanding of the lateral.
Business planning	• Collaborative business planning, again utilising internal business support teams to build a more detailed picture, with the firm identifying opportunities for the lateral to enhance their business off the firm's platform • Assess cultural aspects as well as business. Develop deeper understanding of the individual as well as their financial value.

continued on next page

Stage of recruitment process	Opportunity to improve integration
Due diligence	• Early stage internal due diligence to build a picture of the individual – whether they should be considered, through to particular business or cultural aspects that could aid or hinder integration • Mid-stage due diligence – informal market soundings from clients and wider market, to build into original internal soundings • Final stage due diligence – detailed business and cultural diligence into the lateral to supplement the first two phases of diligence and complete the paperwork
Final stages	• Direct, personal message from firm leadership to connect with the potential new partner while also further promoting the firm culture and any other key messages • Finance director to answer all questions around financial management of the firm, billing etc, so this does not need to be covered upon joining • Social events with relevant practice, sector or client groups, partners, associates or business support teams, especially while on their notice period

Ideally, best practices to prepare for a successful transition would include initiating integration efforts earlier in the acquisition process, instead of waiting until the offer was accepted. Toby Brown, "Trends in the Lateral Partner Recruitment Market", *Thomson Reuters*, 15 January 2020.

4.2 Preparation and buy-in

Heidi Gardner and Anusia Gillespie recommend firms spend 40% of their time on preparing to hire, 30% on recruiting and interviewing and 30% on integration.[5] This represents almost a threefold increase on preparation time and a sixfold increase on integration. Why are these numbers so high? Because

---

5   *Ibid.*

firms currently spend more time recruiting than they do thinking about how best to do it and how then to get the best out of those they recruit.

Part of the preparation process should be the development of buy-in from key stakeholders. Many lateral appointments have failed (or failed to reach their potential) because important stakeholders have not fully bought into the hire. This can be especially challenging with larger firms and how they manage their internal structures (practice vs sector, office vs practice, client team vs region, etc). However, by taking more time to prepare for the recruitment process and develop stakeholder buy-in, the ability to impact integration will be increased.

.3 Interviews can prepare for integration

Every interaction is an opportunity to develop relationships and build cultural understanding.

Some larger international firms use upwards of 45 partners throughout a lateral hiring process while for others the number is considerably fewer. Importantly, a large proportion of the more extensive interviews are based not on competency but on opportunity and synergy, representing more depth and mutual investment in business and integration plans. We found that the partners who had been involved in a more extensive process felt integrated more quickly than those who had not. Essentially, prior to hiring a partner, giving them more human touch points within the firm made them feel at home more easily and quickly.

While the number of partners used throughout a lateral process can be important to developing a broad consensus and support towards the hire, ultimately we found that it is the mindset and the skills of the interviewing partners that make the difference, not their number. If a firm has 40 partners interviewing a potential lateral because they all want a say in the appointment, then a valuable opportunity is being lost to develop 'in-process buy-in'. However, if those 40 partners want to interview a lateral in order to fully understand their practice and their approach to business, and to identify potential synergies and opportunities, then outcomes become very different.

Using interviews as a way to develop information to help integration and build a more rounded business case is a significant opportunity for law firms. In order to develop an understanding around both cultural and business alignment, feedback needs to represent detailed analytical thinking. Capturing this rich information through developing clear feedback loops between all parties involved in the process will both help the selection process and positively shape integration.

.4 Due diligence

There are wide-ranging views on due diligence, from firms who choose to do none at all to those who carry out discreet diligence early in the process using trusted third parties. Broadly speaking, however, due diligence is a contentious subject across firms, with a high degree of scepticism surrounding the value add. Both the cost of due diligence and the quality of the product are raised as reasons not to conduct it, and the arguments can again be wrapped into the context of the conversation: on average, over 60% of laterals do not achieve their stated first-year targets and 40% ultimately fail in a three- to five-year period.

Firms can choose whether and how to carry out thorough due diligence, but high quality due diligence can and should provide firms with a clear understanding of the business and cultural fit of the lateral and can significantly improve integration and the opportunity for sustained success as a result.

Where possible, using partners, associates and business support teams who have worked with or close to a potential lateral can discreetly build an initial picture of their character and capabilities. Identifying alumni of the lateral to perhaps be involved in the onboarding process can save a lot of time and help significantly with the integration process.

Firms that are good at lateral recruitment do extensive due diligence as a matter of course … There is huge value in insightful and objective views on candidates. David Morley, "Comment: A triumph of hope over experience – Lateral hiring needs an upgrade for the post-Covid era", *Legal Business* blog, June 2020.

4.5 The role of non-partners

Our research suggested that through a greater diversity of perspectives in both the recruitment and integration processes, law firms can achieve better rates of success in their lateral partner hires.

While HR teams are currently the most involved in lateral recruitment and integration, this is expected to continue to evolve as new dedicated roles such as lateral partner integration manager emerge.

A business support function that is currently not involved in lateral recruitment and integration processes is business development. No firm interviewed involved their business development teams in either the strategic planning for recruitment or the process itself. Given the amount of up-front market analysis and thinking these teams can do prior to a recruitment process, there is a clear case for their involvement.

Bringing business development teams into the room early will allow them to use their knowledge of the firm and clients to add value to the process, in particular when assessing the business and integration plans. Using business development teams and other internal practice or client services teams to scrutinise, challenge and support business plans is a business-critical step that law firms should include in their process. The involvement of non-partners can reduce the amount of time spent by hiring partners, while also increasing the sophistication of the hiring process itself.

Finally, when considering integration in particular, one other skillset outside the partnership to consider is that of the finance team. More often than not, the responsibility of educating potential laterals on the financial management of the firm falls on the hiring partner; but diversifying responsibility to include the finance director can give the lateral access to an important area of the firm they are considering joining.

Often, those who are pushing for the hire are the ones tasked with diligencing and challenging it as well as integrating it. Law firms need to learn to devolve responsibility and use internal resources better. Why aren't firms using the CFO and business development team as a matter of course to get the right cross-section of support and information from within the business? EMEA practice group head.

The involvement and empowerment of non-partners, particularly within the business support functions, can lead to more informed and diligenced processes while reducing the time commitments currently borne by the hiring partners themselves.

4.6   **Co-creating the business plan**
The general approach currently within the legal industry is that lateral partner paperwork, and business plans in particular, are predominantly written by the lateral partner with input from the firms themselves being limited to minor amendments.

However, when looking at what makes for successful integration, it is both the business and cultural fit that needs to be assessed. Our research suggests that law firms can use the business plan phase of the recruitment process to provide laterals with evidence of the firm's values and culture and therefore test for evidence of alignment.

Law firms can demonstrate a greater level of empathy towards laterals through the business plan and paperwork process, ultimately identifying ways to share the risk in order to protect and support their assets.

Changing the current imbalance comes down to law firms accepting and embracing more accountability toward the creation of a lateral's business plan. Business plans have the potential to become more informative and collaborative, resulting in a smoother, more balanced integration process with greater potential for success.

4.7   **The human and cultural elements of integration**
It is important to view the recruitment process as more than just a transaction; it is an opportunity to develop relationships and begin integration.

Once a lateral has agreed to join a firm there is a sense of relief and relaxation that the deal is done, but there is no end-game to this process; firms must keep up momentum internally to ensure integration is smooth and sophisticated. Alongside the recruitment process, there is an opportunity for firms to continue cultural integration once a lateral is on his or her notice period by using social events to introduce further partners, other fee earners and business support teams. This can remove any feelings of isolation prior to joining while also building a sense of comfort and understanding with the existing infrastructure, meaning early integration is more seamless. Demonstrating empathy to a lateral partner following their resignation is a powerful way to start building cultural integration and provides a stabilising influence in what can be a difficult transition for many.

Utilising the notice period to maintain contact and build relationships is important, as is the impact a firm can make on a lateral's first day. Plan for that first day, using the existing team (associates, business support etc.) such that everyone knows their role and how to positively impact the lateral. Senior associates are currently underutilised in the integration process, particularly within the first few days and weeks. They can help guide laterals when other partners might not have time and this can add to rapport-building and empowerment amongst fee earners.

The role of senior associates in integration is an interesting one: they should be playing a bigger role in helping the partner find his/her way in the new firm Weekly catch-ups on what's going on, going out for drinks, etc. Executive board member, international law firm.

Another simple strategy for initial impact is for law firm leadership to be engaged in their lateral appointments and demonstrate their engagement by being visible and connected to new joiners. For a lateral to have direct contact from the senior or managing partner of their new firm only serves to further integrate the individual into the business and build their understanding and cultural appreciation of the firm.

On a more structural level, firms should have mutually clear expectations in terms of KPIs, of both themselves and the lateral (financially and culturally) and look to have update meetings with laterals on a quarterly basis for at least the first year. Having clear measurables and expectations provides the lateral with comfort and focus upon joining their new firm.

As a lateral you need clear KPIs, systems and processes for the individual as a lateral. Lateral partner, international firm.

There is a need for transparency. 50% of the reasons for failure relate to the fact that expectations are not clearly stated. Co-global head of practice group, international law firm.

Some firms use new partner offsites or bootcamps as another effective tool to integrate and inform laterals. This concept can be used for new laterals along with newly promoted partners to further integrate them into the firm and the partnership, its workings and what being a partner entails. During such exercises, partners receive overviews by Business Development, Marketing, Finance and HR and this provides a good opportunity for new partners to network. Presentations by other laterals who have successfully integrated, sharing their experiences and challenges, can help further humanise the conversation.

The integration process sets the tone for the success or otherwise of the entire opportunity of joining a new firm; it demonstrates the true attitude of the firm to the hire. Lateral partner, international law firm.

While the integration of laterals is on most law firms' agenda, it is easy to lose sight of the positive impact that can be made at a human level for new partners. Having an integration plan is one thing; having aligned messages and behaviours from across the organisation is another. Some small changes can make a big difference if they are made with commitment from firm leaders, with clear levels of accountability and expectations of consistency.

The firm and its leadership are always asking what is the impact on our people? How does this impact on the human level? That is a big difference and for a new partner extremely welcoming and comforting. Lateral hire to elite US firm.

5. Conclusion

The business of lateral hiring seems to have outgrown law firms' thought process and approach to their talent and talent acquisition, due to the aggressive expansion of firms globally and their rush for talent in the last decade. This has resulted in poor levels of success and while some firms are assessing and analysing the issue proactively, the majority are failing to adapt their approach effectively.

Improving lateral success rates and experiences comes down to firms recognising the need to change and innovate, as in other areas. Improvements will all be underpinned by consistency of process and behaviour, accountability towards the firm and each other, and leadership to drive these behaviours down through each level of the business.

Cultural intelligence – an indispensable talent

Peter Alfandary
PRA CrossCultural & Development

1. Introduction

Austrian-American psychologist Paul Watzlawick once stated: "What is true is not what I say but what the other person understands."

Language is full of nuances, mistranslations and 'false friends'. Even between native English speakers, confusion can reign. 'Quite good' to an American means very good. To the British, it implies that something is just okay. When Americans table an idea, they postpone discussing it. The British, on the other hand, put it on the immediate agenda.

Words such as 'benefits' (*advantages* as opposed to *profits*), 'director' (*board member* as opposed to *manager*), 'agenda' (*list of meeting points* as opposed to *diary*) and 'realise' (*become aware of* as opposed to *achieve*), as well as being dependent on context, may mean different things to native and non-native English speakers.

We must avoid the overuse of colloquialisms. Too often in presentations to international audiences one hears British speakers using words or expressions such as 'recoil', 'gutted', 'cram in', 'crib sheet', 'chipper', 'soak up', 'clinch', 'bandwidth', 'air time', 'straight from the off' and 'bee's knees'. For some listeners, each of these words will act as a distraction and each distraction will detract from the overall message. Their use is at best culturally insensitive, at worst damaging to the speaker's credibility.

Idiomatic expressions, used extensively by British and Americans, confuse and are counterproductive. We should avoid throwing 'curve balls' to non-native English speakers or asking them to 'step up to the plate', and we should all stop 'beating around the bush' if we are going to 'hit the ground running' as culturally intelligent lawyers.

Anecdotal evidence clearly points to the fact that a conference call where all the participants are non-native English speakers but are using English as a common language works remarkably well, but that the overall level of the group's understanding actually goes down when Brits or Americans join the same call.

As our profession becomes increasingly international, it is crucial that lawyers understand the nuances and differences of the new markets and jurisdictions in which they are required to operate.

As the legal market becomes increasingly homogenous and difficult to navigate, cultural intelligence (CQ) is becoming more and more important. Defined by two leading researchers and academics, Ang and Earley, in terms of an individual's capability to adapt to situations where there are different or new cultural contexts, CQ is now a crucial skill for any lawyer seeking to work in an international context.

Fundamentally, legal services are still made up of two key elements: the What and the How.

The What is our technical ability as lawyers – regardless of the discipline or practice area in which we operate. Excelling in the What is not only a *sine qua non*, but is now treated by clients as a starting point. Legal excellence has become no more than a base expectation – we are increasingly being judged on how we deliver our services, not just on the services themselves.

As the legal market becomes more saturated, as law schools churn out wave after wave of legal talent, a lawyer's competitive edge is no longer about simply his or her ability to litigate, but rather his or her abilities to build, nurture, manage and deepen client relationships. We are fast approaching a stage where the only real differentiator that most firms now have is the quality of their service delivery; historically, this is a skill in which some lawyers have been sorely lacking.

As markets open, firms merge and the legal profession becomes increasingly international, CQ has become an integral part of any good lawyer's portfolio.

2.   Cultural intelligence and culture

IQ as a measure of intelligence has been with us for over a century.

Some of the very first IQ tests were devised as early as 1905 by two Frenchmen, Binet and Simon. Over the years, IQ testing has had many critics, but it continues to be used in some sectors as a measurement tool.

In the 1990s, the business world partly shifted its focus to emotional intelligence (EQ) – in essence, an individual's ability to combine thinking with emotions so as to understand and empathise with others. Following the work of Daniel Goleman, EQ continues to be seen as an important tool for successful leadership.[1]

CQ focuses not on our intellect or emotions, but rather on our ability to work effectively and efficiently across cultural and national boundaries.

CQ is now a recognised management tool and skill. The subject is vast and the research voluminous. Cultural differences in business have now been studied, analysed, categorised and explained in depth by prominent researchers and academics, in addition to Earley and Ang, including, amongst many others, thinkers such as Van Dyne, Trompenaars, Hampden Turner, Hofstedde, Hill, Livermore, Storti, Lewis, Rosinski, Meyer and Hall.[2]

---

1   Daniel Goleman, *Emotional Intelligence: Why it can matter more than IQ*, Bantam Books, 1995.

What exactly is culture?

In essence, culture is the Who, What, Why and How of our behaviour when viewed collectively by others with whom we interact, as well as by ourselves as part of the group to which we consider we belong. It is, as Hofstede has said, "the collective programming of the mind which distinguishes the members of one group from another".[3] Furthermore, and as Pagel states, we are all "wired for culture".[4]

Culture is like an iceberg. When we first arrive in another country or simply are exposed to another culture, the cultural differences hit us at their most simplistic level and without any noticeable effort on our part. We immediately notice differences in language, dress, smells, signs, climate and food – these represent the visible part of the iceberg.

The invisible part of the iceberg, the mass below the waterline, is much bigger and more significant than its tip.

Dwelling just below the surface are marked distinctions in how we communicate, deal with conflict, manage our time and approach problems. There are deep-rooted differences in perceptions of professionalism, etiquette, right and wrong, and acceptable behaviour.

Lawyers who want to succeed in international markets must constantly ask themselves important questions:

- What makes individuals in this particular culture different from those with whom I normally interact?
- What style of communication do they prefer?

For further information on cultural intelligence (and used as sources for this chapter), see P Christopher Earley and Soon Ang, *Cultural Intelligence: Individual Interactions Across Cultures*, Stanford University Press, 2003; Philippe Rosinski, *Coaching Across Cultures*, Nicholas Brealey International, 2003; Mark Pagel, *Wired for Culture: Origins of the Human Social Mind*, WW Norton and Company, 2013; Penny Carté and Chris Fox, *Bridging the Culture Gap: A Practical Guide to International Business Communication*, Kogan Page, 2008; Jeremy Comfort and Peter Franklin, *The Mindful International Manager: How to work effectively across cultures*, Kogan Page, 2014; Edward T Hall, *Beyond Culture*, Anchor Books, 1997; Fons Trompenaars and Charles Hampden-Turner, *Riding the Waves of Culture: Understanding Cultural Diversity in Business*, Nicholas Brealey Publishing, 1997; Geert Hofstede, Gert Jan Hofstede and Michael Minkov, *Cultures and Organizations – Software of the Mind: Intercultural Cooperation and Its Importance for Survival*, McGraw-Hill Education, 2010; David Livermore PhD, *The Cultural Intelligence Difference: Master the One Skill You Can't Do Without in Today's Global Economy*, Amacom, 2011; Richard D Lewis, *When Cultures Collide: Leading Across Cultures*, Nicholas Brealey, 2018; P Christopher Earley and Elaine Mosakowski, "Cultural Intelligence" in *On Managing Across Cultures*, Harvard Business Review Press, 2016; Ann L MacNaughton and David A Victor, "Conflict Management and Cross-Cultural Awareness", in George E Kronman, Don B Felio, Thomas E O'Connor and Mandy S Kronman, *International Oil and Gas Ventures: A Business Perspective*, American Association of Petroleum Geologists, 2000; Ioannis Papadopoulos, "Introduction to comparative legal cultures: the civil law and the common law on evidence and judgment" (oral presentation on Antoine Garapon and Ioannis Papadopoulos, *Juger en Amérique et en France : Culture Judiciaire Française et Common Law*, Cornell Law Faculty Working Papers 15, 2004); David Livermore, *Leading with Cultural Intelligence: The Real Secret to Success*, Amacom, 2018; Craig Storti, *Figuring Foreigners Out: A Practical Guide*, Intercultural Press, 2000; Daniel Kahneman, *Thinking, Fast and Slow*, Penguin, 2012; Erin Meyer, *The Culture Map: Decoding How People Think, Lead and Get Things Done Across Cultures*, PublicAffairs, 2016.
Geert Hofstede, Gert Jan Hofstede and Michael Minkov, *Cultures and Organisations: Software of the Mind*, supra.
Mark Pagel, *Wired for Culture: Origins of the Human Social Mind*, WW Norton and Company, 2013.

- How do they make decisions, manage their time, analyse problems and deal with conflict?

The answers are less obvious than you might think.

The culturally intelligent businessperson and lawyer must spend time addressing these questions and must strive to become an expert at functioning effectively across cultures. In so doing, he or she can deepen professional relationships with both colleagues and clients.

4. The 21st-century paradox

We live in a world where communication has changed beyond all recognition and expectations.

At this juncture, it is too early to know exactly what the new normal will look like after the COVID-19 pandemic, but it already is (and will increasingly be) a world of virtual meetings, of email, and of social media, where instant reactions, initial views and quick answers are expected of each and every one of us. We live in a world where quality thinking time is in ever-shorter supply.

We also live in a world where English has become the *lingua franca* of the business community and where it is difficult to compete without knowledge of English. Despite the near ubiquity of the common language, communication has not, in fact, become any easier. The globalisation of the English language has given rise to a paradox: we may all speak English, but that does not mean that we are all speaking the same language.

Take, for example, a group of German, Japanese, British, Brazilian, American and French business people, negotiating. They may all be speaking English, but that does not guarantee that they really understand each other.

Worst of all, a common understanding may be assumed: the participants, whether meeting physically or virtually, may have fallen into a 'trap of similarity', that dangerous place where we assume understanding but where in reality we end up with miscommunication, misunderstanding and inaccurate presumptions.

Intercultural miscommunication is a key obstacle to effective cross-border business, a problem that is only exacerbated by the increasing speed of our communications, where we have seconds to react, where replies are expected immediately and where we are afforded precious little time to think.

Competing Across Borders, a survey of global executives published by *The Economist* Intelligence Unit in 2012,[5] concluded that "misunderstandings rooted in cultural differences present the greatest obstacle to productive cross-border collaboration", while at the same time recognising that "effective cross-border communication and collaboration are becoming critical to the financial success

5   Available at: https://eiuperspectives.economist.com/economic-development/competing-across-borders.

of companies with international aspirations". Little has changed in the past eight years.

The legal profession is not immune to this. If our clients are worrying about cultural intelligence, so too should we be. We are not above falling into the trap of similarity. There are no exceptions to the rule – even for lawyers.

5. Lawyers are like everyone else

Now and also in our post-COVID-19 pandemic world, every client and every lawyer joining a video conference call carries an invisible suitcase containing his or her unique cultural baggage.

Macs and PCs provide a useful analogy here. Some of us use Macs and some of us PCs. Each may be used to perform the same tasks, but they are built, designed and programmed entirely differently. In this case, the trap of similarity is the assumption that because the Mac and PC are both computers, they can talk to and understand each other immediately and intuitively. The truth is that communication is possible, but only with additional software.

Some lawyers and some clients are Macs, whereas some are PCs.

CQ is the software that all lawyers now need if they are going to excel at the How.

The good news is that, perhaps unlike IQ, CQ can be taught and is therefore integral to 21st-century talent management.

6. The culturally intelligent lawyer

In order to succeed, lawyers need to develop an increased understanding of the Why involved in cultural differences, along with a greater degree of personal self-awareness and a willingness to adapt behaviour and develop strategies appropriate to a variety of cross-cultural encounters.

Effective talent management in both law firms and in-house legal departments will need to encompass what the leading researchers have identified as four fundamental factors:

- *Motivation:* For lawyers, this refers to the partner, associate or general counsel's drive and energy to adapt cross-culturally and deal with increasingly apparent challenges with clients from different cultures or with lawyers in different jurisdictions.
- *Cognition:* This is the lawyer's level of understanding about culture and how it shapes both the business and legal environment in which others operate. This factor includes an understanding of one's own culture and how it is perceived by others.
- *Metacognition:* This refers to the lawyer's ability to strategise when working with clients and colleagues in other cultures. Despite current market pressures, it means finding the time to observe, prepare and plan for dealing with differences in the way that legal concepts are explained or advice is delivered.

- *Behaviour:* This is the lawyer's ability to change his or her behaviour, use of language and verbal and non-verbal actions when interacting with others.

Advice to an Asian client cannot necessarily be given in the same way as to a US client. A German chief executive or French general counsel may need to be dealt with differently from a Brazilian chief executive or British general counsel. Also, the client's reaction to the same advice may differ depending on his or her culture of origin.

How often have we heard the complaint (in both international law firm and in-house legal departments) that the Paris/London/Moscow/New York/Mumbai/ Frankfurt/Sao Paulo office just do not seem to understand what we really are saying, what we really want and what the client needs ...?

CQ is about suspending judgement. It is about working smarter, particularly with the continual stress we are under as lawyers. It is in times of stress that we need to be most wary, as we all tend to revert to stereotype: the British become more British, the French more French, the Japanese more Japanese, Americans more American.

It is also about understanding not just the differences between legal systems but also how different cultures view crucial issues such as time, deadlines, risk, formality, directness, uncertainty or even the very purpose of meetings.

6.1 Some points of cultural difference

(a) Time management

In some cultures, such as Germany, the United Kingdom and the United States, time is thought of as highly linear. Diaries are respected religiously, meeting times are rigorously adhered to and interruptions are disliked. People concentrate on one activity or relationship at a time and deadlines are observed. These monochronic cultures are diametrically opposed to their polychronic equivalents.

In South America, most of Southern Europe, Africa and parts of Asia, time can be viewed differently and may be seen as more of a guideline than a rule. People may well multitask and can focus simultaneously on multiple relationships. If new circumstances arise, timetables and deadlines may well change, without incident.

Italians or Brazilians do not believe that there is much of a problem if a meeting or conference call starts 15 minutes late. By this time, the American or German will have interpreted the delay as either disrespect or lack of seriousness or professionalism.

(b) **Meetings**

Closely linked to concepts of time are the ways that meetings traditionally, whether in person or online, tend to be conducted in different cultures. In France, for example, meetings have been described by one senior executive (perhaps unfairly) as "intellectual orgies". This may be hyperbolic, but in less time-orientated cultures meetings may well start and finish later than planned and, in extreme cases, may seem like nothing more than ill-disciplined shouting contests or intellectual boxing matches.

Monochronic cultures will tend to have much more structured meetings, where a strict agenda is followed and pre-approved topics are discussed. The purpose of these meetings is to conclude with an action plan that either reflects the decisions taken at the meeting or agreements regarding next steps.

Americans, British and Germans, for instance, will often be surprised at how tolerant their Latin counterparts are of participants who go off point, who digress, talk on their phones or talk among themselves while others are speaking.

It is too early to predict how a substantial increase over the coming years in virtual as opposed to physical meetings will change these behaviours. At the very least a virtual meeting makes it far more difficult to have side conversations during the meeting. Of course (and depending on their own biases) some cultures will view this as a very positive step while others may see it as an impediment to effective brainstorming.

c) **Communication styles**

In 'low-context' cultures such as the United States and the Netherlands, communication will tend to be very direct and unambiguous. Indeed, it may be so direct that it is sometimes misinterpreted as rudeness. In other 'high-context' cultures, such as Japan or the United Kingdom, the unsaid may well be as important as the said. The Dutch or American listener will need to learn the skills and acquire the patience to successfully decode the message.

The British, in particular, need to learn that they are often nigh incomprehensible to the rest of the world. Their indirectness and use of metaphor are not only hard for foreigners to understand, but also often interpreted as hypocrisy. The British use of understatement, humour and self-deprecation is a source of much confusion and misunderstanding. This is hardly surprising when being "a little bit disappointed" means "very angry", when "I am not certain that I completely agree" means "I do not agree" and when the remark, "That is a courageous proposal" means that the suggestion is ridiculous.

d) **Reasoning and decision making**

The culturally intelligent lawyer understands that some cultures, the UK and the US for example, will have a tendency towards a pragmatic, fact-first and fact-led reasoning process rooted in a more inductive way of reasoning and influenced in their history by empirical philosophy. Inductive reasoning starts with an observation of the facts, then looks for a pattern, comes up with an initial hypothesis and then concludes with a theory. The common law legal system, which developed out of case law, is a prime example of inductive reasoning.

In contrast, other cultures – indeed most European ones – may approach a problem in a theory- or principle-led way where the reasoning process is highly analytical and needs to go through a series of logical steps in order to reach a sustainable conclusion. This deductive approach to reasoning finds its origins in the philosophical writings of, say, Descartes or Hegel, and the civil law system, with codification as its basis, reflects this differing approach.

It is with those differences in mind that the culturally intelligent lawyer can begin to understand why some clients and colleagues, for example US and British ones, will usually want an executive summary with conclusions up front, whereas the German or French client will expect to see (and be convinced by) a detailed analysis before being prepared to accept the reliability of the advice. In very simple terms the one is saying, "Just tell me the answer – I'll look at your analysis afterwards if I need to", and the other, "Prove your advice to me by showing me your analysis and then I will trust you and follow your recommendation."

These differences are also often reflected in the time it may take certain cultures to make a decision. In its most simplistic form, a comparison between a 'typical' French and US executive would tend to indicate that while the American would spend, say, 20% of his or her time on reaching a decision and 80% on its actual implementation, the reverse may well be true of his or her French counterpart.

This would tend to explain the often-heard criticism in some European circles about Americans 'knee-jerking' into decisions without having sufficiently analysed the consequences. Conversely, Americans often complain of the European condition of 'paralysis by analysis'. Equally, the contrasting way that failure is (or is not) stigmatised in certain cultures may have a direct effect on decision making. The 'can do' attitude, and the less judgemental view of past failure, so prevalent in the United States should help in understanding the American approach to decision making.

(e) ***Attitudes towards rules and relationships***
The degree to which relationships take precedence over rules presents yet another interesting cultural variation for the international lawyer.

In so-called 'universalist' cultures, rules may tend to be inflexible, regardless of particular circumstances or relationships that foreigners may consider relevant to the issue at hand. By contrast, in 'particularist' cultures, far greater weight may be given to duties and obligations that may arise either from individual relationships or from the specific circumstances prevalent at the time.

One of the founding fathers of cultural intelligence, Trompenaars, illustrated this dilemma with the following example:

> You are a passenger in a car driven by a very close friend. He hits a pedestrian. You know he was driving at 45 km per hour in an area where the maximum speed allowed is 35. His lawyer says that if you testify that he was only driving at 35 km per hour, it will save him from serious consequences. What right does your friend have to expect you to protect him by testifying that he was driving at the lower speed?

Even among lawyers – in all of whom, one would assume, the rule of law is to some extent ingrained – a clear split of opinion very often manifests itself. There are those for whom what is right will always be right and to be fair is to treat everyone alike, and those who lean towards the belief that what is true and fair in one situation might be wrong in another.

f) **Other researched and recognisable cultural variations**

Extensive literature exists to help our understanding of cultural differences, which include a multitude of other categorisations. A non-exhaustive list appears below, all of which are relevant to the culturally aware lawyer. Many factors will be familiar and all are important to think about when dealing with different cultures (whether internally or with clients):

- formality versus informality in relationships;
- short-term versus long-term planning in strategy formulation;
- hierarchy versus equality in management;
- assertiveness versus modesty;
- individualist versus collectivist team behaviour;
- preference for stability versus change;
- harmony versus confrontation;
- discussion-based (with an emphasis on a verbally direct but emotionally restrained approach) versus engagement-based (where the emphasis will be more confrontational and emotionally expressive) negotiations;
- reserved and calm mannerisms versus displays of emotion; and
- preferences for risk versus certainty.

The culturally intelligent lawyer understands and works with all these differences. He or she sees them played out daily, by clients and colleagues across jurisdictions.

The culturally intelligent lawyer has a sound basic understanding of the differences between common law (reflexive) and civil law (legicentric) legal systems.

The culturally intelligent lawyer appreciates the importance of being a 'cultural guide' and will be able to identify and explain foreign concepts in detail without being asked. The culturally intelligent lawyer will explain the concept of discovery to the client who has never litigated in a common law business environment, and will be aware that common law principles of full disclosure may seem as absurd to the client as playing a game of poker with the cards face-up.

The culturally intelligent lawyer is as alive to jurisdictional differences in matters of compliance, corporate governance and contractual principles as to concepts such as good faith, materiality, reasonableness, best efforts and evidentiary truth.

The culturally intelligent lawyer knows that hierarchy and negotiation styles vary greatly across cultures, as do the structure and purpose of meetings. Some cultures respect age and seniority; some favour silence in negotiations; some will be uncomfortable with displays of anger or emotion; and in some the ultimate decider may not even be present at a critical meeting.

Finally, the culturally intelligent lawyer will be acutely conscious of the comparative importance of relationship building from culture to culture. In the role of a business developer, he or she will accordingly vary the 'investment time' spent on winning new work from both existing and prospective clients.

It is indeed a very rich, complex and varied world we live in, and it is one in which the culturally intelligent lawyer must focus on the part of the iceberg that is below the waterline.

7. Stereotypes and culture

In our efforts to become more culturally aware, it is imperative to discuss stereotypes. None of us is without prejudice and cultural stereotypes permeate our thinking much more than we might care to admit.

In the same way that we are all wired for culture, we are also wired subconsciously towards bias, generalisations and stereotyping. We have already observed that in stressful environments, nationalities and cultures tend to revert to stereotypical behaviour, but stereotypes and generalisations can be both dangerous and useful.

They are dangerous because they are over-simplistic and, when misused, can lead to lazy thinking or bigotry. They are useful because – where tempered with the knowledge that they are generalisations and must be thought of as such – they can provide us with essential shortcuts to better understand and interpret the group behaviour of others.

Indeed, an understanding of stereotypes – even if these are untrue, misleading and baseless – is important, in that they can help us better understand the way that others view us. They help us understand preconceptions that people might have of us – preconceptions that, even if based on stereotypical and inaccurate understandings of our respective cultures, still inform the way we are viewed and the ways we will be treated.

Self-awareness is a crucial part of cultural intelligence.

It can come as a surprise to the British to hear that others often perceive them as hypocritical. That perception is primarily the result of the British predisposition to use a coded language that is understated, emphasises indirectness and relies on humour and self-deprecation.

The important lesson for the British to learn is that what they perceive as a normal, polite way of conversing can be viewed as a far more insidious, negative and potentially obstructive form of communication.

Understanding how others perceive us, especially when that perception is incorrect, is a fundamental part of effective communication.

What can go wrong without CQ

Language skills are now a *sine qua non* for lawyers.

Like technical ability, they are only the starting point in our increasingly competitive market. Commoditisation of legal services has become an unstoppable force in our homogeneous world. Differentiation, while still achievable, is ever more elusive.

Without CQ, the 21st-century lawyer cannot excel. Without CQ, expectations between in-house legal departments within the same group but in different countries, or between the different country offices of international law firms, may fail to be met.

Without CQ, local legislation or local procedures may not be properly understood, time and deadlines may be mismanaged, styles of legal advice between lawyers or with clients may become confusing, advice may be misinterpreted or misunderstood, legal concepts may become lost in translation and nuances may be missed or misconstrued.

Stress levels between offices and between lawyer and client, already at record levels, will rise still further and compound misunderstanding. Time will be wasted, legal costs will increase and clients will be dissatisfied.

If we accept that the How is a critical part of the service equation, then we can no longer risk having our lack of CQ jeopardise client service or lead to mistakes.

Practical dos and don'ts for the 21st-century lawyer

CQ is about suspending judgement and remembering that we, like much of our technology, have a pause button. It is about taking a step back. It demands effort, often patience and an element of conscious rewiring.

No list of dos and don'ts can be exhaustive, but suggestions for our profession should at least include the following:

- Do seek clarity by asking questions about the local and legal culture in which you are operating.

- Do think of the questions that the client has not even thought about asking and deal with all jurisdictional surprises in advance.
- Do consider what is the 'question behind the question' and what has prompted the person to ask it in the first place.
- Do take account of others' preconceptions about you.
- Do highlight deadlines, major points, key questions and major risks in your emails, then phone the recipient to ensure that these are clearly understood.
- Do invest time in appreciating colleagues' different ways of 'lawyering'.
- Do ask colleagues about the client's level of cultural awareness and his or her cultural expectations.
- Do listen actively and intelligently and spend more time listening than speaking – most lawyers wrongly believe that the Almighty gave them two mouths and only one ear, whereas a quick look in the mirror will reveal that the reverse is true.
- Don't assume similarity.
- Don't assume understanding – in fact, don't assume at all.
- Don't speak too fast.
- Don't write long paragraphs in emails, each containing a multitude of key points.
- Don't use jargon, idiomatic expressions or colloquialisms.
- Don't make the mistake of believing that adapting your style or behaviour involves a loss of your own cultural identity – it simply means working smarter.
- Don't wait to be asked – a good lawyer offers information and explains the journey that the client is embarking upon.

A final word for the native English-speaking reader: the greatest burden is on you. Now that English has become the *lingua franca* of the legal and the business world, native English speakers have it easy. Never forget, however, that its pre-eminence brings with it obligations and responsibilities.

We need to speak more slowly; we need to be clearer; we need to signpost our conversations and summarise key points – we must ensure that we communicate with precision, clarity and empathy for others.

10. Conclusion

CQ is to be embraced and fortunately – perhaps unlike IQ – it can be taught. It is already on the curricula of some major international law firms and is taught in a number of leading business schools. It is not, however, just a skill to be embraced by major firms or global in-house legal departments. It affects every lawyer working in an international environment.

CQ is an integral part of excellence in terms of client service. It is therefore not an optional talent or a soft skill. It is a critical hard skill and a real talent that we all need to hone.

Lawyers from every jurisdiction need to become cultural guides if they are to become better lawyers.

We all know the fundamental differences between being a simple tourist and being a true voyager. The tourist may return home with little else than a sun tan whereas the voyager does so with new knowledge and new experiences. He or she therefore returns richer, and hopefully wiser.

The 21st-century lawyer needs to be a voyager, not just a tourist.

The final piece of good news is that to help guide them on their voyage, every lawyer possesses an internal GPS, a cultural satellite navigation system.

Our clients are switching on their GPSs. We should all be doing the same.

The author extends thanks to Adam Alfandary for his editorial contributions.

The future of legal talent management: adopting an innovative mindset

Shelley Dunstone
Legal Circles

1. Introduction

What challenges will law firms need to address in managing their legal talent over the next five to 10 years? How will firms need to change and adapt?

There is no single answer. Employment conditions vary from country to country. In some places talent may be readily available and easily replaced, whereas in others there is a shortage. Law firms vary in their challenges and aspirations – there are large firms, small firms and solos, as well as virtual firms, all offering an array of different services. Some have sophisticated approaches to talent management and others have little experience with it.

To begin, two challenges must be acknowledged:

- We are writing for a global audience, and generalisations cannot apply everywhere in the world.
- We are writing about the future, and no one can foresee exactly what challenges will present themselves.

2. Likely future challenges

The factor that has wrought most change on the legal profession in the past decade is technology. Technological change seems likely to continue at a fast pace. Technology is changing the nature of legal work, facilitating and simplifying it, and in some areas reducing the need for lawyers.

In 2018 a study was conducted jointly by the Australasian Legal Practice Management Association and the Centre for Legal Innovation at the College of Law, culminating in The Emerging Legal Professions Survey.[1] To quote the authors:

Legaltech and AI are not going away and will continue to dominate and change lawyer and legal work. Technology and AI are not IT problems, they are a strategic and operational reality for the entire firm or legal department. Law firms and legal departments have tended to adopt a reactive strategy to the advances in technology and need to change this approach. There are real opportunities for lawyers, law

---

1 Available at: www.alpma.com.au/emerging-legal-professions-survey-2018.

firms and legal departments that are willing to work proactively and collaboratively with legaltech start-ups, developers and each other. If lawyers don't engage, they will be increasingly displaced.

This is not to suggest all lawyers should become techies, but rather they will need to understand enough to work with techies and other legal professionals to develop new products that meet client demands. Lawyers also need to understand how technology and AI works and operates in their businesses and be able to interrogate, question or query its operation for client matters.

In Anglo-Saxon jurisdictions, the composition of law firm staff is changing, with professionals coming in from a variety of other sectors. The concept of 'legal talent' encompasses more than just lawyers.

The Emerging Legal Professions Survey observed:

Lawyers have never been, and increasingly will not be, the only income producers in a law firm. Work needs to be distributed to whoever can do it most effectively and efficiently inside (insourcing) or outside (outsourcing) the firm. Those firms that recognise these legal business professional skills and provide equal opportunities for their lawyers and all other legal professionals, will retain great people. Those that do not, will lose them.

Equally, technology cannot be utilised to the full without the right human skills. Technology can be bought, but the best skilled professionals are harder to acquire and retain. Innovation is about more than technology. Leaders of a major workforce solutions company recently stated:

Our own talent development philosophy is to combine this dual focus on potential for soft skills, and knowledge for hard skills: we select people with high learnability (people with a hungry mind) and match their interests to in-demand skills, while understanding that those hard skills may soon become outdated – so the key is that their curiosity remains intact. Technical competence is temporary, but intellectual curiosity must be permanent.[2]

In this chapter, we propose a variety of questions that may provide a catalyst for thinking innovatively about managing legal talent (and for simplicity we will refer to legal talent in terms of lawyers only).

Some of the future challenges for the legal profession are set out in the following sections.

2.1 Attracting and retaining lawyers

Young people seeking employment today have higher expectations of their employers than had previous generations. They pay greater attention to a firm's employer brand, which incorporates its reputation in the marketplace, working conditions and benefits, and opportunities for professional development.

---

2   B Franklewicz and T Chamorro-Premuzic, "Digital Transformation is About Talent, Not Technology", *Harvard Business Review*, 6 May 2020.

Employees (and not just women with children) have been demanding flexible ways of working, and technology is making this possible. The COVID-19 lockdown has demonstrated the viability of remote working, and employees are unlikely to accept old arguments as to why it will not work. New businesses have emerged that hire out experienced lawyers on a temporary or contract basis, and this way of working is becoming a popular, alternative career path for senior lawyers. Younger workers are more inclined to seek a higher purpose in their work and are attracted to employers that demonstrate corporate social responsibility.

Questions to ask could include the following:

- How can we recruit more lawyers with the right qualities and skills?
- How can we help our lawyers grow and develop their capabilities in a way they desire, so that they will stay with us?
- What can we do to make legal practice a more meaningful and fulfilling career for our lawyers?

2 Training

Young people tend to change jobs more frequently and to seek a more varied career than their predecessors. It might become more difficult to hire lawyers with the right type of experience, so law firms will need to become better at training new graduates. However, legal process outsourcing and disruptive technologies are reducing the amount of beginner work that is available for new law graduates. Clients are less willing to pay for junior lawyers to learn at their expense. Yet younger employees increasingly expect and value professional development, including mentoring.

Questions to ask could include the following:

- How can we challenge the conventional wisdom that it takes two years' experience for a new graduate to become productive and profitable?
- What tools can we develop to help junior lawyers to become more productive, more quickly?
- Do our lawyers need training in new technologies?
- How can we get better at mentoring our lawyers?

3 Career development

In some places, reduced barriers to entry are allowing non-lawyer providers to compete in the market for legal services. Commoditisation and 'supermarketisation' of legal services are leading to an expectation of lower prices; but at the same time, lawyers want higher salaries and want to do work that is intellectually challenging.

As more people change careers, age is no longer an indicator of seniority. A new law graduate of mature age might have years of valuable business experience to offer. Lawyers in larger firms have shorter shelf lives: for example, an 'out at 55' policy is becoming more common.

Questions to ask could include the following:

- How can we keep our lawyers intellectually stimulated?
- How can we manage our mature-aged graduates more effectively?
- How can we better harness and utilise the wisdom of our most senior lawyers?

2.4 Legal practice development

It is increasingly necessary for all lawyers to bring business into the firm, but not all have the skills to do so. The internet provides a valuable platform for professionals to promote their services, but there is still much untapped potential for lawyers to utilise social media. There still exists an uneasy tension between personal branding and firm branding, as firms seek to embed clients within the firm, rather than have clients 'belong' to any particular lawyer.

Questions to ask could include the following:

- How can we help our lawyers to build their skills in practice development?
- How much freedom should we give our lawyers to utilise social media in their professional capacities?
- To what extent should our lawyers be allowed to promote themselves, as opposed to promoting the firm?

2.5 Succession planning

For many lawyers, partnership has become a more remote prospect, because the firm is top heavy or unwilling to dilute the partnership equity pool. Equally, for many younger lawyers, partnership does not hold the allure it once did. Many choose to remain employees or leave to work in-house at companies. However, a new generation of partners will need to be found, to keep the firm going and to ensure that outgoing partners are paid fairly for their career-long investment in the firm.

Increasingly, young lawyers are breaking away from traditional firms to establish practices that embody their own values and to practise law in their own way. Technology is enabling these lawyers to work flexibly, on their own terms, and to provide automated legal services that do not require long hours of work. Skilled marketing through social media allows lawyers to attract their own clients, thereby avoiding the need to buy an existing practice.

Questions to ask could include the following:

- How can we provide a satisfying and rewarding career path and create a sense of belonging in the firm for those who are not partners?
- How can we encourage younger lawyers to become interested in partnership?
- What skills development can we offer to equip our lawyers to become our 'succession plan'?

- How can we encourage our young lawyers to channel their efforts into the success of our firm, instead of departing to set up their own?

What is meant by an 'innovative mindset'?
A mindset is a mental attitude that determines how you will interpret and respond to situations. Your mindset is your own unique way of thinking about what is possible.

Innovation involves doing new things, or doing things in new or better ways.

So an innovative mindset is a mental attitude of being willing to try new things.

It is easy to say, "We are innovative", but harder to put innovation into practice, because humans are creatures of habit. It is much easier to keep doing the same things in the same way than to take the risk of trying something new.

Despite the disruption that has developed in recent times, the legal profession as a whole is still fairly conservative. There are ethical rules and considerations that must be observed. Lawyers (at least in common law jurisdictions) are required to follow precedent; they must look to the past to find solutions. But they are not the only ones who are prisoners of precedent. All humans can find themselves stuck in precedent at times, because that is how the brain works.

Throughout your life, your brain takes in pieces of information and arranges them in patterns in your memory. As new information comes in, your brain does a search to see how it might fit with other information already stored in your memory. When you look for an idea, your brain goes straight to its store of similar ideas and retrieves them. The shelves of your brain are stocked with examples of things that you have seen, done or heard of before.[3]

In effect, your brain offers you a selection of templates (or 'precedents' in lawyer-language). This explains why many people find it difficult to think laterally and why brainstorming sessions often produce little in the way of truly novel suggestions. The conversation goes something like this: "What should we do?" "Let's brainstorm some alternatives." "Well, what did we do last time?" "What are our competitors doing?" "What is best practice in this area?" "Let's not reinvent the wheel."

It is not easy to visualise a wholly new way of doing things. And when you do, plenty of people will tell you why your idea will not work. It is seen as safer to follow what others have done.

However, those who persevere with their new ideas attract attention and can build competitive advantage.

There follows an example of a lawyer who has achieved this with his law firm.

William Duggan, "How Aha! Really Happens", *Strategy+Business*, 61, Winter 2010.

3.1 Case study: breaking free from precedent

Kain Corporate and Commercial (Kain C+C) is a law firm with a team of 29 staff (including 20 lawyers) based in Adelaide, Australia, offering services in corporate, commercial and M&A law.

This firm is extremely popular among lawyers seeking employment. One reason for this is the substantial amount of charitable work it undertakes.

The firm's founder, John Kain, says:

Compared to the overwhelming majority of the world's population (and many parts of Australia's population), we occupy a position of rare privilege – materially, socially and in many other respects. With this privilege comes responsibility – to use our good fortune to help those less fortunate.

With this philosophy, he resigned his partnership at an established commercial law firm and set up his own firm based on a unique model, which seeks to achieve two things:

- Do good work to help people in need, in a meaningful and sustainable way.
- Change the way that people think and behave, to encourage them to use their own good fortune to help others.

The vehicle through which this is achieved is the Kain C+C Charitable Foundation, which has the mandate of "unlocking compassion to change our world".[4]

Having a higher purpose at the heart of the legal practice has brought business benefits such as ease of attraction and retention of staff. John says:

The business benefits are a welcome side effect; but that's not why I established this model. I chose to do it because it's the right thing to do ... It does help to create a unique culture, which is now deeply ingrained. It gives our business a soul. Working here is more than just a job.

Each team member makes a fortnightly donation (which is automatically deducted from gross salary) to the foundation. The business then matches those donations, dollar for dollar. But this is only the start. As John says, "It is not a donation-only business. It is only hands-on work that changes the way people think and behave."

Therefore, each team member also commits to spending the equivalent of one day per year performing volunteer work through programmes sponsored by the foundation. Local programmes include providing free legal advice and computer training for homeless people at a *pro bono* clinic and mentoring disadvantaged young people to help them transition to work. The firm's billing targets are adjusted to reflect time spent on foundation projects.

Internationally, the firm has developed the Uganda Project to help the

---

4   To find out more about the Kain C+C model, visit www.kainlawyers.com.au.

plight of children who have been orphaned due to HIV/AIDS, war and disease. A team from the law firm (and from its partner organisations) regularly travels to Uganda to undertake physical work such as building houses and other infrastructure, assisting at a medical clinic, working in an orphanage and donating clothes, books and toys. The visit lasts for two weeks: one week is funded by the firm and the other by the team member. The firm contributes to the travel costs.

In a blog entry published on the firm's website, one of the participants wrote:

It was just like any childcare centre in Australia, with one major disheartening difference – the children we were playing with had no family. I helped feed and play with a young child called Nicole. Soon after, Nicole would not let go of me. The whole time with her I could not stop thinking that my newborn nephew of three weeks would have already received more gifts and affection than she will receive in her lifetime.

The charitable activities also provide leadership development opportunities for the staff. Leading the group travelling to Uganda presents a unique leadership challenge. The work is hard and confrontational. The leader must be able to encourage team members who are out of their comfort zone and may feel upset by what they see. To lead such a group requires maturity and self-assurance.

Better teamwork is another benefit. When someone is away working on a foundation project, someone else must cover his or her work. Staff recognise that they are all part of a single team contributing to good work in the community.

Philanthropy is at the heart of everything the firm does.

John accepts that other law firms also engage in philanthropic or *pro bono* work and allow their staff to take time away from the office to work for charity. However, he says that his firm's model is different: "We don't simply encourage or allow it; we demand it." Instead of having staff members do bits and pieces of charitable work, "we orchestrate all of our efforts to produce a more effective overall result". When job applicants are interviewed, they are told very clearly what the firm's expectations are. Commitment to the philosophy and the work of the foundation is a prerequisite for joining the firm.

At Kain C+C, the foundation work is given the same priority as client work. It is not something that is done in people's spare time. This in itself is a major mindset shift. In most law firms, client work always comes first.

'Mindset' is a way of thinking about what is possible. Where there is no precedent, the assumption is that if something were a good idea, people would already be doing it. It requires vision to imagine that it would be possible to run a law firm like this.

So how did John conceive of the idea for this innovative way of running a law firm? He says that the idea came from his personal conviction that if yo can, you should. He realised that it would be difficult to develop a new mode within an existing business structure. He also recognised that a piecemea approach does not bring about lasting change.

There was no precedent for such a law firm, so he had to make it up as h went along. He says: "Some of my lawyer friends mocked me, but I am no concerned about what other people think. If you are always looking over you shoulder, you will end up with mainstream thinking." Another key was not t worry about making mistakes, "as long as they are not huge mistakes, and w do not repeat them".

It may sound as if this firm does not place a great emphasis on financia success. On the contrary, John has been methodical in ensuring that the firm i run in a business-like way. He recognised that the foundation could be sustaine only if the law firm were financially sound and successful. The firm has corporate structure and is overseen by an independent board which takes a objective view of its business activities.

The foundation, too, is run as a business, with strict corporate governance It applies the following seven criteria in deciding which projects will b supported:

- Hands-on support – involve both financial and hands-on support from the firm or its corporate partners.
- Scalability – be replicable by the firm or its corporate partners in othe locations or contexts.
- Sustainability – be self-sustainable with a continued, long-term impac beyond the firm's period of support.
- Measurability – generate identifiable outcomes measurable by short- an long-term key performance indicators.
- Preventability – address the causes of problems, rather than treating th symptoms.
- Most in need – receive limited government funding or philanthropi support.
- Minimal resources – have low administration costs, solid and prove administration and strong volunteer support.

A major benefit of this approach is the genuine pride of the firm's staff. On lawyer recently related a conversation with a taxi driver about her work. Th public perception of lawyers is not always positive. It is not always easy to tell stranger, "I am a lawyer," because of the reaction that you might receive. Thi lawyer, however, was extremely proud to say that she was a lawyer and to tel the taxi driver about the good work being done by her firm.

4. Competing for talent

Law firms compete against each other for the lawyers that they require. How can an innovative mindset lead to competitive advantage in the market for legal talent? Competitive advantage is derived from two things:

* what you have (your strategic assets); and
* what you do with these strategic assets to create value.

Your strategic assets are your inherent strengths, which usually include intangible things such as core competencies, firm culture and reputation. Competitive advantage is based on strategic assets – enhancing your strategic assets can build competitive advantage.

It is important to be clear about:

* what sort of law firm you have;
* what sort of talent you want to attract; and
* why your targets will be attracted to your firm.

Law firms wanting to improve their competitive advantage in the market for legal talent should develop the following as strategic assets:

* their ability to adapt to a changing environment; and
* their reputation for being innovative with talent management.

5. The role of the leader in promoting innovative thinking

5.1 The challenge

People in organisations are not always receptive to new ideas. Time and other resources are limited. People do not like to take risks that could be perceived as mistakes. The safe, the easy, the usual way and "what we did last time" all exert a powerful pull.

Conformity is a strong human trait which is driven by the desire to be liked and accepted by others. Humans evolved under harsh and uncertain conditions. There was safety in numbers and even the earliest humans formed tribal or kinship groups for protection. Membership of these groups was a matter of survival. When we are genetically programmed to see expulsion from our social group as a dangerous prospect, fitting in becomes paramount.[5]

Suggesting an untried idea, seeming different or eccentric, challenging the status quo – according to our finely tuned instincts, all of these behaviours have the potential to attract scorn, condemnation and rejection.

Solomon Asch's conformity experiments in the 1950s demonstrated people's reluctance to speak up against majority opinion. In these experiments, subjects

---

5   A good book on this subject is Nigel Nicholson's *Executive Instinct: Managing the human animal in the information age* (Random House, 2000).

were placed into small groups. Only one person in each group was a genuine unwitting subject; the rest were confederates planted by the organisers. Each group was shown a drawing of a 'standard' line of a certain length, followed by three other lines of varying lengths. The subjects were asked to identify which of the three lines was identical in length to the standard line. The answer was clearly the second line. However, under directions from the organisers, the confederates unanimously selected the incorrect line. The 'real' subject answered last. Over the course of multiple trials, 75% of the subjects agreed with the incorrect judgement of the majority at least once.

In organisations, this phenomenon is manifested in the following sorts of beliefs:

- "It has always been done this way and it seems to work – why should we risk changing it now?"
- "Everyone else seems to accept things the way they are, so who am I to question them?"

Whereas the purpose of innovation is to stand out, many people would prefer to blend in. Most people strive to earn the approval of their peers, so putting forward an unusual, unproven idea can feel risky.

In a study reported in *Harvard Business Review*,[6] researchers sought to identify the factors that influence employees when deciding whether to bring ideas to their bosses or to withhold them. They interviewed 200 employees of a leading high-technology company – the very place where you would expect to find a flow of creative suggestions. Yet approximately half of the employees indicated that they felt it was not safe to speak up. In particular, they were reluctant to put forward creative ideas for improving products, processes or performance.

When questioned further about this, there were three types of response:

- Some people said they had experienced a hostile reaction from a manager in response to a previous suggestion.
- Some related stories about people who had spoken out publicly and were suddenly gone from the company.
- For many of the employees, it just felt risky. They did not know what would happen if they made a suggestion. Some were worried about embarrassing their bosses in public. Some felt that their suggestions would be resented.

These responses demonstrate that you cannot expect people simply to volunteer their suggestions. Leaders need to invite ideas and develop a climate where people feel comfortable to offer their suggestions.

---

6   James R Detert and Amy C Edmondson, "Why Employees are Afraid to Speak", *Harvard Business Review* May 2007, 23–25.

The researchers commented:

We found the innate protective instinct so powerful that it also inhibited speech that clearly would have been intended to help the organisation. In our interviews, the perceived risks of speaking up felt very personal and immediate to employees, whereas the future benefit to the organisation from sharing their ideas was uncertain.

They concluded:

Making employees feel safe enough to contribute fully requires deep cultural change that alters how they understand the likely costs (personal and immediate) versus benefits (organisational and future) of speaking up.

.2 Give priority to innovative thinking

In his book *The Seven Habits of Highly Effective People*,[7] Steven Covey presents a 'Time Management Matrix' in which activities are classified as urgent or non-urgent and important or not important. He makes the point that our time is usually taken up with urgent things that clamour for our attention. To get ahead, we need to make time for the things that are non-urgent, but important:

We react to urgent matters. Important matters that are not urgent require more initiative, more proactivity. We must act to seize opportunity, to make things happen. If we don't ... have a clear idea of what is important, of the results we desire in our lives, we are easily diverted into responding to the urgent.[8]

Covey tells a story about a professor who fills a big jar, first with rocks, then with gravel, then with sand and finally with water. At each stage, he asks the students: "Is the jar full?" At the end of the demonstration, he asks the students: "What is the point of this illustration?" One student responds: "No matter how full your schedule is, if you try really hard, you can always fit some more things into it!" The professor says: "No, the point is that if you don't put the big rocks in first, you'll never get them in at all."

Thinking innovatively about your talent management is important, though rarely urgent. If you do not make time for it, it will not get done. It will not shout for attention until some crisis occurs. Treat it as a 'big rock'.

.3 Ask the questions that others are not asking

Questions provide a catalyst for innovative thinking. Competitive advantage goes to those who ask the questions that others are not asking.

A number of questions regarding future challenges in legal talent management were posed at the start of this chapter. While there may not be immediate answers to all of these questions, the important thing is that they are asked. This is the first step towards finding innovative solutions.

Stephen R Covey, *The Seven Habits of Highly Effective People*, The Business Library, 1989, pp146–162.
Ibid, p151.

(a)   *An innovation story*

If you were out in a boat on the open sea, how would you know where you were? These days, you would use your satellite navigation system. But 300 years ago, there was no way of accurately determining your position. You could work out your latitude by studying the sun – the higher the sun at noon, the closer you were to the Equator. But there was no way of working out your longitude.

In 1714, after a spate of bad shipwrecks, the British government offered a prize of £20,000 to the person who could devise a practical method of determining longitude at sea.

As years, then decades passed with no solution, many people believed that the problem could not be solved. 'Finding the longitude' became a slang term for any crazy activity or impossible task. Cartoons began to appear in the press showing lunatics doing all sorts of odd things.

Astronomers believed that the answer lay in charting the moon and stars, so that is where most of the research was invested. It was also known that longitude corresponded to time: local time changes by one hour for every 15 degrees travelled to the east or west. So if you knew the time at your starting point and the time at your present location, you could work out your longitude by calculating how far you were from your original starting point. The problem was that clocks did not keep time at sea, because they relied on pendulum mechanisms which were disrupted by gravity and the motion of the sea.

The prize was ultimately won by John Harrison. He suggested that clocks could solve the longitude problem and worked on creating one that did not require a pendulum. People thought that he had gone mad. However, he made it a lifelong project and was finally awarded the prize for his H4 pocket watch.

Where are the 'pendulums' in your business – the things you assume cannot be changed? Question those assumptions!

5.4   Invent problems to solve

The inventor of a product called 'Honey Spread' was interviewed after he had sold his creation to a local food manufacturer. Honey Spread has the consistency of a gel: it does not form sticky strings like runny honey. This consistency is achieved through the addition of pectin. When asked what had inspired him to add pectin, the inventor replied: "It was just one of many things I tried." When pressed further, he said impatiently: "Look, I'm a product developer. It's my job to find problems and solve them. I was just trying to make honey not sticky."

His leap of imagination was not the idea to add pectin. It was asking the question: "How can I make honey not sticky?" How many people would ever think of asking this question? Most people would assume that honey is just sticky; they would not conceptualise this as a problem to be solved.

What questions are your competitors not asking? What problem could you usefully identify and solve?

An innovative mindset for the future

As a leader, you will need to work on cultivating an innovative mindset in yourself, your executive team and the culture of your firm.

Figure 1. How an innovative mindset permeates a law firm

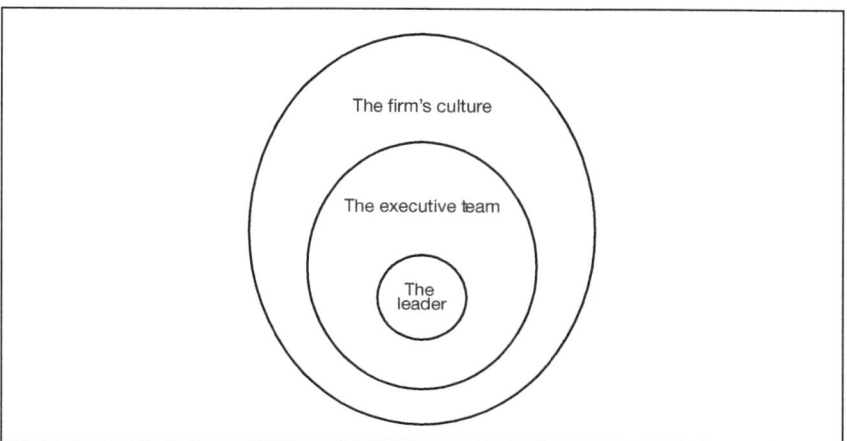

The firm's culture

The executive team

The leader

Source: Author.

.1   Developing an innovative mindset in yourself

Innovation is pioneering. When we seek to innovate, we enter new territory where many answers are unknown, with no precedent for what we should do next.

)   Challenge your worldview

Your worldview is the way that you see the world. It encompasses the framework of ideas and beliefs through which you interpret the world. Your worldview influences the way that you think and behave.

You may regard something as impossible, while someone else considers it to be easily achievable.

To challenge your own worldview, contrast it with the worldviews of others. The more diverse the group, the more diverse the ideas. Mix with other businesspeople. An advisory board can provide fresh perspectives by including people from a range of different disciplines.

)   Take care of yourself

Work on maintaining the spark within you. Do something each day to keep yourself energised, enthusiastic and optimistic.

Delegate work to ensure that you have time to think about the future. Build in some time for recreation and enjoyable interests. Even getting up and going for a walk outside the office can refresh your mind.

Leonardo Da Vinci knew the value of seeing things in perspective:

Every now and then go away, have a little relaxation, for when you come back to your work your judgment will be surer; since to remain constantly at work will cause you to lose the power of judgment. Go some distance away because the work appears smaller and more of it can be taken in at a glance and a lack of harmony or proportion is more readily seen.

(c) Stimulate your mind

Ideas can come from seemingly random sources. Read more books and broaden the range of subjects that you read about. As you read, write down any insights that occur to you. Find some interesting podcasts that you can listen to while you drive, wait or exercise.

(d) Allow time for reflection

Creative breakthroughs arrive unexpectedly, often while you are relaxing or doing something unrelated to your work. You have probably already had the experience of spending a day thrashing out a difficult problem, only to solve it with a fresh idea the following morning. Sleep enables previously unconnected thoughts to come together and produce new insights.

History is full of discoveries that appeared as flashes of insight – but only because the discoverer had been agitating the problem. To produce new insights, the brain needs time to reflect. First, work hard on the problem consciously, then take a break and allow your mind's unconscious processes to do their work.

6.2 Building an innovative mindset among your executive team

Your team will look to you for clues as to how to spend their time and energy. If you want them to put effort into innovative thinking, you must make this clear to them.

'Groupthink' is the enemy of innovation. It is a condition in which group members persuade themselves that their collective opinion is valid, without adequate exploration of other possibilities.

(a) Ask, don't tell

Ideas come from curiosity. Admitting that you do not know all the answers and encouraging others to do likewise leads everyone to explore new possibilities.

Ask 'naïve' questions, commencing with a signal that your intention in asking such questions is to help the group to explore new possibilities. Make it clear that you do not know the answers and it is not a test, but that the questions are intended to act as a catalyst for creative thinking. You might say, for example, "I don't know what the answer to this question might be, but I think it could help us to expand our thinking on this issue ..."

Some individuals will use their forceful personalities to push particular points of view, inhibiting the expression of contrary positions. During discussion, ensure that everyone has a chance to be heard and encourage people to keep an open mind instead of adopting entrenched positions.

Encourage a variety of responses. As the twice Nobel Prize-winning scientist Linus Pauling said: "The best way to have a good idea is to have a lot of ideas."

Try some creative thinking techniques in your discussions – many books are available which offer such approaches.[9] Have patience with the process, because new ideas take time to develop.

b) *Encourage curiosity*

Encourage others in your team to exercise and express their curiosity by proposing their own questions for discussion.

Innovative ideas come from challenging entrenched assumptions. Instead of rewarding the best idea, try rewarding the best question.

c) *Gather the right people at the right time*

Each one of us is the product of our life so far. We have all had a unique childhood, education, working life and experience of the world. We all have different personalities and see the world through different eyes. No wonder it can be so hard to understand each other!

Some people naturally see opportunities and find it easy and enjoyable to think laterally. Others are more likely to tell you why the ideas will not work. Both approaches are necessary, but not at the same time. People who take a negative approach could be valuable when it comes to evaluating ideas and managing risk. But when you are trying to generate a range of new ideas, these people may not be the best to have in the room.

To make good decisions, we need the input of both types of person. We need to anticipate the problems and prevent them from occurring. A focus on risk prevention is not helpful at the idea generation stage, but becomes important later on, when potential obstacles must be identified and addressed.

The key is to know which people are oriented towards opportunities and which are more likely to see the obstacles, and to utilise their respective strengths.

In making this assessment, you could rely on your experience of each individual or use one of the personality testing tools that are available.[10]

A classic is Edward de Bono's *Six Thinking Hats* (Penguin Books, 1985).
0   For example, Team Management Systems' Opportunities–Obstacles (QO2) Profile measures our approach to risk, opportunities and obstacles at work. See www.tms.com.au.

(d)   **Think like a scientist**
Inevitably, you will sometimes encounter resistance to new suggestions. You will not know whether an idea will work until you try it. Set up an experiment or pilot programme; try it in one practice group or with some enthusiastic individuals who are opinion leaders in the firm.

  If the results you hoped for are not achieved, do not give up. Change the conditions of the experiment and record what you learn at each stage.

6.3   Cultivating a culture of innovation in your firm
If you want the people in your firm to think innovatively, you must lead by example. You may in fact be a strong supporter of innovation, but you must actively demonstrate this. People cannot read your mind – they can only observe your behaviour.

(a)   **Set the mood**
Leaders set the tone in an organisation. If a leader is interested only in short term results, people will think short term. If a leader seems downcast or weary that feeling will spread throughout the organisation. Moods and emotions are contagious, so make an effort to keep your mood positive

(b)   **Mix people up**
Get everyone involved in generating solutions. Legal practice can be a solitary sport. Within teams, homogeneity of thought can develop which inhibits the creation of new ideas. Encourage opportunities for diverse groups of people in the firm to come together.

(c)   **Be aware of words, actions, reactions**
To build a culture of innovation, everyone in the firm needs to know and believe that thinking creatively is part of their job and that their ideas will be valued.

  Leaders can easily stifle innovation without meaning to. The things you say the things you do and the way that you react to new ideas all communicate your beliefs about the value of innovation.

  Ensure that you are modelling the behaviours and attitudes that you wish to see in others.

7.   Conclusion
Today's talent management practices were once considered novel ideas. At one time, they did not even exist. Somebody had to be the first to propose these solutions.

  Changing circumstances call for new solutions. Your firm's ability to adapt to change with innovative talent management solutions can build competitive advantage. A reputation for innovative talent management can assist you in attracting the talent you want.

The task of instilling an innovative mindset starts with the leader.

About the authors

Peter Alfandary

Founder, PRA CrossCultural & Development

peter@pra-development.com

Peter Alfandary spent over 30 years as an international law firm partner and now advises large professional firms and corporations on the importance of cross-cultural issues in building successful business relationships.

He runs workshops on this topic and is a regular keynote speaker at conferences and corporate retreats. His TEDx talk on culture has been viewed over 360k times.

Peter holds dual French and UK nationality, was educated at the French Lycée in London, and received his LLB from the University of Kent and his LLM from the LSE.

As senior VP of the French Chamber of Commerce, Peter is highly active in the Franco-British business community.

Peter is an MBA guest lecturer on cultural intelligence at EDHEC business school.

In recognition of his services to Franco-British relations, Peter was made Chevalier and also Officier de la Légion d'Honneur by the French Republic.

Stuart J Barnett

Thought partner & executive coach

stuart@stuartjbarnett.com

Stuart Barnett is an executive coach, mentor, writer and keynote speaker. He specialises in working with senior lawyers, with a focus on personal strategy and leadership development. He has worked with many of the world's leading law firms, including Clifford Chance, Baker McKenzie, Herbert Smith Freehills, Ashurst, King Wood Mallesons, Dentons, Pinsent Masons and Clyde & Co. His articles have appeared in *Lawyers Weekly*, the *Wall Street Journal*, *The Australian* and *The Sydney Morning Herald*.

Marc Bartel

Senior client partner, Board & CEO Services France, Korn Ferry

mbartel@outlook.fr

Marc Bartel leads Korn Ferry's CEO and board practice in France and advises senior leaderships and boards of corporates and law firms on governance and talent issues. Prior to joining Korn Ferry, Marc had led the Paris office of another executive search firm. He has lived for ten years in London, holding various senior management positions (ranging from COO to Asia regional managing partner to deputy CEO) with leading international law firms such as Lovells and Linklaters. Marc began his earlier career as a practising lawyer, initially in Boston and then Paris. He also leads the legal, tax and compliance practice and has performed executive searches across all sectors within the legal/tax and compliance functions.

Marc obtained a business law degree and a master's in comparative law from Lyon University and a master's in comparative jurisprudence from New York University, and is a member of the New York Bar. He also obtained an MBA from the MIT Sloan School of Management.

Laure Carapezzi
HR business adviser, Allen & Overy Paris
laure.carapezzi@allenovery.com

Laure Carapezzi works in the HR department of the Paris office of Allen & Overy.

After several years as a lawyer in competition and business law, Laure joined Allen & Overy in 2017 for her first HR experience.

With her law background and having dealt with many legal sector issues, she quickly immersed herself in the various challenges by bringing an additional perspective to the HR function.

She is particularly interested in diversity and inclusion issues in law firms. She was admitted to the Paris Bar in 2014 and holds a master's degree in law from Nantes University.

Jay Connolly
Global chief talent officer, Dentons
jay.connolly@dentons.com

As part of the Dentons leadership team (global management committee and global board) Jay Connolly is focused on ensuring an exceptional people experience and delivering

the firm strategy. Building a world-leading HR and talent function is one core element. Jay joined Dentons in 2011, bringing extensive experience in talent management and human resources leadership and expertise from a variety of sectors, including professional services and large global corporates.

Prior to joining Dentons, he worked in the US and UK offices of Clifford Chance LLP as a senior member of the global HR leadership team. His career has also included senior HR roles at LEGO Company and Unilever. Jay has lived in the US, UK and Europe and built extensive experience working across the Middle East and Asia.

Kevin Doolan
Partner, Møller Institute
kevin.doolan@mollerinstitute.com

Kevin Doolan is a partner in the professional service firms group at the Møller Institute based at Churchill College, University of Cambridge and is visiting professor at Harvard Law School where he teaches on their executive education programme. He has a particular interest in the pricing of professional services; business development skills for professionals; and in cross-generational working practices.

In 2013 he developed the Harvard Law School case study on pricing services (HLS 13-17) with Professor George Triantis of Stanford Law School, and teaches pricing in the Harvard accelerated leadership programme. In 2015 he created the Harvard Law School case study on business development (HLS 15-12) with Dr Lisa Rohrer of Harvard and Cambridge associate Alexis Caught.

He divides his time between teaching on university programmes and consulting into many of the world's leading law firms.

ꞇelley Dunstone
ꞇincipal, Legal Circles
ꞇelley.dunstone@legalcircles.com

ꞇelley Dunstone is the principal of Legal Circles, consultancy practice which helps lawyers to ꞇhieve their business and career aspirations. She an Australian lawyer and has been a partner ꞇ a mid-sized Australian commercial law firm. addition to Law, she also holds qualifications management and applied finance. She is a life ember of the Australasian Legal Practice anagement Association. Shelley presents at ꞇnferences around Australia and internationally.

ꞇeidi K Gardner
ꞇistinguished fellow, Harvard Law School
ꞇardner@law.harvard.edu

ꞇ Heidi Gardner is a distinguished fellow at ꞇrvard Law School and faculty chair in the ꞇhool's executive programmes. Previously she ꞇs a professor at Harvard Business School. ꞇeidi's book *Smart Collaboration: How ꞇofessionals and Their Firms Succeed by Breaking ꞇwn Silos* became a *Washington Post* bestseller. ꞇamed by Thinkers50 as a Next Generation ꞇsiness Guru, she co-founded the research ꞇd advisory firm Gardner & Co.

Heidi has authored more than seventy ꞇoks, chapters, case studies and articles. Her ꞇoks include *Smart Collaboration for In-House ꞇgal Teams* (2020), *Leadership for Lawyers* (2nd ꞇition, 2019) and *Smart Collaboration for ꞇteral Hiring* (2018).

Heidi has lived and worked on four ꞇntinents, including as a Fulbright fellow, and ꞇr McKinsey & Co and Procter & Gamble. She ꞇrned her BA in Japanese from the University ꞇ Pennsylvania, a master's from the London ꞇhool of Economics, and a PhD from London ꞇsiness School.

Tony King
Director, AGK PSF Training Ltd
tony.g.king888@gmail.com

Tony King is a consultant to law firms globally on people management issues. After qualifying as a solicitor, he lectured at the College of Law (now the University of Law) and then joined Clifford-Turner & Co (Clifford Chance LLP from 1987) as a tax lawyer in 1984. He was involved in all aspects of education, training & professional development at Clifford Chance from 1988 to 2014. After he retired from the firm and in addition to his consultancy, he was a member of the Queen's Counsel Selection Panel (2014–2018) and is currently treasurer of the City of London Law Society and the senior warden of the City of London Solicitors' Company. He is chair of trustees of the charity IPSEA.

Jean-Baptiste Lebelle
Head of HR, Allen & Overy Paris
jean-baptiste.lebelle@allenovery.com

Jean-Baptiste Lebelle is head of HR for the Paris office of Allen & Overy. He has almost 20 years' experience on HR matters in the legal business sector and worked for major law firms in Paris as a headhunter before starting a career as an HR professional. Before joining Allen & Overy, Jean-Baptiste was head of HR of PwC tax & legal services in Paris.

Jean-Baptiste has been particularly involved in recruitment and retention issues for many years, and has worked on implementation of the new approach to performance management.

He graduated from Sciences Po Paris and holds a master's in law from Pantheon University.

He is also visiting lecturer on HR issues for institutions including Sorbonne University and HEC.

About the authors

Sarah Martin

Co-founder, Martin & Levin; associate fellow,
University of Oxford, Saïd Business School;
faculty member, Meyler Campbell
sarah@martinandlevin.com

Sarah Martin is a founder of the leadership
development and executive coaching
consultancy, Martin & Levin.

She is coach to professionals and
executives in international business and works
with senior leaders to design and direct
development programmes. Her focus is on
leadership and women in leadership. Her
clients include professional services firms,
private equity houses and C-suites.

Sarah originally trained as a lawyer,
working in M&A with Allen & Overy and as
senior counsel in the chairman's office of BP.
She has 25 years' experience of business, legal
and governance work at board level.

Sarah holds an MSc in leadership as a
Sloan fellow at London Business School. She
is a graduate and faculty member of Meyler
Campbell, training leadership coaches, and is
an associate fellow at University of Oxford,
Saïd Business School.

Moray McLaren

Founder and partner, Lexington Consultants
moray.mclaren@lexingtonconsultants.com

Moray McLaren has been advising law firms
for over 25 years. A lawyer by training, he
completed an MBA in legal services before
assisting the world s largest law firm on its
global expansion. A partner and co-founder at
Lexington, today he advises top independent
law firms as they review their practice focus,
governance, remuneration and ownership
models. Moray was the inaugural chair of the
strategy working group of the IBA's Law Firm

Management Committee. He is an associate
professor at IE Business School in Madrid and
a member of the Møller Institute at the
University of Cambridge. He recently became a
fellow of the Harvard-affiliated Institute o
Coaching.

Jonathan Middleburgh

Consultant, principal, Edge Consulting
jonathan@middleburghassociates.com

Jonathan Middleburgh is a consultant to law
firms, in-house legal departments and othe
professional services firms. By background a
lawyer, Jonathan graduated with first clas
honours in law from Oxford University and
taught law at the universities of Oxford
Chicago and King's College London, before
embarking on a career at the bar.

After leaving the bar, Jonathan trained a
an occupational psychologist and has a wealth
of experience nurturing leadership talent in
both law firms and legal departments. Fo
several years he was a senior director at Huron
Consulting Group, specialising in lega
management consulting, and is now a
principal of Edge Consulting, an international
consultancy focused on the legal sector and
professional service firms.

Jonathan has coached numerous lawyer
in a wide range of international and domestic
(UK) law firms, legal departments and Fortune
500 companies. His coaching focuses primarily
on issues around behavioural change. He also
has a niche specialisation in resolving
entrenched conflict among senior lawyers.

Rebecca Normand-Hochman
Founder and director, Institute of Legal Talent
& Leadership
normand-hochman@legaltalentandleadership.org

Rebecca Normand-Hochman is a leadership
consultant and coach who brings research-
based people management strategies to the
legal sector.

Since 2010 she has been working with
leaders and partners of international law firms
in Europe to help them improve the way in
which they select, integrate, develop, engage
and retain talent. She also supports
partners who are under pressure to
develop their teams' entrepreneurship
capabilities and helps them find the right
leadership style.

As a former international finance lawyer,
Rebecca knows the complex challenges that
lawyers face. She has also experienced the
specific 'herding cats' management and
leadership challenges of everyday legal
practice.

Combining broad legal and human capital
backgrounds and practical experience, she
offers consulting and coaching to law firm
leaders, leadership teams and partners looking
to develop working cultures in which lawyers
realise their full potential.

In parallel with her client work, Rebecca
is the founder and a director of the Institute
of Legal Talent & Leadership, which carries out
research and publishes thought leadership on
the human and organisational aspects of the
practice of law.

Simon Pizzey
Business coach
simonpizzey@live.co.uk

Simon Pizzey is a business coach who has
worked with clients in the legal sector. The
focus of his coaching work has been on
leadership, personal development and
performance.

Simon is a solicitor who began his career
specialising in dispute resolution. He then
became managing partner of two law firms,
providing strategic leadership, managing the
businesses and developing lawyers and staff.

Simon brings a deep-seated empathetic
approach to the coaching relationship and can
offer valuable insights. He holds an MBA in
legal practice from Nottingham Law School
and is a graduate of the Meyler Campbell
business coach programme.

Larry Richard
Founder and principal consultant,
LawyerBrain LLC
drlarryrichard@lawyerbrain.com

Dr Larry Richard is the founder and CEO of
LawyerBrain LLC, a consulting firm that serves
premier law firms and corporate legal
departments in the areas of leadership, change
management, teams and collaboration, talent
selection and development, feedback,
motivation and lawyer resilience and
wellbeing.

Larry is recognised as the leading expert
on the psychology of lawyer behaviour. A
graduate of the University of Pennsylvania Law
School, he was a litigator for ten years before
earning his PhD in psychology from Temple
University. Since then, he has gathered and
analysed personality data on thousands of
lawyers and consulted with hundreds of legal

providers on a wide range of complex behavioural issues.

Prior to founding LawyerBrain, Larry chaired the leadership and organisation improvement practice at legal specialty consultancy Hildebrandt International for seven years. Before that he was a partner at Altman Weil, another prominent legal consultancy.

Known for his ability to distil cutting-edge scientific principles into actionable recommendations for improving lawyer performance, Larry is a frequent presenter at professional conferences and a sought-after keynote speaker, as well as a highly sought-after consultant to leaders of law firms and corporate legal departments.

Robert Sharpe
Consultant psychologist
rs@robertsharpe.com

Dr Robert Sharpe manages his own consultancy practice, providing both clinical and coaching services to individual, team and corporate clients in the oil, retail, banking and legal sectors. His 25-year consultancy to Allen & Overy, working with 16 of its global offices in that period, included coaching over 40 senior associates, mostly non-UK nationals, into partnership.

In other sectors, he has worked with Citibank, Marks & Spencer, Unilever, Esso, Mobil and other A-list companies for periods of five to 25 years. He enjoys such long associations, accumulating a depth of knowledge as to how various sectors operate. He has authored four books and numerous chapters and professional papers and is a gifted mathematician, having matriculated in pure mathematics before switching to the mathematics of human thought and

behaviour. He says he is lucky to have spent his career doing exactly what he would do if he had to do it all over again.

Tom Spence
Co-founder, Donoma Advisors
tom@donoma-advisors.com

Tom Spence is a co-founder of Donoma Advisors, a specialised consultancy firm for the legal sector based in London. He has advised law firms internationally through both management consultancy and talent advisory services for over 10 years, working with clients across four continents. Prior to establishing Donoma Advisors, Tom co-founded another legal sector-focused talent advisory business.

His advisory work centres on helping law firms deliver better results from their talent acquisition and growth strategies, leveraging his consultancy experience in actively assessing how firms can improve their future lateral hiring and integration.

Tom is a chartered management consultant and a member of the Chartered Management Institute, and sits on the London & South East Committee of the Institute of Consulting.

Caroline Vanovermeire
Director, Effra Consult Ltd; Global talent director, Dentsu International
caroline.vanovermeire@effraconsult.com

Caroline Vanovermeire has a strong track record in strategic and operational talent management. She has built a reputation for coming up with creative and future-proofed solutions to address complex business challenges whilst remaining pragmatic, efficient and commercial.

Caroline attended the strategic talent management programme at Harvard Business

chool on the invitation of Professor Boris
Groysberg. She is an accredited ICF coach at
'CC level and obtained a master's in
sychology from the Catholic University of
euven and a master's in HR management
rom Antwerp University.

She is the founder of Effra Consult,
consortium of best-in-class business, digital,
IR, change, innovation and leadership
rofessionals who partner with professionals
o achieve the outcomes they need. She is also
lobal talent director at Dentsu International.

About Globe Law and Business

Globe Law and Business was established in 2005, and from the very beginning, we set out to create law books which are sufficiently high level to be of real use to the experienced professional, yet still accessible and easy to navigate. Most of our authors are drawn from Magic Circle and other top commercial firms, both in the UK and internationally.

Our titles are carefully produced, with the utmost attention paid to editorial, design and production processes. We hope this results in high-quality books which are easy to read, and a pleasure to own. All our new books are also available as ebooks, which are compatible with most desktop, laptop and tablet devices.

We have recently expanded our portfolio to include a new range of journals and Special Reports, available both digitally and in hard copy format, and produced to the same high standards as our books.

We'd very much like to hear from you with your thoughts and ideas for improving what we offer. Please do feel free to email me at sian@globelawandbusiness.com with your views.

Sian O'Neill
Managing director
Globe Law and Business

www.globelawandbusiness.com

Related titles

Leadership for Lawyers

Essential Leadership Strategies
for Law Firm Success
Second Edition

Consulting Editors **Heidi K Gardner** and
Rebecca Normand-Hochman
on behalf of the International Bar Association

Mentoring and Coaching for Lawyers

Building Partnerships for Success

Consulting Editor Rebecca Normand-Hochman
on behalf of the International Bar Association

Recruiting and Retaining Lawyers

Innovative Strategies to Attract,
Develop and Retain Legal Talent

Consulting Editor **Rebecca Normand-Hochman**
on behalf of the International Bar Association

Go to **www.globelawandbusiness.com**
for full details including free sample chapters

Get instant access with our eBooks

Globe Law and Business

Your eBooks are now delivered through VitalSource Bookshelf. Read them online in a browser as soon as your order is complete or offline on your computer or device of choice by downloading the Bookshelf app. It's free and boasts a range of features that we think will enhance your reading experience, such as text zoom, read aloud, notes and annotation facility and much more. To purchase a digital edition, please visit www.globelawandbusiness.com and add your eBooks to the basket at checkout.